How to Avoid Strategic Materials Shortages

How to Avoid Strategic Materials Shortages

DEALING WITH CARTELS, EMBARGOES, AND SUPPLY DISRUPTIONS

BOHDAN O. SZUPROWICZ

21st Century Research

A Wiley-Interscience Publication

JOHN WILEY & SONS, New York · Chichester · Brisbane · Toronto

Library of Congress Cataloging in Publication Data:

Szuprowicz, Bohdan O   1931–
  How to Avoid Strategic Materials Shortages

  "A Wiley-Interscience publication."
  Includes index.
  1.   Strategic materials.   2.   Geopolitics.
I.   Title

HC79.S8S98   355.2′4   80-24431
ISBN 0-471-07843-3

Printed in the United States of America

10 9 8 7 6 5 4 3 2 1

To my father Jakob Szuprowicz

a lifetime warrior against socialist imperialism

The supreme excellence is to subjugate the armies of your enemies without ever having to fight them.

Sun-Tzu in *The Art of War*
written in the fifth century B.C.

PREFACE

Following the tremendous success of the Organization of Petroleum Exporting Countries (OPEC), many developing countries that supply strategic and critical minerals to the West realized they had the potential to exert political and economic blackmail. As a result business and political leaders in most industrialized countries have been concerned about politically motivated shortages and supply disruptions of strategic materials, vital to industry and national security, that must be imported from unstable regions of the Third World.

This book discusses the geopolitics of most strategic and critical materials, centering on the crucial question of access and alternative solutions. The book's purpose is to outline political, economic, and technological factors that must be continually monitored to assess the vulnerability of governments, industries, military establishments, and individual corporations to sudden unexpected and prolonged shortages or embargoes of strategic and critical materials supplies.

The world seems to be entering a period of intensified economic competition, involving many new third world mineral supplying countries. This book identifies major potential actors and correlations of forces in this "resources war." The worst-case scenarios suggest possible outcomes, their impact on business and industry, and possible solutions.

Although the earth's crust and oceans contain an abundance of all minerals required by mankind for centuries to come, the perversity of nature placed the economically exploitable concentrations of minerals in widely scattered locations, with truly rich deposits very few and far between. The overwhelming control of the Soviet Union and southern African countries over most of the global reserves of such strategic materials as gold, diamonds, chromium, platinum, palladium, rhodium, cobalt, manganese, beryllium, and antimony is developing into an ominous geopolitical threat to the industrialized countries of the West.

The production and reserves overhang of these two regions is so huge and mineral markets so volatile that there are strong disincentives to explore and invest in other parts of the world without special inducements, guarantees, and government support. Thus the United States, western Europe, Japan, and even China and their respective industries are at the mercy of political and economic forces in control of those areas.

The elements that might induce formation of a strategic materials "supercartel" are now in place, and if such an international structure develops even in part, it could have disastrous effects on the unprepared. This unusual correlation of forces also presents the Soviet bloc with the opportunity of the century to win political and economic concessions unwarranted by normal market forces, without resorting to military action.

This book is designed to provide essential and easily understood information to policymakers in all walks of life. If it is considered "too technical" by the politicians and "too political" by the engineers, they have merely recognized a purposeful attempt to bridge the range of interests contained between the two extremes. It should prove particularly useful to business executives, marketing and purchasing managers, production planners, government leaders, economists, military strategists, intelligence officers, politicians, international trade analysts, bankers, investment analysts, scholars, teachers, inventors, design engineers, and dictators.

Initial chapters of the book define strategic materials, identify political events that influence their availability, quantify import dependence of major end-user countries of the West, and indicate the importance of the issues to economic growth and national security. Several subsequent chapters discuss in detail strategic materials supply positions of major international groupings such as the Soviet bloc, southern Africa, China, the Pacific Basin, and Latin America.

Alternative solutions to shortages and supply disruptions, stockpiling policies, and politics of undersea resources are next examined to assess their potential contributions in case of a crisis. A need to recognize potential problems and develop appropriate foreign policies is advocated in anticipation of future events. From a strictly business-oriented point of view I examine various investment opportunities that may develop as a result of political and economic changes associated with persistent resource wars and shortages.

The final chapter of the book provides practical suggestions about how to assess the vulnerability of countries, industries, supplier and end-user corporations to strategic and critical materials shortages and supply disruptions and how to compare such organizations for investment purposes. All this is presented on the assumption that contingency planning will give an advantage to those who are prepared for the worst.

In the course of researching and writing this book many organizations and individuals were extremely helpful with their special insights into specific geopolitical situations and constructive criticism of potential scenarios and alternatives. Invitations to express many of my views during seminars and conferences and the benefit of resulting public discussion and comment were particularly valuable. Special thanks must go to Mrs. Jerry Harris of the Council on Religion and International Affairs for numerous introductions to diplomats, businessmen, military strategists, scholars, and journalists; to Roberta Martin and Ed Winckler of the East Asian Institute at Columbia University for repeated invitations to speak at their seminars; to John Cunningham, International Division Director of American Management Associations, for providing a forum to present the issues to the business community; to Ed Dyckman of the Department of Defense (DOD) for arranging participation in the DOD Interagency Materials Availability Steering Committee meetings at the Pentagon; to Gary Lloyd, Director of the Business Council for International Understanding; to the organizers of Defense Technology '79, National Aerospace and Electronics Conference, the Infotech Conference, and the Georgia World Trade Institute for opportunities to place the issues before their audiences.

I am also extremely grateful for the personal comments and observations of many persons concerned with the issues involved. Special thanks are due to Robert Haavind, editor of *High Technology*, who was the first to undertake the publication of my discussion of this subject. Rene Le Moal of *Usine Nouvelle* in France, Mark Winchester of the Center for International Business, Trevor Sykes of *The Bulletin* from Australia, Alexander Ross of *Canadian Business*, and the editors of *Japan Economic Journal, Il Mondo* in Italy, *Purchasing*, and *Datamation* have also been helpful in publishing and reviewing my articles. Dr. K. P. Wang of the U.S. Bureau of Mines contributed very valuable observations on the minerals industries of China and the Far East. Professor Frank Barnett, Director of the National Strategy Information Center, introduced me to the concepts of Trioceanic Alliance and the need to expand the scope of the North Atlantic Treaty Organization (NATO). Dr. J. L. Steyn and his South African colleagues contributed invaluable insights into the policies of South Africa. Krys Mackiewicz of Great Britain deserves very special thanks for demonstrating the unusual potential in the question of Afghanistan. Other diplomats, businessmen, and officials, too numerous to mention by name, from Australia, Canada, China, France, Germany, Iraq, Israel, Japan, Malawi, Poland, the Soviet Union, the United Kingdom, and Taiwan also left their mark on the process of formulating the concepts and scenarios presented in this work.

A particularly insightful contribution was made by my father, Jakob Szuprowicz, a professional artillery officer, whose lifetime includes participation in the Bolshevik Revolution, World War I, the Polish-Russian War of 1920, and several theaters of World War II. I am especially grateful for the opportunity to draw freely from his personal memoirs, which provide invaluable observations and comparisons of the motivations of the "levantine mind" in conflict and competition with the precepts of the Western set of values.

Last but not least my most sincere appreciation is due to my wife Majusia not only for her unwavering enthusiasm to support this project but also for her patience and endurance in tolerating all the inevitable annoyances and aggravations that such an undertaking must entail.

BOHDAN OLGIERD SZUPROWICZ

North Bergen, New Jersey
January 1981

CONTENTS

How to Avoid Strategic Materials Shortages

CHAPTER
ONE

What Are Strategic Materials?

Raw materials such as oil, iron ore, copper, aluminum, chromium, rubber, and many others are the lifeblood of modern industries. Most occur in the form of minerals or natural resources in practically every part of the world. Theoretically the earth's crust and the seas are believed to contain enormous reserves sufficient to satisfy the needs of the whole world for centuries to come.

In practice, however, mineral deposits that are economically exploitable with currently existing technologies are often concentrated in only a few regions of the world. Moreover many of the highly industrialized countries that are primary consumers of those raw materials often do not possess sufficient deposits of all the necessary minerals within their territorial boundaries. Japan is a good example of an economy with rapidly growing needs that must rely almost entirely on the imports of most of its raw materials from overseas.

When basic industries of a country become significantly dependent on supplies of such raw materials from foreign sources these become strategically important to the economies of those countries. Conversely an industrialized nation that possesses all the necessary raw materials within its own borders can consider itself truly self-sufficient. The United States until the late 1950s and the Soviet Union at present are two rare examples of such self-sufficient superpowers. China, Brazil, and southern Africa as a region are possible future groupings where such conditions may develop.

Not all the raw materials are of equal strategic importance to all the countries at all times. Even when a particular mineral is critical to one industry it may not be of importance to another unless it in turn depends on the output of the other industry. As a result the definition of what is a truly strategic and critical material will vary not only from country to country but also among industries and even enterprises within each country.

The concentration of global oil resources in the Middle East and the OPEC cartel focus the world's attention on oil as the most strategic and critical material in the world. But oil is only one form of energy, and although up to a point it is indispensable to all countries and all modern industries it is not necessarily the most strategic or critical of them all.

Other minerals, less known than oil, are of immense strategic importance. These include chromium, cobalt, gold, titanium, tungsten, platinum, diamonds, or uranium. In recent years most of those minerals have been the subject of violent price and supply fluctuations often more unstable than the oil markets.

A QUESTION OF ACCESS AND PRICE

Among the 194 countries of the world there are three basic groups of nations that have differing vital interests in the supply and consumption of raw materials. These include the industrialized free market economies, the centrally planned economies dominated by the Soviet Union, and the developing countries of the Third World.

The industrialized free market economies are the largest users of all raw materials and account for about 70 percent of global consumption by volume. Those countries are also the largest producers of raw materials, accounting for about 45 percent of all such output in the world. This means that already 25 percent of the world's consumption of all raw materials must be imported by the industrialized free market economies from sources outside the territories under their political control (Figure 1.1).

As a result access to sources of raw materials and secure means of transportation to end-users is of paramount importance to industrialized free market economies. The price of raw materials under certain conditions may not be the decisive factor, particularly in the case of minerals whose sources are relatively few and for which substitute materials are not readily available. Such conditions are conducive to the formation of cartels that can unilaterally dictate the prices in full knowledge that continuing supplies even at escalating prices are of the utmost importance to the end-users.

By comparison the Third World countries produce about 30 percent of the world's raw materials. This is in fact somewhat less than the total production in the industrialized free market economies. However, the Third World countries consume only 6 percent of all the raw materials used in the world. In effect most Third World countries are large exporters of raw materials and of paramount importance to them is their ability to obtain the best price for their exports. This objective is often coupled with a desire to obtain financing and technology to establish more advanced minerals processing and end-user industries within their own countries. This objective becomes extremely important when one realizes that the world will need one billion new jobs before the year 2000, most of which must be created in Third World countries.

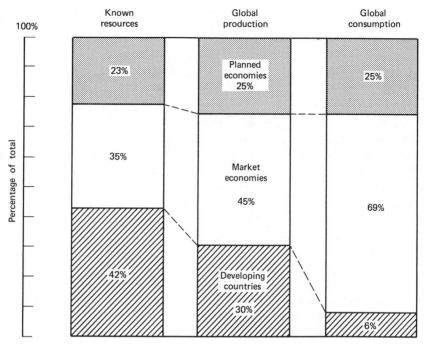

Figure 1.1 Comparative raw materials resources, production, and consumption in three basic groups of nations in the world. Source. **Based on estimates in the article "Crisis in Mineral Resources" in** SEMA Review **published by Metra Consulting in Paris, France, September 7, 1979.**

This basic imbalance between raw materials positions of industrialized free market economies and Third World countries is further aggravated by the fact that known world resources of raw materials are considerably larger in Third World countries than in the realtively more depleted industrialized free market economies. Developing countries are now believed to contain about 42 percent of all known resources. By contrast the market economies account for only 35 percent of such resources, but it must be kept in mind that these assessments are not static and continue to change, depending on political and economic factors at work.

Resources are discovered where exploration is taking place, and some observers believe that the relatively large known resources in developing countries resulted from anticipated low costs of their exploitation. If prices of raw materials in these countries were to increase to unreasonable levels it is believed that additional exploration in such vast industrialized countries as Australia and Canada would considerably increase the overall known resources of the free market economies.

Centrally planned economies present a more balanced picture of raw materials resources, production, and consumption and give the appearance of relative self-sufficiency and independence of external sources of raw materials. They account for 25 percent of global consumption and produce approximately the same percentage of the world's raw materials. Known resources of the centrally planned economies are believed to be about 23 percent of global resources, but further exploration of such vast territories as Siberia, Afghanistan, Mongolia, China, and Vietnam are likely to result in an increase of these countries' share of the world's resources.

As a result centrally planned economies, and the Soviet Union in particular, are practically self-sufficient in raw materials, which puts them in an advantageous position relative to the rest of the world. They do not have to be concerned about access to any foreign sources, and they centrally control their production levels to meet their internal demands. When world prices for a particular commodity are depressed because of slackening demand or recession the Soviets can benefit from cheap imports and can even reduce their domestic production if necessary. When prices escalate the Soviets are in a position to increase their own output and export raw materials in exchange for hard currencies and high-technology equipment and know-how.

More important, raw materials self-sufficiency and central control of production provide the Soviet Union with the means to exercise political and economic leverage in various countries of the world. This new-found political power may be increasingly coming into play in the future, particularly in disputes between industrialized free market economies and Third World countries about access and prices of raw materials.

NATIONAL ECONOMY AND SECURITY CONSIDERATIONS

On a national level each country has a different raw materials demand and supply framework, although fuels and the so-called basic materials such as steel, copper, aluminum, nickel, lead, zinc, and tin are universally consumed in varying quantities by all countries. On the other hand the economy's nature and its status as a political and military power will determine which materials are considered strategic to the nation as a whole and which are only critical to the existence of specific industries.

Several factors influence the supply and consumption of various raw materials in any particular country. These include the existence of mineral deposits, availability of capital and technology, sufficient energy supplies, transportation infrastructure, industrial and military demand, and export potential (Figure 1.2).

Political power is probably the most important factor influencing raw materials supply and demand in most countries, although it may not appear to be so at first glance. This is so because political power controls such other factors as exploratory rights, labor costs and availability, environmental re-

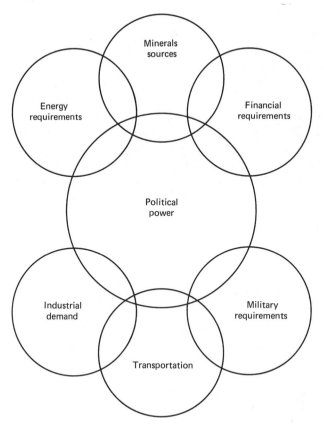

Figure 1.2 Major factors influencing raw materials supplies.

strictions, capital investment, energy supplies, rights of way, taxation, import and export duties, foreign trade organizations, and industrial development.

The degree of dependence and interaction between these various factors influencing the supplies of all raw materials vary, depending on the type of political control in a particular country. In the centrally planned economies this interaction and control are extreme, and politics dominate all other factors. In free market economies and particularly in the United States most factors come into play independently, and numerous alternatives may exist at any one time leading to various conflicts of interest and excessive foreign dependence.

In Third World countries politics plays a much greater role than in the free market economies. This is so because in many instances the mining and production of raw materials is a major industry in those countries that lack the diversity of industrialized economies. Exports of raw materials provide foreign exchange that is required to pay for imports of equipment and technology to keep the economy in operation and maintain political power.

National security in the case of the superpowers such as the United States and the Soviet Union is perceived to be dependent on a large military establishment and high-technology industries. These in turn depend on supplies of strategic materials that may or may not be the same as those required by the civilian economy.

Ideally a superpower should be self-sufficient in all the strategic materials or have assured sources of supply in foreign countries friendly or allied to its policies. Other industrialized economies, which are not self-sufficient in raw materials, must choose to become client states of either the superpowers or other geopolitical groupings such as OPEC to assure themselves of adequate supplies of all the strategic materials required to maintain the growth of their economies.

The economies of east European countries are closely linked to the availability of fuels and raw materials from the Soviet Union. Characteristically only Romania, which has its own significant oil resources, has been showing a modicum of independence from the Soviet Union. The same argument could be applied in the case of China which broke its close relationship with the Soviet Union and embarked on self-sufficiency policies of development only after it became clear that China possessed significant oil resources of its own.

Any Western political initiatives to "loosen" the Soviet grip on eastern Europe would have to assure those countries the energy and raw materials supplies to run their economies. Following World War II when the United States was still a self-sufficient superpower and western Europe had greater control over its raw materials supplies this may have been a more realistic proposition. Since then the free market economies have become increasingly dependent on imports of their raw materials from Third World countries whose political objectives are not only volatile but also may differ significantly from those of the West.

There is a very basic difference between raw materials policies of the centrally planned economies and those of free market economies. In the Soviet Union raw materials supplies are allocated according to centrally planned objectives for specific industries and the military establishment. It is basically a wartime measure designed to overcome shortages by establishing priorities.

By contrast free market economies in general and that of the United States in particular have developed in an environment of abundant natural and capital resources. Under those conditions government leaders, industrial end-users, the military establishment, and raw materials suppliers all follow their own independent objectives with regard to raw materials supply and consumption. Materials managers and design engineers are primarily concerned with raw materials prices and physical characteristics. Now they are beginning to face the problems of shortages and availability as paramount in their planning and budgeting.

HOW TO IDENTIFY STRATEGIC AND CRITICAL MATERIALS

If there exists the possibility of a severe shortage or outright supply disruption of a material that cannot be readily substituted in an industry then it must be considered as being strategic or critical to the end-users. This is particularly true if such a material originates from foreign sources outside the political control of the country in which end-users and their industries are located. Oil is an obvious example, particularly in the case of countries that do not possess any domestic resources of this mineral.

Unexpected price escalations may also play havoc with production schedules in cases when the end product contains a large proportion of materials whose prices increase significantly. On the other hand even drastic price increases of materials that are used in very small quantities in some products may not be critical to end-users. In such cases availability of such indispensable materials and unexpected shortages regardless of price may nevertheless create severe problems to the end-user industries.

Numerous danger points signal the criticality of each particular material to end-users that can be determined in advance. These range from the number and location of supply sources to various characteristics of the material that may threaten excessive regulation of its production and its eventual disappearance from the market. Many of these danger points are listed in Table 1.1. Assignment of relative values and weights to these characteristics for each specific material can also lead to the development of the Strategic Materials Vulnerability Index that is discussed in more detail in Chapter 15.

The existence of several danger characteristics with regard to a particular material does not in itself imply that the material's supplies will be inadequate in the future. Whether these danger points will have a disruptive effect on the supplies depends on other events and conditions of a political, economic, and social nature. Most of these are completely beyond the control of the end-user regardless of whether the materials originate from domestic or foreign sources. Many such events are also beyond the control of materials traders and distributors who are the intermediaries between the actual producers and the end-users and whose business objectives are often at variance with those of the materials-consuming industries.

Those "trigger" events and conditions are often political in nature but are not necessarily unpredictable. Materials managers whose enterprises depend on strategic and critical materials that exhibit many danger characteristics would do well to become familiar with the sources of their materials and the political climates of those environments. They can protect their organizations from serious loss of revenues or work disruptions by assessing politi-

Table 1.1 Materials Availability Danger Points

1. Single supply source
2. Lack of domestic reserves
3. Lack of substitute materials
4. Inadequate world reserves
5. High import dependence
6. Supplies by allocation
7. Price controls
8. Excessive energy requirements
9. Irregular and infrequent supplies
10. Import and export controls
11. Environmental restrictions on use
12. Health and safety impacts on production
13. Very high military usage (over 95%)
14. Declining use of material
15. Technological development threat
16. Low volume of total sales
17. Low level of production
18. Poor usage visibility
19. Low recycling potential
20. High existing or potential taxation

cal risks involved well in advance and prepare alternative action plans. In a world of materials shortages this course of action is the sine qua non of survival.

The events and conditions that must be monitored for this purpose both on the domestic scene and in foreign countries include labor costs, strikes, civil unrest, wars, cartels, boycotts, embargoes, terrorist activities, revolutions, new legislation, taxation, as well as acts of God in distant places such as droughts, floods, fires, and earthquakes.

ENERGY RESOURCES

Energy resources are most often associated with oil, but in fact these exist in various alternate forms in different countries. They include oil, natural gas, coal, lignite, and biogas, as well as hydroelectric, nuclear, geothermal, solar, tidal, and wind power. Oil provides the most convenient source of energy, but there are many countries that to this day rely primarily on coal as their major energy source. These include China, South Africa, India, Czechoslovakia, Poland, and East Germany.

There are about 30 countries in the world that appear to have significant energy resources, although not necessarily in the form of oil. Among those are the major producers, consumers, and exporters of energy in the form of oil, natural gas, or coal. Besides OPEC members these countries include most of the industrialized powers and populous-developing countries like China, India, Mexico, Brazil, Indonesia, and Nigeria (Table 1.2).

The more significant energy have-nots of the world are France, Japan, and Italy. At the same time these countries are big energy consumers. It is therefore not by accident that nuclear power development programs are well ad-

Table 1.2 Proved Energy Reserves in Selected Countries Ranked by Crude Oil Reserves in 1978

Country	Crude Oil (billion barrels)	Natural Gas (trillion ft.^{3})	Coal (million metric tons)
Saudi Arabia	166 OPEC	94	0
Kuwait	66 OPEC	31	0
Iran	59 OPEC	500	200
Soviet Union	35 state owned	1,020	256,000
Iraq	32 OPEC	28	0
Abu Dhabi	30 OPEC	20	0
United States	28	205	178,600
Libya	24 OPEC	24	0
China	20 state owned	25	98,900
Nigeria	18 OPEC	42	100
Venezuela	18 OPEC	41	1,000
Mexico	16 state run	32	900
United Kingdom	16	27	45,000
Indonesia	10 OPEC	24	1,400
Canada	6	59	9,400
Norway	6	24	na
Algeria	6 OPEC	105	na
Qatar	4 OPEC	40	0
Egypt	3 state run	3	neg
India	3	4	33,700
Oman	2	2	0
Syria	2	2	0
Brazil	1	2	8,100
Ecuador	1 OPEC	4	0
Romania	1 state owned	9	400
West Germany	neg	6	34,400
South Africa	0	0	26,900
Poland	neg	5	21,800
Yugoslavia	neg	1	8,500
North Korea	0	0	8,500

Source.   National Foreign Assessment Center, ER 79–10274, August 1979.

vanced in those countries. That, however, creates another dependence on sources of uranium for nuclear fuels, making that metal a strategic energy resource.

Over 50 countries are now in the process of developing nuclear power that has the added attraction of nuclear weapons development potential. This makes uranium doubly strategic as a raw material to most countries in the world.

Energy resources and related problems have been widely discussed for years as a result of the emergence of OPEC as a new form of an international economic and political power center. The main objective of this book is to explore the problems associated with possible shortages or supply disruptions of critical nonenergy resources such as metals and minerals that are also vital to the operation of modern economies.

Nevertheless availability of adequate energy supplies is also of great significance to the minerals and metals production cycle and must be taken into account. Energy in one form or another is indispensable in exploration, mining, processing, refining, and transportation of raw materials. The different metals in their finished form can indeed be rated according to the amount of energy that is required to produce a unit amount of each (Table 1.3).

High cost or shortages of energy in a particular country or region will increasingly play a role in determining which metals will substitute for others and where production may be discontinued. In the United States, for example, 4 percent of all the energy consumed is used to produce aluminum alone. But recovery of aluminum from scrap can be accomplished with only a fraction of that energy; therefore as prices of energy continue to escalate organizations that are heavy end-users of aluminum may find it profitable to engage in large scrap recovery operations. By the same token any reduction

Table 1.3 Relative Energy Requirements in Metals Production

Metal	Relative Requirements of Energy per Ton of Finished Metal
Iron	1.00
Copper	2.76
Steel	2.84
Aluminum	12.15
Magnesium	18.50
Titanium	25.80

Source. U.S. House of Representatives, Committee on Science and Technology, *Materials Policy Handbook*, June 1977.

of imports of bauxite or alumina from which aluminum is extracted may set into motion reciprocal actions of exporting countries.

Alternatively energy-rich countries such as Bahrain in the Persian Gulf have developed aluminum refining capacity in their own territory based on cheap and abundant local energy supplies. Such developments may further reduce domestic aluminum production capacity in other countries where energy is much more expensive and may lead to strange new arrangements between countries that have the energy and those with deposits of strategic minerals.

There is a discernible trend among energy-rich states toward the development of energy intensive industries in their own territories. But if these countries do not possess sufficiently large markets to absorb the output of such industries there is the danger of disruption of existing markets in other countries through exports of products at significantly lower prices to capture market shares. Interestingly the centrally planned economies can protect themselves by strict foreign trade monopolies under central political control, but the free market economies are vulnerable to domestic output declines and unemployment in several threatened industries. Steel and textile industries are good examples of that type of industrial setback.

The Persian Gulf states provide about 70 percent of oil consumed in the industrialized countries of the West. There are some political analysts who now believe that revolutions similar to that which occurred in Iran in 1979 may change the political climate in such major oil-producing countries as Saudi Arabia or Kuwait in the near future. This could mean further reductions of oil exports from the Persian Gulf with a serious impact on the cost of the production of metals and minerals in Third World countries that rely on imports of energy.

BASIC METALS AND RAW MATERIALS

Over 70 percent of the total value of the world's production of the top 50 most valuable minerals is represented by energy resources, and at least 23 percent constitutes metallic minerals. The remainder are minerals such as diamonds, salt, phosphates, asbestos, sulfur, mica, fluorspar, graphite, and asphalt.

Several of the metallic minerals are produced in great quantities in the form of ores from which the basic metals in most common usage are extracted. These include iron ore, copper, aluminum, nickel, tin, zinc, and lead. Production of some of the metals, including iron, copper, aluminum, zinc, and lead, reaches million of tons per year on a global basis. These basic metals are critical to many industries because they are used in such large quantities (Table 1.4).

Aluminum, in the form of bauxite, and iron ore are respectively the third

Table 1.4   Basic Metals Reserves of the World

Metal Ores	Rank of Relative Abundance	Largest Reserves Areas
Iron ore	4	Soviet Union, Brazil, Canada, Australia, India, United States
Copper	26	United States, Chile, Canada, Soviet Union, Peru, Zambia, Zaire
Aluminum	3	Australia, Guinea, Brazil, Jamaica
Nickel	23	New Caledonia, Canada, Australia, Indonesia, Cuba
Tin	54	China, Thailand, Malaysia, Bolivia
Zinc	24	United States, Canada
Lead	36	United States

and the fourth most abundant elements in the earth's crust. The other basic metals are considerably less abundant, and together with all other elements constitute only a few percent of the earth's crust. Nevertheless the volume of the earth is so huge that millions of tons of all those metals can be produced every year.

Despite the fact that aluminum and iron ore are so abundant there still exists the possibility of a producer's cartel because these metals are very widely used and because their ore deposits are very uneven and the highest-grade areas are concentrated in only a few countries.

Iron Ore

This mineral is the primary source of iron and steel, basic to any industrial system. Major use in construction, shipbuilding, railroads, machine tools, automobiles, heavy equipment, agricultural machinery, and numerous consumer appliances makes this metal the most common in the world.

However, over 31 percent of high-grade iron ore reserves is believed to be located in the Soviet Union, which is by far also the largest producer of iron ore in the world, accounting for almost a third of the total. Another 45 percent of iron ore reserves is located in Brazil, Canada, Australia, and India. The United States is believed to contain only about 6 percent of global reserves and is a net importer of iron ore from abroad.

China is actually the second largest producer of iron ore in the world after the Soviet Union, but the quality of Chinese ores is low. China is also a major importer of some ores from Australia and steels from Japan, West Germany, and other countries.

The resulting steels that are produced from iron ores in the steelmaking process are widely used for industrial and military applications. High-quality steels are alloys that also require large quantities of manganese, chromium, nickel, molybdenum, vanadium, and smaller amounts of other metals. Any shortages of these alloy metals could pose very serious problems to many of the high technology industries that require the use of special quality steels.

Aluminum

The use of aluminum in the world now exceeds the use of any other metal except iron. Construction industries are the largest consumers of aluminum, and transportation, packaging, electrical, and telecommunications industries are also major users of the metal.

Transportation use includes aircraft manufacturing, for which aluminum is critical. Civilian jet transports and helicopters are also important in the export trade of major aircraft manufacturing countries, including the United States, France, the United Kingdom, Germany, and the Soviet Union. Military aircraft are major weapons systems and also contribute to the export trade of all major aircraft manufacturing countries. These applications make aluminum a very strategic material, particularly to those countries that do not possess bauxite deposits within their territories.

Geographically major high-grade bauxite reserves are located in Australia, Guinea, Brazil, and Jamaica that together account for 75 percent of all known reserves. The bauxites are subjected to hydrometallurgical processing to produce alumina that in turn is reduced to aluminum by an electrolytic process which consumes very large quantities of energy in the form of electric power. Although aluminum may be substituted by magnesium, production of that metal requires even larger quantities of energy.

The United States is the largest producer of primary aluminum metal from imported bauxite and alumina. The Soviet Union is the second largest aluminum producer from its own domestic bauxites, and it also imports some aluminum from other producers. Japan, Canada, West Germany, and Norway are the next largest aluminum-producing countries.

Copper

After oil, coal, and natural gas, copper production accounts for over 6 percent of the value of all the minerals produced in the world. Copper is one of the first metals known and used by mankind, and the importance of this metal lies in its excellent characteristics as a conductor of heat and electricity.

Copper is indispensable for use in electric power transmission, communications, generators, motors, transformers, switchgear, heat exchangers, condensers, air conditioning, refrigeration, tubing and piping, bearings, and military cartridge and shell casings. It is one of the most strategic materials and can substitute for many other metals, although it is itself hard to replace.

The United States and Chile are estimated to contain 40 percent of the world's copper reserves. Canada, the Soviet Union, Peru, and Zambia are believed to account for another 32 percent of the total. However four developing countries—namely, Chile, Peru, Zambia, and Zaire—account for over 80 percent of copper exports in the world. Poland is another country that recently developed its significant copper deposits. Copper is the third most important raw material moving in foreign trade after oil and wheat and accounts for about 3 percent of global exports of all primary products.

It is worth noting here that in the recent past Chile experienced a Marxist government, Zaire was the subject of the Katanga secession war in the 1960s and two subsequent Shaba province invasions of the copper-producing areas, Zambia received significant foreign aid from China, and Peru received economic aid from China and significant military and economic aid from the Soviet Union.

Nickel

This metal is one of the most versatile alloying materials used in the production of stainless steels and corrosion resistant superalloys capable of withstanding very high temperatures. Nickel can be substituted in almost every use but only at increased cost or loss of product performance.

The metal has numerous strategic applications and is essential in military uses, including nuclear applications, jet engines, aircraft frames, submarines, armor plating, gun barrels, and rocket motor casings. About 90 percent of nickel is consumed in the form of alloys; the remaining consumption consists of use in electroplating, electrical equipment, machinery, vehicles, catalysts, batteries, fuel cells, ceramics, and household appliances.

As much as 25 percent of known nickel reserves of the world are in New Caledonia, a French Overseas Territory located in the South Pacific northeast of Australia. Canada is believed to account for 15 percent and the Soviet Union for 14 percent of world reserves. Indonesia has 13 percent; the Philippines and Australia, about 9 percent each; and Cuba, 6 percent of the total.

The Soviet Union is now believed to be the largest producer of refined nickel, having surpassed Canada in the mid-1970s. Japan, Australia, New Caledonia (with France), and Cuba are the next largest refined nickel producers. The Soviet Union is financing a $600-million expansion program of Cuban nickel production that may make Cuba the third largest nickel producer by 1985. This would give the Soviet bloc control of 60 percent of the world's nickel production, and if the demand of the Council for Mutual Economic Assistance (COMECON) does not absorb this output attempts to export large quantities of nickel to the West could seriously affect the stability of nickel markets.

Tin

Tin is considered essential to an industrial society, and for many of this metal's applications there are no completely satisfactory substitutes. At least one-third of all the tin is used in the manufacture of cans and containers. Other important uses are in solders, babbits, and bearing metals, brass and bronze, tinning, foils, ceramics, pigments, and miscellaneous chemical uses. About 20 percent of the tin used in the United States is reclaimed from scrap.

Major tin reserves exist in South East Asian countries. Indonesia is estimated to contain 24 percent of world reserves; the People's Republic of China has 15 percent; Thailand, 12 percent; Bolivia, about 10 percent; Malaysia, over 8 percent; and the Soviet Union and Brazil, about 6 percent each. Nigeria, Australia, Zaire, and Burma also possess some tin.

Malaysia is the leading primary tin producer in the world, accounting for about 40 percent of the total, followed by the Soviet Union, which produces about 17 percent. Thailand, Indonesia, Bolivia, and China are the next largest tin producers, ranging from 16 to 8 percent of the world's tin output.

Tin is uniquely the only metal subject to an international agreement between producing and consuming countries. The International Tin Council (ITC) exists since 1956 and in 1976 United States joined the Fifth International Tin Agreement for the first time. The council seeks to secure long-term balance between production and consumption of tin by establishing a floor and a ceiling price. This is effected by maintenance of tin "buffer stocks" and by applying export controls on tin producers.

Zinc

Zinc is the third most commonly used nonferrous metal in the world after copper and aluminum. It is versatile and essential in modern living. Principal use is in automobile die castings, typewriter chassis, housings, galvanizing iron and steel products, as alloying element in brass, in rubber, and as paint pigment. No adequate substitute is known for zinc in its use in galvanizing steel. Brass sheet as cartridge brass is used in large quantities to manufacture small arms ammunition shell casings for sporting and military use.

Highest zinc reserves are in the United States and Canada, which are estimated to contain about 27 and 20 percent of global reserves, respectively. Other major zinc reserves are in Australia, Peru, Japan, and the Soviet Union, but zinc mining also is significant in Mexico, Zaire, Italy, Germany, and Poland.

The Soviet Union is the largest producer of refined zinc, followed by Japan, Canada, and the United States. Poland, West Germany, Australia, Belgium, France, Italy, Spain, Finland, and Mexico are among the larger producers. In total at least 30 countries produce zinc, which means that many alternative sources of the metal exist.

Despite this wide occurrence and production zinc is only the twenty-fourth most abundant metal in the earth's crust, but it is being used in relatively large quantities. It is estimated that if current rates of consumption continue existing known reserves will not be sufficient to meet global demand during the 1990s. On the other hand it is also held that new and significant reserves of zinc may come into play in the future if the usage of zinc continues unabated.

Lead

The principal use of lead is in storage batteries, bearings, gasoline antiknock additives, and in the electrical industries. Lead is also used in paints, solder, type metal, and some brasses and bronzes. More strategic uses include ammunition and as shielding against nuclear radioactivity.

Nickel-cadmium batteries are now also in use and could substitute for lead, but the cost is high and the supply of nickel and cadmium in an emergency may be more critical than that of lead. However, in the United States 40 percent of lead is being recycled. In terms of the amount of nonferrous metals consumed, lead ranks fourth after aluminum, copper, and zinc (it is often coproduced with zinc).

The United States is estimated to contain 37 percent of global lead reserves, followed by Canada with 13 percent and Australia with 12 percent. Nevertheless in 1978 the Soviet Union was the largest smelter lead producer, having just surpassed the United States in 1977. Australia, Japan, Canada, Mexico, and Bulgaria are also major lead-producing countries. At least 22 countries are significant lead producers.

Environmental legislature such as the Clean Air Act Amendment of 1977 and the Occupational and Safety and Health Administration regulations affect the use and price of lead through strikes and supply disruptions. These may lead to a further shift from use of lead in nonessential applications such as has already occurred in gasoline additives and paints. On the other hand increasing terrorism and the possibility of nuclear threats or even wars may result in a run on lead as one of the best nuclear radioactivity shielding materials.

HIGH-TECHNOLOGY MATERIALS

Since World War II many new materials have been introduced to develop high technology industries that are new such as nuclear power, space vehicles, rockets, supersonic aircraft, jet engines, electronics, petrochemicals, telecommunications, lasers, cryogenics, solar systems, microwaves, and xerography (see Figure 1.3).

Many of the metals on which those industries critically depend did not enter into commercial production until it became obvious that previously existing materials could not perform satisfactorily in extreme temperature, pressure, or corrosive environments. Large-scale use of titanium, for example, did not occur until the development of the aerospace industry. Similarly the use of zirconium is closely related to the development and mass production of nuclear reactors. For the same reason uranium became strategically important as a nuclear fuel, weapons material, and a source of plutonium (a manufactured element that does not occur in nature).

During the 1940s materials such as beryllium, cobalt, hafnium, selenium, silicon, and titanium went into production for the first time on a commercial basis. During the 1950s and 1960s technological advances demanded introduction on a commercial basis of such exotic new materials like bismuth, columbium, germanium, tantalum, tellurium, vanadium, and zirconium. The arms race of the cold war, the venturing of people into space and the development of satellites, and now the space race with man on the moon and interplanetary probes did much to fund and promote these developments.

Over 30 different metals besides the basic materials previously discussed can be identified with high-technology applications. In current research and development almost all the elements are being constantly evaluated either on their own or in combinations with other elements in search of cheaper or more effective substitutions. Because most of the high-technology products have more often than not specific military applications all the materials in this category automatically become strategic in nature. It is not by accident that most in fact can be found in the strategic stockpile maintained by the General Services Administration of the United States.

However, except in the case of gold, cobalt, magnesium, platinum metals, silver, titanium, tungsten, and uranium most of the high-technology metals are little known. This is so because relatively small quantities of these materials are used, and in most cases each represents only a fraction of a percent of the total value of all the minerals produced in the world. Similarly many of those very strategic materials are seldom visible in the international trade statistics. More often than not the exports and imports of these materials between producing and consuming countries are obscured under overall trade classifications such as "nonferrous metals" or "other minerals and ores."

Cobalt, for example, which is vital to the manufacture of jet turbine blades and high-performance magnetic alloys, was for many years readily available in world markets. It was not until repeated rebel invasions of the Shaba province in Zaire, which produces 60 percent of the world's cobalt, that end-users of the metal began seriously considering political and technological alternatives to further threats of shortages and price escalations.

Material	Aerospace	Aircraft	Catalyst	Cryogenics	Electronics	Fiber Optics	Gyroscopes	Instruments	Jet Engines	Magnetohydrodynamics	Microwaves	Nuclear Reactor	Optics	Rockets	Semiconductors	Solar Systems	Superalloys	Thermonuclear Fusion	Xerography
Beryllium	●	●				●		●				●							
Bismuth												●							
Cadmium		●											●						
Cobalt	●		●	●		●			●			●					●		
Columbium			●	●	●				●			●			●		●		
Cesium											●								
Europium					●														
Gallium					●														
Germanium					●			●					●						
Gold					●	●									●	●			
Hafnium						●				●									
Indium		●						●						●					
Iridium								●					●						
Lithium															●	●		●	
Magnesium	●	●																	
Niobium																	●		
Osmium																			
Palladium	●				●			●						●					
Platinum			●					●						●					
Rare earths			●			●									●				
Rhenium			●																
Rhodium																			
Ruthenium																			
Selenium																			●
Silicon													●		●				
Silver					●														
Tantalum	●				●							●							
Tellurium																		●	
Thorium												●							
Titanium	●	●															●		
Tungsten	●							●				●		●					
Uranium	●	●	●									●						●	
Yttrium			●		●							●				●			
Zirconium												●							
Vanadium																	●		

Figure 1.3   Major uses of high-technology materials.

DEFENSE INDUSTRIES AND MILITARY MATERIALS

Various metals and minerals used specifically for military applications such as ammunition, armor plate, explosives, gun barrels, missiles, nuclear weapons, rocket motors, satellites, small arms, and submarines are strategic in the fullest meaning of the word. Some like aluminum and copper are also basic materials to the economy, but others like barite, opium, or shellac have very precise use in the military establishment without corresponding application in the civilian economy. On the whole most materials critical to the military equipment and its supporting industrial complex are the same as materials required by high-technology industries (see Figure 1.4).

From the point of view of an industrial manager and an international politician it is important to realize which materials are critical to the military establishment. In times of crises or wartime emergencies those are the materials that will first come under government control, and shortages of such materials may develop rapidly.

At the same time selective price controls may be imposed on trade involving such materials, and supplies may be based on allocations or some other form of rationing to prevent hoarding and profiteering by private interests. This is particularly true in the case of those materials that must be imported from abroad as a result of limited or nonexistent domestic production because it is relatively easy to police the movement of such materials through government-controlled institutions such as customs and export controls. Chromium, cobalt, germanium, manganese, and natural rubber would be good examples of such critical materials.

THE MOST CRITICAL MATERIALS FOR THE UNITED STATES

For many decades until the 1950s the United States produced more raw materials than it consumed. This was true in the case of oil, of which the United States was a major exporter in the first half of this century, as well as in the case of other minerals. Although many minerals have also been imported in earlier decades, the low cost of foreign supplies was the main reason for that action.

Those conditions do not exist today anymore, and the United States has become a raw materials deficit nation. At present it is the largest producer in the world only of copper, molybdenum, and natural gas, among the major materials. It is the second largest world producer of coal and lead and the third largest producer of oil and zinc. On the other hand the United States continues to be the largest consumer of most raw materials and as such is increasingly being perceived by resource-rich Third World countries as a tar-

Figure 1.4 Major military uses of critical materials.

Material	Aircraft	Ammunition	Armor Plate	Cartridge Casings	Detonators	Drugs	Explosives	Fuels	Gun Barrels	Helicopters	Helmets	Jet Engines	Missiles	Night Vision	Nuclear Reactors	Nuclear Shielding	Photography	Rocket Motors	Satellites	Shipbuilding	Small Arms	Space Navigation	Stainless Steels	Submarines	Water Treatment	Thermonuclear
Aluminum	●		●										●					●								
Antimony		●																								
Asbestos																	●									
Barite		●			●																					
Beryllium	●								●			●	●		●							●				
Chromium		●	●						●				●										●			
Cobalt	●												●													
Columbium	●											●	●					●					●			
Copper		●		●																	●					
Germanium														●												
Gold																		●								
Hafnium															●											
Iodine													●			●										
Lead		●																								
Manganese																							●		●	
Molybdenum													●								●			●		
Nickel	●		●						●				●					●					●	●		
Opium						●																				
Petroleum								●																		
Potash							●	●																		
Quinine						●																				
Rubber	●																									
Shellac		●																								
Silver																	●									
Tantalum	●																	●								
Tellurium																										●
Thorium	●											●			●											
Titanium	●											●	●													
Tungsten	●												●					●					●			
Uranium							●								●				●					●		
Vanadium	●											●			●											
Zinc		●															●					●				
Zirconium															●			●								

get for exploitation of their unique supply positions in one or more raw materials.

To be sure the United States continues to produce most basic and critical materials, but in many instances domestic consumption far outstrips domestic production, and the country must increasingly rely on imports from foreign sources.

At the beginning of 1980 the United States imported 50 percent or more of its apparent demand of about 20 of the most important basic and critical materials. These include natural rubber, manganese, diamonds, cobalt, chromium, tantalum, titanium, platinum, palladium, rhodium, ruthenium, aluminum, tin, fluorspar, nickel, gold, germanium, indium, mercury, beryllium, zirconium, tungsten, zinc, and oil.

It it clear that most of those materials are critical to the high-technology industries and to the military establishment. But a high import dependence in itself is not the best measure of the real criticality of those materials. What matters also are the number of foreign suppliers and their political ideology and stability, availability of alternative sources, potential domestic reserves, substitutes, and stockpile position. On the other hand the magnitude of import dependence is becoming a more important factor every day as OPEC continues to escalate the price of oil and as stability in many Third World countries is being undermined by nationalistic aspirations of various revolutionary leaders often assisted in their "liberation" struggles by the countries of the socialist camp.

Considering several such factors the U.S. Army War College Strategic Studies Group applied a quantitative test to a number of non-oil minerals that appeared vulnerable to political and nonmarket forces from foreign suppliers. This strategic materials vulnerability study showed that the United States is particularly vulnerable to potential supply disruptions of chromium, platinum metals, tungsten, manganese, cobalt, aluminum, titanium, tantalum, nickel, mercury, and tin. Simultaneous disruptions of supplies of several of those, particularly of chromium, platinum, cobalt, and nickel, could create an extremely serious economic situation for the United States. Because of a unique concentration of supplies of chromium, platinum, and cobalt in southern Africa and the Soviet Union and negligible reserves of those same materials in the United States, western Europe, and Japan such a possibility should not be ruled out (Table 1.5).

GOLD, SILVER, AND PLATINUM METALS

Primarily known for its monetary and jewelry applications gold is also an essential industrial material. It is used in integrated circuits in electronics, for reliable connectors in computers, as shielding in spacecraft, and in brazing alloys for bonding turbine blades to rotors in aircraft jet engines.

Table 1.5   The Most Strategic Materials for the United States

Material	U.S. Army War College Vulnerability Index	Major Supplier Countries
Chromium	34	Soviet Union, South Africa
Platinum metals	32	Soviet Union, South Africa
Tungsten	27	Canada, Peru
Manganese	23	Brazil, Gabon
Aluminum	22	Jamaica, Canada
Titanium	20	Australia, Canada
Cobalt	20	Zaire, Canada
Tantalum	16	Zaire, Brazil, Canada
Nickel	14	Canada, Norway
Mercury	11	Canada, Mexico, Spain
Tin	6	Malaysia, Thailand

The use of gold in electronics is the most important industrial use of the metal and in the United States is estimated to account for 6 to 7 percent of fabricated gold. Over a dozen countries consume gold in their electronics industries, notably Japan, Korea, and the Netherlands. It is also believed that the most important industrial use of gold in the Soviet Union and other centrally planned economies is in the production of electronic devices.

The importance of gold in electronics stems from the fact that modern solid state electronics devices operate on very low currents and voltages. These devices require reliable connectors, contacts, switches, and components that will remain uncontaminated and clean throughout the life of these devices. This is particularly important in the production of printed circuit boards, connectors, terminal keyboard contacts, and miniaturized circuitry. As a result of escalating gold prices in recent years platinum, palladium, silver, and other metals have been partially substituted in some products, but sometime this is done at the risk of lower product performance and reliability.

Gold plays a strategic role in electronic equipment used for military applications. The U.S. Department of Defense operates a program to recover gold from military scrap, and other government agencies are free to participate or operate their own gold recovery programs.

Total industrial consumption of gold in 1977 in the United States amounted to 1.2 million troy ounces of which less than 1 million were considered to be critical applications. There is little threat of a shortage of gold for strategic use in a country like the United States because of the huge gold reserves held by the U.S. Department of the Treasury that in 1977 amounted to 278 million troy ounces. In addition several million ounces of gold are held in commercial and private bullion stocks.

Nearly half of all the gold that has been mined in the world is held in the form of reserves by governments of countries such as the United States, West Germany, Switzerland, France, Italy, the Netherlands, Japan, and the United Kingdom. The cumulative world production of gold at the end of 1977 was estimated at about 2.8 billion troy ounces. This can be visualized as a cube comparable in size to a five-story building 55 feet long and wide. Of this total South Africa supplied 40 percent and to this day remains by far the largest producer of gold in the world (see Figure 1.5).

Another way to understand the scarcity of gold on earth is to imagine that all the existing gold were distributed in equal amounts to the four billion people in the world. In such a case every person would receive only 0.7 ounces of gold worth about $500 at early 1980 gold prices—not enough to buy even a single Krugerrand.

South Africa produces about 60 percent of the global gold output from the operation of 40 large underground mines controlled by seven large corporations that work very closely with each other. The second largest gold-producing country is the Soviet Union whose output is estimated to be in the order of 17 to 20 percent of the world's total gold supply and is controlled by a state monopoly. Canada and the United States are the next two largest producers of gold, accounting for about 6 and 4 percent of global production, respectively. Other significant gold-producing countries include Australia, Zimbabwe, the Philippines, Ghana, Colombia, Mexico, Japan, India, Zaire, and Nicaragua (Table 1.6).

Estimated reserves of gold depend on the price of gold. As the price increases this automatically reclassifies certain gold resources into reserves that could be economically exploited at predominating prices and costs of pro-

Figure 1.5 Total amount of gold mined from the earth. At the beginning of 1980, the cumulative amount of gold ever mined in the world if stacked in one place would be no larger than a five-story building measuring 55 feet on each side.

Table 1.6   Major Gold-Producing Countries of the World and Their Estimated Gold Reserves and Resources

Country	Percentage of Global Reserves	Percentage of Global Resources	1978 Gold Production (troy ounces)
South Africa	48.0	52.0	22,900,000
Soviet Union	21.0	15.7	8,840,000
Canada	3.7	3.4	1,670,000
United States	9.0	12.6	970,000
Australia	3.0	2.9	660,000
Rhodesia	1.2	1.3	590,000
Philippines	1.5	1.3	590,000
Ghana	0.3	1.6	480,000
Colombia	na	na	280,000
Mexico	1.0	1.3	240,000
Japan	0.4	0.5	180,000
India	na	na	90,000
Zaire	na	na	80,000
Nicaragua	na	na	70,000

Source.   U.S. Handbook of Economic Statistics, ER 79–10274, August 1979; and U.S. Bureau of Mines, *Gold,* Mineral Commodity Profile, MCP-25, October 1978.

duction. On that basis South Africa contains about 50 percent of global gold reserves or resources, whichever way one looks at it. The Soviet Union remains as the country with the second largest gold reserves and resources in the world.

As a result South Africa is expected to remain the dominant factor in world gold production, although industry observers feel that South Africa's gold production will trend downward in the future. Similarly the Soviet Union is playing an increasingly important role as a gold-producing and supplier country. In recent years the Soviet Union has been benefiting from the sales of gold for hard currencies, increasing its proceeds from $725 million in 1975 to $2.67 billion in 1978.

Silver

The major use of silver is in photography, electronics, silverware, and jewelry, but photography is by far the most important single silver-consuming industry and accounts for about 35 percent of the total consumption of silver.

Because of its importance to photography and electronics silver is considered a strategic material, and the United States maintains a supply of silver in its strategic stockpile. On the other hand the United States is a major producer of silver often as a by-product of basic metals production such as copper, lead, and zinc. From that point of view there is little concern about any potential disruptions to the supply of silver.

This is not the case for the industrial countries of western Europe, most of which depend on imports of silver from foreign sources. Japan, with its rapidly expanding electronics and photography industries, is also a large consumer, although it has only minor silver reserves.

The Soviet Union is believed to have the largest silver reserves in the world, amounting to 26 percent of the total, followed by almost equal reserves of the United States that are estimated at 25 percent. Mexico, Canada, and Peru are countries with the next largest silver reserves, amounting to 14, 12, and 10 percent, respectively. With over 60 percent of the silver reserves located in the western hemisphere, mostly in North America, there is little threat that a strategic shortage could develop; this is so because the reserves appear to be sufficient to supply the needs of all NATO countries.

Platinum Metals

Platinum group metals consist of platinum, palladium, iridium, rhodium, ruthenium, and osmium, all of which exhibit outstanding anticorrosive characteristics and are extremely rare. Iridium is the most corrosion-resistant element known and is usually alloyed with platinum to make high-temperature tools.

Platinum metals are important in several of the high technology applications, particularly as catalysts in petroleum cracking and refining processes. Platinum is also used in catalytic converters to reduce pollution from automobile exhausts. Platinum metals are used as electrical contacts, cathode emitters, and in electronic devices, as well as in high-reliability aircraft spark plugs.

The Soviet Union has been the largest producer of platinum group metals for years and has been a major exporter, supplying between 20 to 25 percent of international exports of platinum. Soviet production accounts for over 51 percent of total global output, whereas South Africa produces another 43 percent of the world's output of platinum metals. Canada is the third producing country, but its production accounts for less than 6 percent of the world's total.

Platinum metals are among the most strategic materials imported by the United States, western Europe, and Japan because practically all the supplies must come from either the Soviet Union or South Africa. Platinum metals are used in only small quantities when compared with many other critical materials, but where their particular characteristics are critical there are no practical substitutions.

INDUSTRIAL DIAMONDS

Strategically important to industries that make tools for modern machines are industrial diamonds, which are particularly adaptable to automatic cutting and grinding processes. Such diamonds are used in many grinding wheels to shape and sharpen tungsten carbide cutting tools. Industrial diamonds are also used for turning, grinding, boring, and drilling hard metals, ceramics, and glass and for rock drilling bits. These in turn are quite indispensable in oil exploration.

Of strategic importance are also diamond dies that are required for drawing very fine wires of diameters smaller than 0.0008 inches. Such superfine wires are required for use in semiconductors, integrated circuit connectors, microammeters, timing devices, magnetic field coils, precision fuse elements, and ignition wire primers.

Industrial diamonds resources are concentrated in Zaire, which is estimated to contain 73 percent of all such resources in the world. South Africa and Botswana are each believed to have about 7 percent of the world's resources, and the Soviet Union and Ghana have 3.7 percent each.

Major producers of all types of diamonds measured by the number of karats per year include Zaire, the Soviet Union, South Africa, Botswana, and Namibia in that order. Other producers include Angola, Ghana, Sierra Leone, Lesotho, and Tanzania. Initial sales of over 50 percent of all the diamonds produced in the world every year are strictly controlled by De Beers and its consolidated companies. De Beers is considered to be a de facto cartel whose primary objective is to maintain a floor price on diamond output sales.

Synthetic diamond grit and powder are also produced in great quantities by General Electric and Du Pont companies in the United States and in other countries, including Ireland, Sweden, South Africa, Japan, and the Soviet Union. In recent years China also announced a capability to manufacture synthetic diamonds because it is not certain that natural diamonds are found in China in any significant quantities and it has been importing such diamonds from abroad.

However, synthetic manufacture of some diamonds requires the use of wonderstone, a raw material from South Africa that is used in the manufacture of synthetic diamonds in the United States.

Estimates of the Bureau of Mines suggest that world reserves of industrial stones are not sufficient to meet global demand by the year 2000 if current consumption trends continue. As a result it is expected that large-scale synthetic diamond production will increase both in the United States and abroad as the simplest and most cost-effective solution. Under such circumstances countries that control the supplies of wonderstone or other suitable raw materials required for the manufacture of synthetic diamonds will become important strategically to the consuming nations.

NUCLEAR MATERIALS

One of the most strategic and controversial raw materials in the world today is uranium, the nuclear fuels derived from uranium, and plutonium, a prime nuclear weapons material. Despite antinuclear sentiments, protests, and demonstrations a surprisingly large number of countries is constructing nuclear power plants to produce part of their energy requirements from the atom.

At least 55 countries of the world have a total of 775 nuclear reactors in operation, under construction, on order, or in planning stages to go into operation before 1985. In addition at least 18 countries are planning to operate their own uranium enrichment or plutonium separation plants. Governments and nuclear industries of many countries are committed to spending hundreds of billions of dollars to develop nuclear power.

One of the attractions of nuclear power plants and nuclear fuel–manufacturing capability is the political prestige suggestive of the potential for developing nuclear weapons. The very existence of a nonproliferation treaty only confirms this trend among governments big and small, and many political analysts are convinced that whereas nuclear weapons proliferation may be delayed by various political and economic measures it is unlikely that it can be halted unless the existing nuclear powers literally destroy their nuclear arsenals and nuclear weapons establishments. Needless to say such a development is not very likely to take place after the tremendous investments that have been made by several countries in nuclear weapons and nuclear power development.

At present China, France, India, the United Kingdom, the United States, and the Soviet Union are considered to have nuclear weapons capability by virtue of demonstrated ability to engineer nuclear explosions. Of those countries all except the United Kingdom possess some uranium resources within their own territories.

Standing in the wings of the nuclear stage are a group of Third World countries that are believed to be working toward the achievement of nuclear power status—often driven by political and energy incentives. Some of those countries are even believed to already possess the nuclear weapons capability or to be within grasp within a very short time. These include Argentina, Brazil, Egypt, Iran, Israel, South Korea, Pakistan, South Africa, Taiwan, and perhaps even Yugoslavia. Some African political and social scientists are also advocating nuclear power status for such key African countries as Nigeria and Zaire to give these important African states a voice in global politics to which Western powers will have to pay more attention.

There is yet a third group of countries that are industrialized and heavily dependent on imports of energy from abroad to whom nuclear power provides an immediate and important source of energy. These include Czechoslovakia, Japan, France, Germany, Italy, Spain, Sweden, and Switzerland. All could develop nuclear weapons without much trouble because each has an advanced scientific and technological establishment capable of that. So far all have chosen not to build their own nuclear weapons, but it is questionable how long this resolve will last if various Third World states become armed with nuclear weapons and start threatening vital interests of industrialized nations.

The two countries considered to already possess nuclear weapons are Israel and South Africa that are rumored to have been collaborating in nuclear research for some time. In September 1979 a large explosion was registered by intelligence satellites off the coast of South Africa, and it was speculated that this was a South African test of a nuclear weapon. In February 1980 the Western media suggested that Israel and South Africa collaborated for some time in a joint nuclear weapons program and indeed tested their first nuclear bomb off the coast of South Africa.

Whereas these suggestions have been categorically denied by both countries the fact remains that each has a nuclear program and capabilities to build nuclear weapons. The collaboration of the two countries makes a lot of sense geopolitically for both, because each must develop independent energy sources and a national security apparatus. Israel has the technology and wide access to Western know-how, and South Africa controls more than adequate uranium resources and large areas of land and sea regions suitable for remote testing of nuclear weapons.

Among the industrialized nations all except Germany also have some uranium resources in their territories that give them additional incentives to develop nuclear industries of their own.

As a result of these dual politicoeconomic incentives many countries that possess uranium resources feel that the time will come when they will play an important role in global politics. Aside from the major nuclear powers uranium is already being produced in Argentina, Brazil, Australia, Canada, Czechoslovakia, Gabon, Italy, Japan, Mexico, Namibia, Niger, Portugal, South Africa, Spain, and Sweden. In addition countries with uranium resources include the Central African Republic, Greenland (Denmark), Finland, India, Angola, Turkey, Yugoslavia, and Zaire. Uranium will undoubtedly be found in other regions as its price rises and the importance of its existence increases because it is quite widely distributed in the world.

At present the United States is the largest uranium producer in the world, with a capacity to produce about 35 percent of the global uranium output. The Soviet Union is believed to be the second largest uranium-producing country with its output estimated at 28 percent of the world's total, although no official statistics about Soviet uranium mining are known. Canada, South Africa, and France are the next three largest uranium-producing countries. Niger, Namibia, Australia, and Gabon are the next significant uranium-producing countries. The new uranium mine at Rossing in Namibia is believed to be the largest single uranium mine in the world, and this gives a special strategic significance to the emerging country of Namibia.

Since the OPEC oil embargo in 1973 uranium mining and prices as well as nuclear power development received a shot in the arm following a prolonged decline in nuclear power development targets and much political opposition. Interestingly the Soviet Union, threatened with a declining oil production during the 1980s, is promoting nuclear power within the Soviet bloc countries without political opposition. Although the Soviet Union and Czechoslovakia both produce uranium the extent of their resources is unknown, and the Soviet bloc may be trying to secure for itself future uranium supplies to keep its nuclear power programs on stream. Soviet-Cuban penetration into southern Africa regions such as Angola and Mozambique, with the possible Marxist takeover of neighboring Namibia would be one possible solution for future COMECON uranium supplies.

Thorium Resources

Among nuclear materials thorium is another possibility as a nuclear fuel for the future. Thorium could come into importance as a fuel for high-temperature nuclear reactors, although developments in this area are in prototype design stages. Nevertheless it is important to keep in mind those countries that at present are known to possess thorium resources. The major producer of thorium at present is Brazil, but thorium reserves have been discovered in Canada, Egypt, India, South Africa, Sri Lanka, Turkey, and the United States.

NONMETALLIC STRATEGIC MATERIALS

Nonmetallic minerals other than the energy minerals such as coal and oil account for only between 5 to 6 percent of the total value among the top 50 most valuable minerals produced in the world. The most important of those are salt, potash, diamonds, phosphates, asbestos, sulfur, kaolin, fluorspar, pyrite, talc, boron, limestone, barytes, mica, feldspar, nitrates, soda, graphite, and asphalt.

Diamonds, already discussed earlier in this chapter, are the best known as having specific strategic value, but fertilizer materials that include potash, phosphates, and nitrates are also of crucial importance in the production of fertilizers in countries concerned about increasing the productivity of their agriculture. Limestone and fluorspar are important to the steelmaking process; asbestos is vital in high-temperature thermal insulation, in shipbuilding, and for electrical insulation; talc finds uses in electronics, precision insulators, and ultrahigh frequency transmitters.

Not all the materials are strategically important, since some are available from many sources and there are many natural and synthetic substitutes. Perhaps the best assessment of the most strategically critical can be made by an analysis of the United States strategic stockpile that includes among nonmetallic materials asbestos, diamonds, fluorspar, graphite, iodine, mica, opium, sapphire, ruby, talc, and sulfur.

NATURAL RUBBER

Natural rubber is the traditional strategic material even though since World War II synthetic rubber has substituted for natural rubber in most applications. Nevertheless natural rubber continues to be very important in about 10 to 15 percent of all rubber applications because it has a lower heat buildup under stress, greater resistance to cracking, and better adhesive qualities than synthetic rubber. Because of these properties natural rubber is much better suited for airplane tires, truck tires, radial tires, and surgical gloves and adhesives. All these applications are important in military uses, but in addition escalating prices of oil, which is the raw material for making synthetic rubber, may soon eliminate the price advantage that synthetic rubber has over natural rubber.

Malaysia is the leading producer of natural rubber, accounting for about 45 percent of the world's total. Indonesia is the second largest producing country, with about 27 percent, and Thailand is third, with about 14 percent. India and Sri Lanka are also significant producers, with small amounts coming from West Africa and South America.

As a result all the industrialized countries depend totally on imports of natural rubber primarily from the southeast Asia region. Because of continued unrest in that area, even though supplies of natural rubber have been meeting world demand, the price has been going up. Another indication of this material's importance is the fact that the United States continues to maintain natural rubber in its strategic stockpile.

GRAINS AND FOOD AS STRATEGIC COMMODITIES

The most important agricultural commodities include wheat, corn, rice, soybeans, coffee, cotton, palm oil, sugar, tea, beef, and lumber. Fish and fishing rights may also play an important role in international relations and as a reciprocal concession between countries.

As a result of the grain trade embargo to the Soviet Union in 1980, imposed because of that country's invasion of Afghanistan, a lot of attention has been given to the use of grain as a weapon to achieve political objectives. These proposals stem from the fact that the Soviet Union, China, east Europe, the OPEC countries, and many Third World countries are all net importers of grain and food. It is believed by some political analysts that such grain and food embargos would influence the foreign policies of some of those countries.

Actually China and the Soviet Union are very large grain and food producers, comparable in total output levels of those of the United States. However, the loss of grain as a result of poor management of crops, lack of proper storage facilities, and less-intensive use of fertilizers and mechanization contribute to creating demand deficits despite relatively large production levels. Imports of grains by such countries, although they appear massive because of central buying, represent only a few percent of their total consumption and will probably decline in the future with improved harvesting techniques and higher productivity.

In addition supplies and demand for grains depend on the weather, a very unpredictable factor. Grains and foodstuffs are also highly perishable commodities by comparison with minerals that can be stored in the ground by simply not being mined.

REFERENCES

Behrmann, Neil, "Strategic Metals," *Barron's Weekly*, 5 February 1979.

Brooks, David B., and P. W. Andrews, "Mineral Resources, Economic Growth, and World Population," *Science*, 5 July 1974, Vol. 185, No. 4145, p. 13.

Central Intelligence Agency, "Nuclear Energy," Research Report E 77–10468, Washington, D.C., August 1977.

General Services Administration, "Strategic and Critical Materials: Descriptive Data," Washington, D.C., December 1973.

Hurlich, Abraham, "Planet Earth's Metal Resources," *Metal Progress*, October 1977, p. H1.

Kahn, Herman, William Brown, and Leon Martel, *The Next 200 Years*, William Morrow & Company, New York.

King, Michael, L. "Natural Rubber Price Rises Despite Boost in Output and Tire Industry Recession," *Wall Street Journal*, 13 February 1980, p. 38.

Library of Congress, Science Policy Research Division, *Materials Policy Handbook*, U.S. Government Printing Office, Washington, D.C., 1977.

Meadows, Donella H., and Dennis L. Meadows, *The Limits to Growth*, Potomac Associates, London, 1977.

National Foreign Assessment Center, "The World Oil Market in the Years Ahead," Special Report E 79–10327U, Washington, D.C., August 1979.

OECD Nuclear Energy Agency, "Uranium, Resources, Production, and Demand," Organization for Economic Cooperation and Development, Paris, August 1973.

Szuprowicz, Bohdan O., "Soviet Squeeze on Strategic Materials," *Datamation*, October 1978.

van Rensburg, W. C. J., and D. A. Pretorius, *South Africa's Strategic Minerals*, Valiant Publishers, Johannesburg, 1977.

Wu, Yuan-li, "Raw Materials Supply in a Multipolar World," Crane, Russak and Company, New York, 1973.

CHAPTER TWO

Why Shortages Will Occur in the Future

There is little question that the earth's crust and seawater contain an abundance of all the minerals that theoretically could be considered infinite, relative to mankind's present and future demand. The real question is not whether adequate resources of these minerals exist but how quickly the various sources of supply will become available. This is so because the relative abundance of a given material has very little relationship to its concentration in a deposit of its ores.

This raises two points that are crucial to the availability of materials. The first point has to do with the existence of known reserves, rather than total resources, that can be exploited with currently available technology at an economic price. The lead time to develop a new mine is several years, and the investment required is often in the hundreds of millions. The second point is even more important than the first. It has to do with the political control of the region in which such exploitable reserves exist or are believed to exist.

To understand the ramifications of these statements it is necessary to distinguish clearly between reserves and resources of a given mineral. *Reserves* are estimates of the amount of a mineral that can be economically and legally extracted from an identified body of known resources. *Resources* on the other hand are usually larger estimates of the total amount of a mineral whose extraction is only potentially feasible in the future.

Reserves of many minerals continue to increase as more exhaustive exploration takes place. But the fact remains that because of the perversity of nature a high proportion of the most important minerals reserves in the world are concentrated in relatively few areas. This creates the framework where realization of these facts is conducive to the use of political power to gain control of these areas.

An analysis of the countries which are the leading producers of the most important minerals of the world shows that a little over 20 political entities control the bulk of the production of over 30 of the most critical materials required by modern economies. Among those countries the Soviet Union, the United States, Canada, and Australia are significant producers of minerals among the industrialized states, whereas most of the others are developing countries. This applies to South Africa as well that is really a developing country when rated by standard per capita yardsticks.

As these countries become more aware of their important or sometimes dominant supply position they demand a redistribution of wealth and initiate steps to better themselves by raising mineral export taxes, duties, and prices and engaging in industrial development programs often designed to process their minerals locally to add value to their products and obtain even higher prices in export markets (see Table 2.1).

It is quite true also that reserves of many of the most important materials exist and are even being exploited in many other countries of the world. But the percentage of these other reserves relative to world demand for those materials is rather small.

To put it in perspective it is worth keeping in mind that among the most important minerals produced in the world 50 to 90 percent of each comes from the first three largest producing countries. This range narrows to about 60 to 95 percent if the first five largest producing countries are taken into account. This is another way of looking at the concentration of minerals production capabilities among just a few countries.

This concentration of important minerals production is similarly paralleled by the existence of minerals resources since it is obvious that the largest producing areas are located in regions where the resources were originally discovered. What this means is that the opening up of very large new mineral mining areas is more often than not going to take place in the same countries that are the leading minerals producers today. This fact creates only additional incentives for politicians and nationalists to devise means to obtain exclusive control of deposits and processing plants within their countries and to try to obtain the best return on the sales of their minerals because many of the producing countries of the Third World have practically no markets at all for these resources within their own territories.

Thus the uneven concentration of resources in a relatively few countries, along with sharp differences in ideology, living standards, income levels, and forms of governments, creates a fertile ground for international instability. This in turn must lead to increasing and often planned disruptions in minerals availability designed to achieve political and economic objectives without regard to normal laws of supply and demand.

THE OPEC IDEA

Because it has been aimed at oil, which represents over 70 percent of the value of all the minerals produced in the world, the OPEC cartel has be-

Table 2.1 Largest Producers of the Most Important Minerals in the World

Country	Largest Producer in the World of	Second Largest Producer of	Third Largest Producer of
Soviet Union	Oil Iron ore Manganese Chromite Nickel Tungsten Platinum Titanium Magnesium Lead Zinc Cadmium Beryllium	Natural gas Lignite Copper Cobalt Gold Tin Diamonds Asbestos	Coal Bauxite Molybdenum Mercury Uranium
South Africa	Gold Uranium Vanadium	Manganese Chromite Platinum	Diamonds Asbestos
United States	Natural gas Copper Molybdenum	Coal Lead Uranium	Oil Zinc
Canada	Silver Asbestos	Nickel Molybdenum Zinc	Gold Platinum
Australia	Bauxite		Nickel Lead Cobalt
Zaire	Cobalt Diamonds Tantalum		
China	Coal	Iron ore Tungsten	
Malaysia	Tin Rubber		
Bolivia	Antimony		
East Germany	Lignite		
West Germany	Germanium		
Saudi Arabia		Oil	
Brazil		Manganese	Iron ore
Indonesia		Rubber	
Norway		Magnesium	
Chile			Copper Molybdenum

Table 2.1   (Continued)

Country	Largest Producer in the World of	Second Largest Producer of	Third Largest Producer of
Albania			Chromite
Thailand			Tungsten
			Tin
			Rubber
Guinea			Bauxite
Gabon			Manganese

Source.   Developed in 1980 by 21st Century Research from basic production data published by the National Foreign Assessment Center and the U.S. Bureau of Mines in several documents during the last few years.

come one of the most important political and economic forces in the world. It is probably going to be a major force in global politics for the rest of this century, and although it will reshape old alliances and political groupings it is also putting a lot of ideas into the heads of politicians and nationalists struggling for power in most of the countries of the Third World.

The inescapable fact is that OPEC countries—which contain about 320 million people, comprising about 8 percent of some of the world's most impoverished, illiterate, and backward populations—have been able to dictate oil production and price levels to the most powerful and wealthiest nations of the world for the last seven years (see Table 2.2).

The OPEC cartel has been so successful that some industry executives are now resigned in the realization that it may continue for the rest of this century unless a major conflict radically alters the map of the world. Step by step the OPEC countries were able to obtain ownership of the oil fields, control of pricing and oil production levels from the largest and most powerful corporations in the world, including Exxon, Mobil, Texaco, Gulf, Socal, British Petroleum, and Royal Dutch/Shell. Now the OPEC countries are beginning to direct their attention to the task of securing control of the refining and marketing of oil that is the last vestige of power left with the international oil companies. All this was achieved with the complete approval and participation of the respective governments of all those countries.

The success of the OPEC cartel has been more than duly noted by the other Third World countries for two reasons. One was an immediate and painful effect on the trade balance of developing countries that must import oil to meet their energy needs. There seems to be some belief that this has put those countries in the camp of the irate industrialized nations of the west by virtue of having to suffer a common humiliation and price escalations. This need not necessarily be true, because many of those countries may regard themselves as on their way to undertake a similar type of action

Table 2.2   The OPEC Cartel Countries

OPEC Country	Oil Output (millions of barrels per day)	Population (millions)	Major Ethnic Group	Literacy Rate (percentage)
Saudi Arabia	9.77	7.8	Arab	15
Iraq	3.31	12.2	Arab	20 to 40
Iran[a]	3.18	35.5	Persian	37
Venezuela	2.47	13.1	Latin	74
Kuwait	2.27	1.1	Arab	40
Nigeria	2.15	80.0	African	25
Libya	2.13	2.8	Arab	35
United Arab Emirates	1.85	0.8	Arab	25
Indonesia	1.61	140.0	Asian	60
Algeria	1.04	18.4	Arab	25
Qatar	0.53	0.18	Arab	25
Ecuador	0.22	7.8	Latin	57
Gabon	0.20	0.5	African	below 80

Source.   International Energy Statistical Review, February 1980; and National Basic Intelligence Factbook, GC BIF 79–002, July 1979.
[a] Before the formation of the Revolutionary Islamic Republic in 1979 Iran was the second largest OPEC oil-producing country, with an oil output over 5.00 million barrels per day.

against those who control whatever resources are being mined in their territories. To them although painful in the pocketbook the OPEC cartel is also an inspiration and proof positive that superior know-how, technology, and military power must make way to a clever and bold raw materials supply control action.

The second reason is that some of those countries are significant producers of one or more important non-oil minerals that are indeed the lifeblood of modern industries. In parallel with oil most industrialized nations of western Europe and Japan must import their raw materials from Third World countries. Now the United States is also becoming increasingly dependent, but it must be remembered that the OPEC cartel did not really start any significant action until the United States developed a fairly substantial foreign oil import dependence in the early 1970s. Because the import dependence of the United States continues to grow and that of other NATO countries is already very high the stage is clearly set for the formation of other non-oil or even oil and minerals cartels and international marketing organizations.

Whereas OPEC controls about 52 percent of the world's oil production it probably would not have found it so easy to impose its will on the Western world if it were not for the existence of another oil cartel that controlled at least 26 percent of the global oil production and large areas of potential energy resources. The Soviet Union is in fact the largest single oil producer in the world and controls its production through a state oil monopoly. Between OPEC and the Soviet Union almost 80 percent of oil produced in the world is outside the control of normal market forces.

It could be argued that if the Soviet Union were not a closed centrally planned economy considerable capital would have found its way there, resulting in larger and more efficient oil and natural gas production than has been achieved by the Soviet Union so far. This would have also provided another large exporter of oil to the world at large, larger than what the Soviet Union is capable of exporting at its present production levels. The decline in Soviet oil production that is now being predicted for the 1980s may have been prevented by more advanced Western oil technology and additional capital. This decline if it occurs will also affect the power of the OPEC countries, since it will create an even larger demand for their products and will allow them to escalate their prices even further.

NON-OIL MINERALS PRODUCERS CARTELS

Minerals other than oil are also subject to producers cartels or quasi-cartels, some of which have been in operation for many years, but none achieved the success of OPEC. By comparison with oil all other minerals present a rather paradoxical situation to the importing countries. On the one hand availability of such raw materials as chromium, cobalt, tungsten, or uranium is highly critical to numerous industries. On the other hand even though those materials are essential their import volumes and values are relatively small and almost negligible when compared with oil. As a result politicians and economists tend to ignore and neglect the issues, particularly when they are being assured by various experts that alternative sources and substitutes will sooner or later defeat any attempts to cartelize non-oil minerals supplies.

There is widespread belief among industry observers that the threat of cartels in other minerals is considerably less and shorter term than the OPEC oil cartel. Large global resources, technological progress, substitution, and recycling are important limitations on the extent of cartelization that is possible. Economic analysis will show a price ceiling on most non-oil minerals beyond which escalation is not possible without end-users actually abandoning the use of some materials. It is therefore argued that most cartels are doomed to failure because their major objective is to continue sales of minerals at inflated prices. Nevertheless even short-lived cartels can cause severe shortages and put an unwary manager out of business.

But this is only one way of looking at the cartel potential from a purely rational and economic point of view, ignoring its political leverages. Most studies of cartels concentrate on a single commodity such as copper or aluminum and consider the impact of a specific cartel on a particular country such as the United States, which, as countries go, is still relatively well endowed with many natural resources and raw materials.

Even so some observers point out that if a cartel came into being with the control of several strategic materials such as chromium, platinum, nickel, and cobalt simultaneously such collusion would have extremely serious effects on the economy of the United States. The chances of such a multimineral cartel are of course considerably smaller than those for the formation of a cartel in a single commodity. Nevertheless some potential exists, particularly among southern African countries that are predominant producers of those and other immensely strategic materials.

There is another factor in cartelization that is often overlooked by many analysts who take the strictly business approach. It has to do with the "resources overhang" of a particular country or region. For example, the chromium resources of Zimbabwe and South Africa are so immense relative to the rest of the world that it is extremely risky for anyone to invest in developing other less economic sources even when the prices escalate. Under such circumstances there always remains a threat of a sudden planned price reduction to prevent the profitability of alternative sources long enough to discourage any investment. Only government-supported projects could withstand such politicoeconomic leverage on a longer-term basis.

Cartels are actually a fact of life in international business and have existed for years in raw materials as well as in manufactured commodities and products. A 1974 study by the Organization for Economic Cooperation and Development on restrictive business practices identified several hundred export cartels in Germany, Japan, the Netherlands, Spain, the United Kingdom, and the United States. These cartels take the form of National Export Cartels, grouping manufacturers of a particular product in a country, and International Export Cartels, which are arrangements between producers of the same commodities or products in several countries.

Although antitrust legislation prohibits cartels in the United States this legislation has no effect outside this country nor has it any power over foreign corporations that do not enter into cartel activity on the territory of the United States. In any case most governments are quite eager to assist their industries to gain an advantage in export trade by whatever means are available to them. In Germany a Federal Cartel Office exists to formally register German export cartels. Japanese government support given to various industries vis-à-vis foreign competition in the form of joint research and development or restrictive import practices is also well known.

In the communist world the ministries of foreign trade in each country consist basically of several import-export cartels operated by the state that control 100 percent of their countries' domestic markets and often put pressure on outside firms doing business with them by demanding reciprocal purchases of goods that the countries themselves have not been able to sell in the world's markets.

International non-oil producers cartels or cartel potential exists in several commodities. These include bauxite (aluminum), copper, tin, iron ore, gold, diamonds, zinc, uranium, chromium, mercury, lead, cobalt, tungsten, nickel, antimony, and phosphates. In addition any metal or mineral produced as a by-product would automatically be affected by any cartel action in any of these commodities.

Intergovernmental Council of Copper Exporting Countries (CIPEC)

The Intergovernmental Council of Copper Exporting Countries (CIPEC) is one of the best examples of a cartel-like organization in non-oil minerals. It came into being in 1967 and was organized by Chile, Peru, Zambia, and Zaire—the major copper-producing countries in the Third World. In 1974 CIPEC took its first price control action by announcing cuts in copper production of up to 15 percent among its member producing countries. Also between 1967 and 1974 the governments of Chile, Zambia, and Peru either nationalized or obtained controlling interests in copper mines from their foreign owners and operators. Since 1974 Indonesia, Australia, New Guinea, Mauretania, and Yugoslavia became new members or associate members of the organization that claims control over 38 percent of world's mine copper output and 72 percent of the export trade in copper mine and smelter products. The CIPEC organization is not regarded as a successful cartel organization so far, because copper price instabilities continue and production in developed countries remains quite significant relative to CIPEC's share of copper output.

Copper production is also important as a source of significant quantities of by-products such as gold, silver, molybdenum, nickel, platinum, selenium, tellurium, palladium, and rhenium. The Zaire copper mines, which are among the largest in the world, are also a major producer of cobalt. The 1977 and 1978 rebel invasions of those regions from Angola disrupted the production of copper, thereby assisting CIPEC to tighten the copper markets. But more important these disruptions had a much more severe effect on the supplies of cobalt, resulting in a very short supply of the mineral that still exists. Any further disruptions of Zaire cobalt sources would further aggravate the cobalt supply situation in the free world.

International Bauxite Association (IBA)

In aluminum there exists the International Bauxite Association (IBA) whose member countries include Australia, the Dominican Republic, Ghana, Guyana, Guinea, Haiti, Jamaica, Sierra Leone, Surinam, and Yugoslavia. Over 65 percent of the world's bauxite is produced by those countries that also account for 80 percent of the world's trade in bauxite and alumina. During past aluminum shortages, suppliers of the refined metal resorted to allocation, thereby indicating the seriousness of the situation and the power of a cartel if it came into full bloom in this commodity. Because the use of aluminum is growing relatively fast there is concern that IBA may develop into a global cartel, but there is also a limit to which bauxite prices can go up. The reason for the limitation is that an aluminum-from-clay extraction process has been developed that could eventually make even large aluminum consumers like the United States almost completely self-sufficient.

International Tin Council (ITC)

In the case of tin major producing countries, including Malaysia, Thailand, Burma, and Bolivia as members of the International Tin Council (ITC), have entered into a series of five-year agreements with the consuming nations with the objective of stabilizing tin supplies and preventing wide price fluctuations. The ITC establishes a floor and ceiling price for tin and enforces it by applying export controls on producing countries and by maintaining a "buffer stock." The organization is only partially successful because although it has been able to maintain the floor prices during demand periods, tin prices have risen above the established ceilings and producers increased exports beyond limits to take advantage of higher prices and market demand.

The Uranium Cartel

Another international cartel case in a strategic mineral surfaced in 1976 when 29 uranium-producing companies were accused of price fixing after uranium oxide prices escalated from $6 a pound to about $40 during the preceding two years. The uranium cartel came into being in 1972 and included leading producers in Australia, Canada, South Africa, Britain, and France. One reason advanced for the cartel's formation was the 1964 ban by the United States on imported uranium for enrichment as fuels for domestic nuclear reactors.

The Special Case of Gold

In the case of gold nearly 60 percent of global output is controlled by several large corporations with interlocking directorships and mutual shareholdings that constitute an effective producers cartel. Much of the world's newly mined gold, including that from the Soviet Union, is sold through Swiss banks in Zurich, whereas its price is traditionally "fixed" by five major bullion dealers in London. Between 1968 and 1973 an International Gold Pool maintained a two-tier price system for gold that has been discontinued. Because of its unique monetary role it is difficult to talk of a gold cartel, particularly when nearly half of all the gold ever mined in the world remains locked up in government vaults of major industrialized countries. What must be kept in mind, however, is the continuing instability in South Africa that could eventually lead to a takeover of that country by Marxist forces. The fate of new gold and world gold markets would then come under a completely different set of rules, resulting in extremely serious consequences for many countries.

Other Potential Cartels

Some analysts believe that quasi-cartels, or as they are sometimes called "commodity associations," will continue to form in other raw materials more often than not with the encouragement and even participation of various governments. There is a good potential for cartels in iron ore, chromium, and tungsten, although groups in mercury, and lead have also been reported to exist. When cobalt was in short supply after the 1978 invasion of Zaire there were reports that a cobalt cartel was in the making. In 1978 even zinc producers were believed to have been eyeing the prospects of forming a cartel, and soon after the OPEC quadrupled its oil prices in 1973 Morocco led a short-lived cartel action as a leading exporter of phosphates that are a critical ingredient in the production of fertilizers.

Third World politicians and diplomats will often argue that such cartels or commodity associations are necessary political devices and learning processes for many developing countries, and they predict that more of them will come into being in the future. These views are based on more fundamental beliefs that natural resources belong only to the people of the countries in which they occur and cannot be owned by foreign entities at any price. This does not in itself preclude foreign investment and know-how inputs, but because of these basic tenets such investments must be assessed relative to other opportunities available to the owners of the capital who are always looking for more secure areas, some of which may turn out to be in the developed countries.

STATE MONOPOLIES

In all communist countries and many Third World countries control over the production of raw materials and the export of such lies with a single ministry or state-owned corporation. This is particularly true in the case of oil production and distribution as, for example, the Petroleos de Mexico organization in Mexico and similar state-run firms in most countries outside the free market economies of the industrialized world.

In the case of non-oil minerals there is more often than not a ministry that supervises the operation of one or more companies engaged in the production, mining, processing, and distribution of specific materials.

In many cases some small countries produce and export only a single mineral that provides a major contribution to the balance of trade and the national income. Production of bauxite in Jamaica would be a good case in point. In such instances government control of such an industry seems justified because it impacts a large proportion of labor in a city or the country. Severe fluctuations in employment as a result of unstable markets for many raw materials could pose serious problems for such a government if it did not have some control over the industry. It may be a case of foreign markets ruling the governments of those countries or local governments protecting themselves by reacting to foreign markets. Political control in those countries provides the means to influence the raw materials supplies of other countries.

The Soviet Union is the best example of state monopolies and has the most advanced administrative structure for all mining industries because it produces practically all the minerals required by a modern economy. As such it has a model organization for any other state monopoly and freely offers assistance to developing countries in organizing their minerals industries. There is little question that such restructuring usually takes place along state monopoly lines.

The Soviet state monopolies consist of ministries of ferrous and nonferrous metallurgy that are responsible for the exploration, mining, and production of all non-oil minerals. This is accomplished by specialized administrations and industrial associations of producing units throughout the country. Foreign trade in these minerals is accomplished by corresponding foreign trade organizations specializing in one or more minerals that are supervised directly by a separate ministry of foreign trade.

Between the centralized Soviet state monopoly and a private Western firm operating in various parts of the world there is a wide range of organizations with various degrees of government participation. What is important for the Western end-user of raw materials to remember is that state monopolies or state-owned producers and suppliers perform an important function in their respective governments, namely, that of earning foreign currency and often contribute significantly to the national incomes. As such state monopolies are very sensitive to any political developments in those countries.

As a result the interests of state monopolies are primarily centered on maximizing their revenues in the short run and not necessarily on providing end-users in foreign industries with an orderly and assured supply of their critical materials. The profitability of an Ohio manufacturer of equipment using critical materials from abroad is of no interest whatsoever to the producers of such materials. In cases of national emergency or when additional revenues must be raised raw materials producing monopolies are the first to be required to find ways of increasing their incomes to shore up the economy or a government through taxation and special export duties.

In many of the relatively poor Third World countries it is useless to think of increasing revenues by increasing taxation of the population. The reason for this is because the people simply would not have the wealth to contribute in such a program. On the other hand any action directed against the richer industrialized consumers in foreign countries is politically very acceptable and may be the only alternative to extract additional revenues. To a shaky government that wants to cling to power a state monopoly is a handy instrument to implement such a policy.

NEW INTERNATIONAL ECONOMIC ORDER (NIEO)

This concept emerged in the form of a declaration adopted by the United Nations General Assembly in 1974. It specifies certain principles on which a new economic order should be founded to eliminate the widening gap between developing and developed countries. This is not just a program for redistributing the wealth of the world. It also seeks the power to determine the rules that will govern the movement of goods, services, technology, and capital across international boundaries.

The program of action focuses, among other considerations, on sovereignty over natural resources, raw materials, technology transfer, industrialization, and multinational corporations as areas for immediate "remedial" action. This declaration or NIEO has become a shorthand label to denote the demands of developing countries. During 1980 a special session of the United Nations General Assembly assessed the progress in the implementation of these programs.

The North-South Dialogue, a synonym for the Conference on International Economic Cooperation, was held between 1975 and 1977 and was one result of these new concepts. The four commissions of this conference dealing with energy, raw materials, development, and finance underscore the major thrusts of this action.

Interestingly the Soviet bloc countries keep their distance from the North-South Dialogue, claiming that the economic imbalance between the free market industrialized countries and the developing countries of the Third World is a direct result of the former colonial relationship for which the communist countries take no responsibility. This position, however, does not prevent the Soviet bloc from voting with the Third World countries against the Western world on issues of the North-South Dialogue. When Henry Kissinger as Secretary of State proposed an international resources bank designed to encourage raw materials production in developing countries through private investment the proposal was defeated. Third World countries prefer to promote proposals that will allow state control of all investments and operations that touch on raw materials. Such attitudes and voting blocs lead to deepening discords between industrialized nations and developing countries and confrontations between the East and West.

More specific proposals to deal with the problem of international commodities were put forward at the United Nations Conference on Trade and Development (UNCTAD) IV meeting in Nairobi in 1976 and are better known as the Integrated Program for Commodities. Five basic steps in this program propose the establishment of a series of international commodity agreements and buffer stocks, a common fund to finance those buffer stocks, compensatory financing to cover shortfall in export earnings, long-range international commitments to buy commodities at agreed prices, and increased processing of raw materials in producing countries.

Developed countries agreed to discuss the buffer stocks and the common fund portions of this program, but several meetings since then have ended in discord, with the industrialized countries being accused for the failure to reach agreement.

The International Commodity Agreement is a proposal to include consumer and producer countries for the purpose of stabilizing prices or supply not unlike the concepts of the ITC, but this agreement would cover many mineral and agricultural commodities. The common fund idea calls for initial $6 billion in financing to be advanced by industrialized countries for buffer stocks. Later proposals for overall industrial development in Third World countries have been asking for a global fund of $300 billion by the year 2000 to be provided by the rich countries for the benefit of developing nations. The objectives are to assist the developing countries to increase their share in the world's industrial output from 7 percent at present to 25 percent by the year 2000. The problem is that unless world industries continue to grow at a healthy pace such an increase in the developing world can only occur at the loss of industrial outputs in the Western world.

Sets of rules for doing business with developing countries that are currently being discussed by the UNCTAD conference brings forth another set of proposals that are certain to create further discords. It is not clear whether state-run multinationals will be considered the same way as privately owned companies that invest in the Third World. The Soviet Union, for one, stubbornly refuses to consider its state monopolies on the same footing as Western multinationals operating in Third World countries.

Developing country governments are also insisting that their domestic enterprises should get preferential treatment vis-à-vis foreign subsidiaries. They also want to have the option of forming international cartels while excluding cartel activities by foreign multinationals. What it all means is that greater international regulation is coming into play, resulting in second thoughts by many corporations about investing in countries with such mounting restrictions or hostile sentiments. A lower level of investment is another contributing factor to future shortages and supply disruptions from some countries.

These United Nations proposals legitimize in the eyes of many Third World country leaders any action that will bring their countries closer to gaining full control of their raw materials production, processing, and marketing. By the same token any bilateral business arrangements made in this climate that may be entered into by a single country with a foreign corporation is open to attack by other Third World countries and could lead to unrest and the deposition of a leader who condoned such a move even if it were a good business proposition to both parties concerned.

This United Nations framework is little understood by corporate end-users who pursue traditional business arrangements in the Third World unaware of these new developments. Nor is the appointment of black Americans, namely, Andrew Young and Donald McHenry, as ambassadors to the United Nations particularly helpful to the business world as the Carter Administration would like us to believe. Third World leaders are aware that black Americans do not represent the views or interests of corporate America. They are apt to dismiss such appointments as political cosmetics designed to secure black votes in America, since they do not believe such people have any real authority to speak for the business and investment community that will have to make the hard decisions in the end. All those developments within the United Nations forum are eagerly observed and exploited throughout the Third World even though they do not carry any force of law. As a result the movements to obtain control of corporations and enterprises operating in various countries are growing in force, and the United Nations proposals provide a rallying point and objectives against which leaders and revolutionaries in the Third World are measuring each other.

TERRORISM AND SABOTAGE

International terrorism has been escalating during the 1970s, and there are many indications that this trend may continue for the rest of the century. Terrorism is usually directed against human beings and what they represent, with the objective of gaining worldwide publicity. Of the total of over 3000 terrorist incidents during the 1968–1978 decade 1130 occurred in western Europe, but North Americans were by far the most numerous victims, accounting for over 42 percent of all victims in all such terrorist attacks. Western Europeans were the second most common targets of terrorists, accounting for about 32 percent of all the victims (see Figure 2.1).

Terrorism may take the form of kidnaping, taking of hostages, letter bombing, arson, explosive bombing, armed attack, hijacking, assassination, thefts and break-ins, sniping attack, occupation of facilities, and sabotage. Terrorist activity is an indication of tension or forthcoming change in a coun-

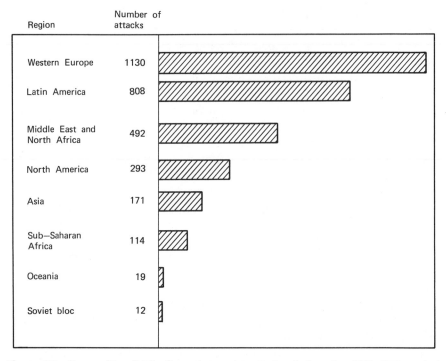

Figure 2.1 **Geographic distribution of terrorist attacks during the 1968–1978 period.**
Source. **National Foreign Assessment Center, Washington D.C., March 1979.**

try or a region, and one of the effects of terrorist activity is the reluctance of foreign corporations to invest or continue operations in a country where such conditions exist.

Sabotage includes the destruction of machinery, offices, plants, and mines and of such transportation facilities as bridges, tunnels, and railroads, among others. It can directly affect the supply of raw materials for short periods if it is directed at the production or transportation facilities. Sabotage occurs also during labor strikes, civil unrest, revolutions, and wars and may in connection with such events cripple even large operations for long periods of time.

Terrorist groups are getting larger, better organized, and sometimes have tacit approval of the governments of countries in which they operate. This is clearly demonstrated by the attack on the American embassy in Teheran by a group of 400 militants and by the rebels who repeatedly attacked Kolwezi copper mining regions in Zaire from their bases in Angola in 1977 and 1978. The attack on the Islamic shrine of Mecca in Saudi Arabia in late 1979 is another example of a relatively large group in operation. It is likely that this form of terrorism will increase with the collaboration of governments because it clearly produces results.

More than half of all the terrorist attacks occurred in the industrialized countries of western Europe and North America during the 1968–1978 decade, although Latin America and the Middle East were second and third in the numbers of attacks after western Europe. However, war and rebellion, with associated terrorism, sabotage, and all other disruptions in normalcy, have been going on in many parts of the Third World during the same time.

Much of the unrest and revolutionary atmosphere derives from the process of decolonization, the emergence of nearly 100 new nations in the last 25 years, and public demands for new economic order as voiced in the forum of the United Nations. Nationalism, coupled with religious and cultural forces, is given priority in those areas over rational business-oriented posture advocated and practiced by the industrialized countries of the West.

THIRD WORLD INDUSTRIALIZATION

This is a very important objective to many Third World countries but particularly to those with large underemployed populations. This is true in the case of Argentina, Brazil, Mexico, Nigeria, Egypt, Zaire, South Africa, Iran, Pakistan, Indonesia, India, and China. One of the most obvious ways to create employment in those countries is to process the raw materials locally and sell refined products for higher prices.

It is logical to expect that countries with dominant positions in one or more raw materials will continue to demand development of local industries either with the assistance of the end-users of their raw materials or, if such assistance is not forthcoming, with other state monopolies or organizations, including those from the communist countries that may be willing to accept the conditions of cooperation and that are driven more by political rather than economic motives.

However, the debacle of Iran, which was rich as a result of its oil exports, showed that industrialization and modernization pose additional problems to the balance of backward and primitive societies in the process of development. The revolution in Iran and its aftermath are also a warning to Western nations that economic solutions however reasonable they may appear to the Western mind cannot assure future political stability nor can they assure the certainty of raw materials supplies from Third World countries.

GOVERNMENT REGULATION

In developed economies government regulation inescapably restricts development of even known resources for reasons of limitation of space, environmental pollution, and health and safety hazards. In Third World countries governments use all the means at their disposal to maximize the revenues from the exports of raw materials they cannot possibly consume in their own countries. These may take the form of taxes, duties, export licenses, tariffs, and trade quotas or allocations, depending on the needs of the moment.

All those regulations have the effect of delaying the availability of raw materials from more profitable sources, increasing prices, and in some instances may even cause shortages or discontinuance of operations, where excessive taxation and restrictions make the production unprofitable. End-users have very little knowledge of these particular regulations, but their supplies are nevertheless directly affected by them.

An interesting case in point is the disappearance of the ferrochrome industry from the United States even though chromite is one of the most strategic raw materials. As a result of import duties imposed on raw materials imports it became unprofitable for U.S. processors to import chromite. Instead ferrochrome facilities came into being in South Africa, and imports now are in the form of that semiprocessed manufacture, whereby it escapes the duties on chromite. On the other hand foreign countries benefit from obtaining technology and industry and can demand and get increased value for their exports.

EMBARGOES AND MILITARY ACTION

These events are the signs of war and are common among Third World countries. The main problem is their unpredictability. This is so because good advance intelligence could save many businesspeople a lot of money and frustration. For example, the 1956 Arab-Israeli war closed the Suez Canal for almost 20 years and created a serious disruption in the transportation of oil from the Persian Gulf to the consuming nations.

Perhaps even more important to business was the closure of the pipelines from Saudi Arabia and Iraq through Jordan, Israel, and Syria to the Mediterranean ports. The confrontation between Israel and the Arab states has taken a tremendous toll in the cost of additional shipping and port facilities without substantially increasing the security of the oil sources as events in Iran and Afghanistan have clearly demonstrated.

Wars and revolutions have been under way in recent years in a few countries, particularly in the Third World. These include the Western Sahara, Chad, the Central African Empire, Eritrea, Ethiopia, the Yemens, Uganda, Angola, Mozambique, Namibia, Zimbabwe, Thailand, Cambodia, Vietnam, and the Philippines. Now Iran and Afghanistan are also included in this list. Many political analysts are wondering which country will be next. This concern is also borne out by the fact that the Third World countries have been increasingly spending badly needed developmental capital on military equipment and the buildup of their armed forces. Some may condition the availability of raw materials on the willingness of end-user countries to provide military assistance and technology.

RESOURCES WAR POLICIES

The Third World has become a "development battleground" in the much more basic conflict between the East and West. Those who are naive enough to believe that with the advent of détente the Soviet bloc has relinquished its goal of global socialism think that education, foreign aid, and modernization will lead to the democratization of the Third World and establishment of business-oriented economies steered into the modern era by reasonably new and enlightened leaders. The theory of convergence remains alive even as the hopes and expectations of one country after another are shattered with the wars and revolutionary changes that afflict so much of the Third World today.

Third World countries are caught in the middle of this East-West struggle and are encouraged by the Soviet bloc to "liberate" themselves still further from capitalist and racist oppression and exploitation. Raw materials are the major, and often the only, means available to those countries to engage in this conflict by exerting pressure on the end-users of raw materials who depend on them.

It is probably safe to say that as the demands and proposals of the NIEO are further promoted and popularized this conflict will escalate even further, creating more raw materials shortages, supply disruptions, and loss of capital and influence.

Within the East-West struggle context the Soviet bloc countries have several advantages over the capitalist nations. The most important of these is the fact that the Soviet Union is almost self-sufficient in most raw materials. As a result the industries of the Soviet Union and eastern Europe are unaffected by raw materials shortages to any significant degree, whereas the West has to react constantly to the effects of wars, revolutions, or boycotts in Third World countries.

In addition because of their political stance the Soviet bloc is willing to supply all Third World countries with military equipment and assistance in the name of helping liberation movements. In comparison the United States and some Western powers refused to sell arms to African or Latin American countries, but they are really in a no-win situation no matter what decisions are made. If the West provides military aid to Third World countries it is immediately accused of supporting oppressive and puppet regimes designed to exploit those countries. If military equipment is denied by the West it stands equally accused as giving assistance to white regimes such as that of South Africa by preventing the arming of other African countries that wish to destroy it.

Such attitudes and indecision in the West led to the paradoxes where American dollars paid for Nigerian oil end up in Moscow and Prague as payment for Soviet MIG fighter planes and Czechoslovak jet trainers. This is not to mention the loss of sales to Western aircraft suppliers. A similar situation also developed in Peru, a major copper supplier, when refusal of military sales to that government resulted in a Soviet military package, including supersonic SUKHOI jet interceptors.

Another player in this global resources war is China, which, even as a relatively poor country, engaged in several foreign aid programs in the Third World. An analysis of recipient countries in Africa, Europe, the Middle East, eastern Europe, and Latin America reveals that much of Chinese economic and military aid was extended to Third World countries with certain mineral resources that China had to import after its break with the Soviet Union in 1961.

In an era of nuclear confrontation a resources war conducted in Third World countries through proxies such as Cubans or revolutionary movements is an excellent alternative to outright war, particularly if the "correlation of forces" favors the Soviet bloc as it does in the 1980s.

This is somewhat different from the use of aggression to obtain strategic resources—best demonstrated by Nazi Germany and Japan in their concepts of the "1000 Years Reich" and the "Asian Co-Prosperity Sphere." At that time the Western world and particularly the United States were self-sufficient in raw materials and the outcome of the struggle was predictable as soon as the allies were able to deny access to major strategic materials sources to Nazi Germany and Japan.

Today, primarily as a result of decolonization, the global situation is reversed. The Western powers are now the nations lacking secure domestic raw materials sources, and at the same time they are committed to non-aggression and the promotion of democratic processes. The Soviet Union, now self-sufficient in its own right, is in a position to play the role of protector of Third World resources.

It would be extremely foolish on the part of Western politicians and strategists to think that any power finding itself in this position will not use it to further its own economic and ideological goals. This is particularly applicable as the world rests assured that the alternative is the specter of nuclear confrontation, because that is what keeps the West at bay in the face of Soviet expansionism.

STOCKPILING AND BUFFER STOCKS

Until recently the United States was the only country with a significant strategic materials stockpile designed to provide critical materials for key industries in the event of a prolonged war lasting up to three years. Perhaps it is the sign of the times but lately such countries as Japan, France, West Germany, Italy, and Great Britain have begun building their own stockpiles either openly or secretly. This action if it accelerates as a result of the escalation of international tensions between the United States and either Marxist or rightist dictatorships in Third World countries that are major raw materials suppliers could lead to a large jump in prices and widespread short-term shortages.

This could particularly be the case if accelerated stockpiling by western Europe, Japan, and even China is accompanied by the establishment of additional international commodity agreements that call for buffer stocks to be maintained by such organizations on behalf of the producing countries. Since these arrangements tend to maintain the floor prices of commodities but have not always been able to keep the ceiling prices, countries building their costly stockpiles have many incentives to acquire those raw materials before these commodity agreements come into operation.

Such a situation if it develops in the future could set off a period of intense stockpiling, coupled with price escalations and shortages, because producing countries would tend to limit production when they know that a strong stockpiling activity is underway.

TRANSPORTATION AND SHIPPING DISRUPTIONS

These events take place without being explicitly directed at raw materials supplies at times. For whatever reason bridges and tunnels are blown up, railways and rolling stock destroyed, airports bombed, and highway traffic hijacked such will immediately affect raw materials supplies that are the main users of public transportation systems.

In the case of oil pipelines tankers and loading facilities are big and vulnerable targets, particularly in Third World countries. The disruption of the traffic of oil tanker shipping lines from convenient bases is also a real possibility; however, whereas a real threat exists at such points as the Strait of Hormuz in the Persian Gulf or even along the coasts of such countries as Yemen, Mozambique, or Angola, any interference with international shipping by Soviet or any other navy would be an act of war.

Short-term shortages are more likely to develop as a result of local sabotage of rail or road transport. In 1979, for example, a key bridge was destroyed on the TAZARA railway linking the mining regions of Zambia with the port of Dar es Salaam in Tanzania on the Indian Ocean. This had the effect of drawing down inventories of raw materials at the port and affected the shipments to end-users who chose that route.

Other delays in shipments and cost increases resulting from the destruction of the Benguela railway during the Angola crisis of 1975 and the closing of the Rhodesia-Mozambique rail link for some time during the war in Rhodesia are also good examples of potential problems of this type—some of which can be quite lengthy.

REFERENCES

"Any More OPEC's?," *Economist,* 10 February 1979, p. 32.

"Cartels, Anyone?," *Economist,* 27 May 1978.

Chemical Bank, "New UNCTAD Rules Will Regulate Investment in Developing Countries," *Report from Europe,* January 1980.

Kolbe, Robert A., "World Minerals Pacts May Boost Price Levels," *Purchasing,* 16 September 1975, p. 35.

Lipper, Kenneth, "Cartels Are No Solution," *Foreign Policy,* No. 30, Spring 1978, p. 157.

Mandelbaum, Michael, "A Nuclear Exporters Cartel," *Bulletin of the Atomic Scientists,* January 1977, p. 42.

OECD, *Export Cartels,* Organization for Economic Cooperation and Development, Paris, 1974.

Szuprowicz, Bohdan O., "The Danger of a Supercartel in Strategic Materials: It Could Make OPEC Seem Tame," *Canadian Business,* November 1979.

Szuprowicz, Bohdan O., "Fear Soviet Supercartel for Critical Minerals," *Purchasing,* 8 November 1978.

Szuprowicz, Bohdan O., "Menace Sur le Cobalt?," *Usine Nouvelle,* No. 47, 18 October 1979.

Szuprowicz, Bohdan O., "Menace sur les Minerais Strategiques?," *Usine Nouvelle,* No. 38, 20 September 1979.

Szuprowicz, Bohdan O., "Russian Drive to Control Africa's Strategic Minerals," *Bulletin,* 15 May 1979.

"The Target of Terrorists: U.S. business," *U.S. News & World Report,* 26 November 1979.

"Third World—Cockpit of Turmoil," *U.S. News & World Report,* 25 June 1979.

"U.N. Conference of Poorest Countries Ends in Discord," *New York Times,* 10 February 1980.

U.S. Department of State, *International Relations Dictionary,* Washington, D.C., 1978.

Varon, Benison, and Kenji Takeuchi, "Developing Countries and Non-Fuel Minerals," *Foreign Affairs,* April 1974.

Growing Import Dependence
of the West

The seriousness of all the potential threats to the availability of raw materials in the future comes into better focus when the degree of import dependence of the United States, western Europe, Japan, China, and the Soviet bloc are compared.

In the case of oil the import dependence is well known, and from time to time it makes news as gasoline prices escalate, supplies are cut, rationing and taxes are threatened, and government bans on nonessential driving come into force during periods of real crisis.

The Western industrialized countries are also dependent to a high degree on imports of many other strategic materials such as aluminum, iron ore, chromium, cobalt, nickel, copper, tungsten, manganese, tin, lead, platinum, uranium, zinc, and rubber, to name a few. Shortages and price escalations in those materials also occur but are not widely publicized, because in most cases these are industrial materials and such knowledge would not be good for business. Nevertheless shortages and uncertainties of supplies are particularly frustrating to producers of products that critically depend on such materials.

Japan and West Germany are the two most dependent countries in the world, but France, the United Kingdom, Italy, and several smaller western European countries are in the same boat. The United States until the 1950s was almost self-sufficient, but during the last 30 years the import dependence of the United States has increased dramatically and added considerably to Western demand for Third World resources.

THE END OF AN ERA

With the election of Robert Mugabe as Marxist president of Zimbabwe in March 1980 a new era dawned not only on southern Africa but also on the

Western world as a whole. Zimbabwe is estimated to have 33 percent of the world's reserves of high-grade chromite, unquestionably the most strategic mineral for all the free market economies, Japan, and China.

Much of the future of the Western world's high-quality steel industries is now subject to the whims of a Marxist ruler of a new black African country because of the West's almost complete dependence on imports of chromite from Zimbabwe and South Africa. There is a parallel here between the election of Mugabe and the earlier election of Salvador Allende in Chile. In both cases Marxists have been elected by means of a democratic process. Chile is a major supplier and producer of copper, but copper is available in several countries, including Canada and the United States, two of the largest producers in the world. Zimbabwe plays a much more important role in the global chromite supply; therefore the impact of the election of a Marxist ruler in that country is considerably more severe.

In the case of Chile copper supplies were under control of an ideologically hostile government, but alternatives abounded and only a small proportion of Western imports were affected. In the case of Zimbabwe the alternatives are in South Africa, which automatically is further threatened as far as its own stability is concerned. Aside from Zimbabwe and South Africa other alternative sources of chromite with comparable production levels are in the Soviet Union and Albania. This is what makes the developments in Zimbabwe so crucial to the West.

Actually the era of relative abundance has slowly reached its end in stages beginning shortly after World War II. The world was split into two major political groupings, each intent on its own industrial and social development. At that time the Marshall Plan helped to rebuild the devastated European industries that have now developed into a giant economic machine of their own. By 1978 the European Community accounted for 20.2 percent of the world's gross national product (GNP), almost equal to the 21.8 percent represented by the United States. At the same time the communist countries developed their economies and now account for 23.2 percent of the world's GNP or slightly more than the United States.

Since the end of World War II one by one countries of the Third World, particularly in Africa, obtained independence from the former colonial powers, namely, the United Kingdom, Belgium, the Netherlands, France, Italy, Spain, and Portugal. Two important aspects of this process must be kept in mind. First, the United States, not being a previous colonial power, has a relatively poor understanding of what that status meant to the colonial powers. Second, the process is now just about complete for major Third World countries, and what colonies remain are small enclaves of no strategic consequence in raw materials supplies.

The decolonization process was accompanied almost everywhere by various degrees of civil strife and power struggles in the newly independent countries. Much of the unrest is blamed on the fact that when colonial powers were drawing up the borders of their colonies in the late nineteenth century these were decided without concern for the ethnic and tribal divisions that existed in the primitive world.

As a result tribal wars and wars of liberation have plagued the newly emerging nations during the last 30 years, leading to the establishment of armed forces and an increasing demand for military equipment and technology by several nations that could not afford such. When Western countries were reluctant to sell military equipment to various developing countries this also created an opening for the Soviet bloc to offer arms and know-how assistance. Another effect was the establishment of military production in some Third World countries such as Egypt, India, Pakistan, Israel, Brazil, Argentina, and South Africa.

At the time these developments took place the old colonial powers had to maneuver between changing regimes of the left—sometimes backed by the Soviet bloc or China—and dictatorial and military governments and try to continue to maintain reasonable business relations with those countries. Such was necessary because they knew that their growing economies were dependent on critical raw materials from those countries. Now the growing dependence of the United States is becoming another unsettling factor in the old geopolitical equation.

RELATIVE IMPORT DEPENDENCE OF MAJOR COUNTRIES

To fully appreciate the growing import dependence of the Western countries and the geopolitical implications of these developments it is necessary to examine in more detail the relative import dependence of the major countries and regions involved. An overview of the relative import dependence of Japan, western Europe, the United States, China, and the Soviet Union is presented in Table 3.1. The table shows in each case the approximate percentage of apparent consumption in each country, represented by imports from all foreign sources for 16 major strategic materials.

This import dependence varies from year to year as a result of purchases or sales of specific quantities of materials between exporting and importing countries, and this variance can be considerable from one year to the other. The average dependence presented in this chapter is based on the latest data covering the imports and consumption of the countries in question during the late 1970s. It is impossible to be more precise since reports from the different countries are not uniformly available at the same time.

It is easy to see why Japan and the European Community countries are considered the "resource have-nots" of this world. With few exceptions those two highly industrialized regions must import between 90 to 100 percent of their demand of the basic raw materials. This is also true in many cases of demand for the high-technology and strategic materials required for produc-

Table 3.1 Strategic Materials Import Dependence of Several Countries (Amount of Imports as Percentage of Apparent Consumption)

	Japan	European Community	United States	China	Soviet Union
Oil	xxxxxxxxxx	xxxxxxxx	xxxxx		
Iron ore	xxxxxxxxxx	xxxxxxxx	xxx	xx	x
Aluminum[a]	xxxxxxxxxx	xxxxxxxxx	xxxxxxxxx	xxxx	xxx
Diamonds	xxxxxxxxxx	xxxxxxxxxx	xxxxxxxxxx	xxxx	
Rubber	xxxxxxxxxx	xxxxxxxxxx	xxxxxxxxxx	xxxxxx	xxxxxxxxxx
Platinum	xxxxxxxxxx	xxxxxxxxxx	xxxxxxxxx	xxxxxxxxx	
Tungsten	xxxxxxxxxx	xxxxxxxxxx	xxxxx		xxx
Cobalt	xxxxxxxxxx	xxxxxxxxxx	xxxxxxxxxx	xxxxxxxxxx	xx
Uranium	xxxxxxxxxx	xxxxxxxxx			
Copper	xxxxxxxxx	xxxxxxxxx	xx	xxx	
Manganese	xxxxxxxxx	xxxxxxxxxx	xxxxxxxxxx		
Chromium	xxxxxxxxx	xxxxxxxxxx	xxxxxxxxxx	xxxxxxxxxx	
Nickel	xxxxxxxxx	xxx	xxxxxxxx	xxxxxxxxx	
Tin	xxxxxxxxx	xxxxxxxxxx	xxxxxxxx		xxxxx
Zinc	xxxxxxxx	xxxxxxxx	xxxxx		
Lead	xxxxxxxx	xxxxxxxxx	x	xxx	x

Source. National Foreign Assessment Center, U.S. Joint Chiefs of Staff, 1978, U.S. Bureau of Mines, and other data compiled by 21st Century Research.
[a] Includes imports of bauxite, alumina, and aluminum. *Note:* Each "x" represents 10% of apparent consumption met by imports from all sources.

tion of military goods and equipment. Neither Japan nor the European Community as yet have been able to organize significant stockpiles of strategic materials.

It is equally startling to see that the Soviet Union is almost self-sufficient in raw materials of all types. Even in the cases of the few imported minerals the Soviet Union possesses known reserves and could if necessary develop them at a higher cost. It appears that at specific points in time international price levels make it very attractive for the Soviet Union to import aluminum, cobalt, or tin, but this does not necessarily indicate a mandatory import dependence for the long run. The only truly strategic material the Soviet Union must import is natural rubber.

The Soviet bloc as a region also shows comparative self-sufficiency, although individual countries of eastern Europe are no better off in raw materials reserves than their counterparts in western Europe. However, eastern Europe depends to a very high degree on imports of raw materials from the Soviet Union. Only now with predictions of the possible peaking of Soviet oil output during the next few years the eastern European countries may have to start competing for oil and other raw materials in the Third World to a more significant degree. This fact does not ease the supply situation in the long run and creates incentives for the Soviet bloc to support and assist the development of Marxist-run countries in the Third World.

In addition the Soviet Union and the eastern European countries have a certain advantage in bargaining for the resources of the Third World when they need them. They are able to offer barter deals, exchanging machinery and military equipment for raw materials and agricultural products without the need to conduct transactions in hard currencies required by Western countries.

China, despite widespread beliefs that it is self-sufficient in raw materials to become a superpower in the future, is not yet able to produce domestically all the required materials it needs, and the country's self-sufficiency in this respect is considerably less than that of the Soviet Union. By comparison with the West, China is nevertheless considerably better off and depends on imports of only about 15 critical materials. Interestingly in the case of chromium, cobalt, nickel, and platinum, China's import dependence appears to be very similar to that of Japan, western Europe, and the United States.

The United States, once almost entirely self-sufficient, is still in a somewhat better position than Japan and western Europe that have never experienced self-sufficiency except in a few minerals such as coal in some European countries. But the United States is considerably worse off than either China or the Soviet Union on two counts. First, it depends on imports of more strategic materials because of depleted or nonexistent domestic resources. Second, the U.S. economy is the largest in the world, and as a result even relatively lower import dependence levels of the United States translate into much larger absolute demand on foreign sources of supply.

During the last 20 years this growing import dependence of the United States developed as additional demand over and above equally growing demands of western Europe and Japan—the traditional raw materials importers from Third World countries. This means there is increasing competition for raw materials in the Third World available to the West.

IMPORT DEPENDENCE OF THE UNITED STATES

The United States actually depends on imports of 50 percent or more of its demand of almost 30 different metals and minerals. Oil is the most important by value and by volume, but many of the other materials are critical to numerous industries. These materials are imported from about 30 different countries; in some cases the countries are not necessarily the most important producers of each material. This provides a certain amount of diversification of sources but not to the same degree as that practiced by Japan or Germany. Countries of the Third World by far dominate the list as major suppliers of critical materials to the United States (see Figure 3.1).

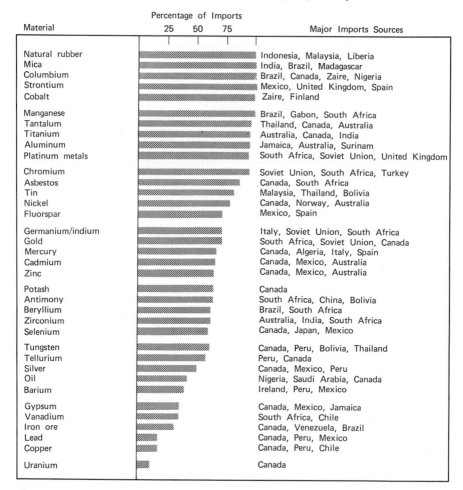

Figure 3.1 **Essential materials imported by the United States and major sources of imports.** Source. **Based on data of the U.S. Bureau of Mines for the 1976–1978 period.**

Among developed countries only Canada and Australia are significant suppliers of minerals to the United States. Canada is a natural partner because of its proximity to the United States and is traditionally the largest trade partner as well. If Canada and the United States were considered jointly as a North American partnership the combined resources would considerably lessen the import dependence of the North American continent as a whole relative to other developed regions of the world.

But even so the North American continent would be lacking any significant reserves of some of the most critical materials, including cobalt, manganese, platinum, chromium, tin, aluminum (bauxite), gold, antimony, and vanadium. This deficiency is an important stumbling block on the path to renewed self-sufficiency of the North American continent in the short term.

One reason why more attention is not being given to the question of non-oil strategic materials import dependence is because they represent a relatively small volume of the overall imports. Excluding large volumes of iron ore, steel scrap, and steel products, the nonferrous ores and metals account for only about 4 percent of the total imports. If iron and steel imports, as well as rubber, asbestos, and industrial diamonds, are included the value of all those imports combined rises to about 10 percent of the total—still only a quarter of the value of oil imports alone (see Table 3.2).

Although the United States also exports some products in those categories it had a trade deficit of over $5 billion in non-oil minerals in 1978. This trade deficit is likely to get worse in the future, but for now the spectacular trade deficit is in oil, where it reached a high of over $40 billion in 1977 and was about $38 billion in 1978. Oil-price escalations in 1979 and early 1980 by the OPEC nations have again increased that deficit into the $50 to $60 billion region.

As a result government officials and legislators must concentrate on problems arising from the escalation of oil prices, and little attention is given to all other critical materials, even though many of those are imported to supply a much higher proportion of national demand than oil. This means that critical non-oil materials end-users and materials managers are left to their own devices to assure the uninterrupted supply of those materials to their own enterprises. In the long run this may prove to be a blessing in disguise, although government support in some foreign areas would prove beneficial even today.

What is perhaps of even greater significance is how the existing import dependence of the United States will change in the future. In this respect certain studies performed at the Bureau of Mines during the 1970s shed some light on the subject, although it must be understood that conditions with regard to reserves and economic recovery change constantly.

Table 3.2 Value of Imports of Oil and Minerals by the United States in 1978

Imports	Value (millions of U.S. dollars)	Percentage of Total
Oil	39,109	22.7
Iron ores, pig iron, scrap, and steels	8,105	4.7
Nonferrous ores and metals	6,755	3.9
Rubber, asbestos, industrial diamonds	1,071	0.6
Total	172,025	100.0

Source. U.S. Department of Commerce, 1979.

In that research supplies and demand patterns of over 90 metals and minerals have been examined. The percent of primary domestic production relative to primary demand was determined for several years, starting in 1950 through 1971; and projections were made for the year 2000.

According to that analysis the United States was almost completely dependent on imports for all of its domestic demand of 12 minerals in 1970, including cesium, chromium, columbium, hafnium, rhodium, rubidium, scandium, strontium, titanium metal, zirconium, corundum, and mica sheet. By the year 2000 it was forecasted that complete import dependence will increase to at least 20 materials because of the depletion of domestic resources.

More important, the analysis also showed that whereas in 1970 the United States produced more than its own requirements of about 32 different minerals, by the year 2000 this country's mineral production rate was projected to fall below the expected demand at that time. As a result the import dependence of the United States will increase, and the United States will be self-sufficient then in only four minerals, namely, boron, bromine, molybdenum, and rare earths metals.

Looking at this analysis in another way over 60 metals and minerals produced in the United States in 1970 will continue to be in production in the year 2000, but in all cases the output, even if it increases in total volume, will supply a smaller percentage of the total demand than in 1970. This means increasing imports of most of those materials in the future.

Among important materials in this category is copper whose surplus domestic production in 1970 was forecasted to drop significantly by the year 2000 when the United States may have to import over 50 percent of its demand. Aluminum, whose import dependence is already very high, is expected to increase to almost 100 percent by the end of the century. Another important expectation is increased import dependence in iron ore, projected to increase from about 30 percent presently to over 60 percent by the year 2000. All these materials are very important in their impact on the balance of trade, because all three are traded and consumed in great quantities.

Other minerals whose import dependence is expected to increase significantly by the year 2000 include beryllium, cadmium, germanium, selenium, silver, titanium metal, tungsten, vanadium, and zinc. Two minerals that were produced in abundance in the United States in 1970 are sulfur and uranium. By the year 2000 the requirements for those materials may also have to be met by imports of 50 and 60 percent, respectively.

VULNERABILITY OF JAPAN

Because it relies almost entirely on imports for all basic minerals and energy Japan has developed into a very competitive factor in the global minerals and metals markets. Despite the lack of its own domestic raw materials

Japan is a leading country in mineral processing and metals production, using primarily imported materials. It has been the policy of the Japanese government, working closely with Japanese industries, to discover and develop new mineral deposits all over the world to help solve what is sometimes known in Japan as the "resources problem."

Japan is extremely well aware of its vulnerability to foreign raw materials availability and has often taken the initiative to assist other countries in the exploration, development, and production of various minerals. In some cases Japanese consortia are willing to enter into agreements to furnish manufactured goods and services in return for raw materials (see Table 3.1).

About 50 percent of Japanese imports are made up of raw materials, whereas 25 percent of its exports constitutes processed mineral and metal products. The total value of Japan's mineral output, including the value added from processing imported materials, is estimated at about 10 percent of the Japanese GNP, which was $980 billion in 1978. These industries include iron and steel, fuels, nonferrous metals, and nonmetallic minerals. They represent some of the largest and most modern refineries, smelters, and processing plants in the world.

In this sector Japan is a major producer of aluminum, copper, ferronickel, steels, titanium, tungsten, and zinc—all from imported ores and raw materials. In some metals Japan produced as much as 15 percent of the global output and is a major exporter of refined metals. As such Japan is highly vulnerable to any disruptions of raw materials supplies and is operating its minerals processing industries in a highly planned and efficient manner (see Table 3.3).

Because of this basic vulnerability Japan is the most formidable competi-

Table 3.3 Japan's Role in Global Minerals Industries

Major Materials	Percentage of World Output
Aluminum, refined	7
Copper, refined	10
Ferronickel	10
Lead, refined	5
Magnesium	6
Oil products	7
Steel ingot	15
Steel products	15
Titanium metal	13
Tungsten	1
Zinc, refined	13

Source. U.S. Bureau of Mines, 1977.

tor for the world's raw materials, and it has had a very long time to develop strategies and tactics that will protect its interests. Many of those strategies and tactics are based on concepts of sudden shock, secrecy, flexibility, deception, and above all the surprise of competitors and potential enemies. These are the concepts and teachings of Sun Tzu, the ancient Chinese military strategist, later adopted in the 1938 operations manual of the Imperial Japanese Army, both of which are part of the executive training of Japanese managers.

Japan conducts its pervasive global operations through highly competitive private trading and operating companies that often work jointly in developing foreign projects. The Japanese government supports Japanese companies in these efforts by establishing suitable foreign trade policies, providing tax incentives, low-interest funding, assuming some exploration and development risk, regulating domestic production and trade, and suggesting suitable stockpiling objectives. In comparison with other industrialized countries Japan is like an armed fortress that is always expecting a siege and has widely diversified sources of its essential raw materials.

STRATEGIC MATERIALS REQUIREMENTS OF WESTERN EUROPE

Western Europe is a large consumer and refiner of minerals and metals, but its high-grade ores are now depleted as a result of the 200 years of heavy consumption since the Industrial Revolution. As a result heavy industries in Europe are now concentrating on the coasts to take advantage of imported raw materials. In this respect western Europe is similar to Japan, which also operates its large processing plants on the coast.

Western Europe as a region is a very large processor of minerals and metals, in most cases accounting for up to 20 and 30 percent of the global output, but much of this production is based entirely on imported raw materials. As a result western Europe is a large competitor of Japan and the United States for the supplies of the same raw materials from Third World countries.

Europe has a long history of mining and metallurgy going back into prehistoric times. About 540 BC silver began to be mined in Greece, and during the Golden Age of Pericles about 450 BC silver was the mainstay of the government of Athens until the mines were exhausted; this fact contributed to the decay of that city-state.

At present western Europe is a leading producer of refined metals such as aluminum, copper, lead, zinc, and steel—but mostly from imported minerals and ores. In addition it is almost entirely dependent on imports of all the other critical materials such as cobalt, chromium, nickel, and titanium, for which Japan and the United States are also competing (see Table 3.4).

Table 3.4   Western Europe's Role in Major Materials Production

Material	Percentage of World Output	Major Producing Countries
Aluminum, refined	26	Germany, Norway, France, United Kingdom
Copper, refined	19	Belgium, Germany, Spain, United Kingdom
Lead	32	Germany, United Kingdom, France, Italy, Belgium
Zinc	32	Germany, Belgium, France, Italy
Iron ore	14	France, Sweden, Norway, United Kingdom
Steel	25	Germany, Italy, France, United Kingdom
Coal (including lignite)	13	Germany, United Kingdom, France, Spain
Oil	1.5	Norway, United Kingdom, Germany, Austria
Petroleum products	24	France, Italy, Germany, United Kingdom

Source.   U.S. Bureau of Mines, 1977.

Because so many vital industries in western Europe depend on supplies of imported raw materials import dependence is taken very seriously in most European countries. Disruption of supplies to Europe affects global metals markets. This is so because Europe plays such a large role in basic metals production. Such a disruption also affects the European end-user industries that depend on metals for the production of machinery and equipment, the mainstay of European exports. Shortages of critical materials in western Europe could easily lead to serious unemployment and political unrest in many countries.

Having lived with these realities for several decades western Europe, like Japan following its rapid industrialization, developed its own methods for assuring security of supplies of critical materials. Partially this includes a much larger diversification of sources of supplies than is practiced by the U.S. enterprises. Western Europe also shows a much greater degree of political pragmatism when dealing with foreign suppliers.

Now that the United States is also becoming a major importer of raw materials and is handling its own import dependence problems rather badly, European politicians and business executives are beginning to question the wisdom of excessive reliance on American security guarantees and techno-economic prowess.

EUROPEAN COMMUNITY MATERIALS POLICIES

During the 1940s and 1950s western European countries were themselves rebuilding their economies and were assisted greatly in this task by the Marshall Plan. At that time the United States was still an almost self-sufficient economy, particularly in energy, and could itself supply many raw materials as well as capital and technology. The European countries, devastated by war and threatened by communist takeovers in eastern Europe and civil unrest and social change in their own countries, were eager to accept American economic assistance and its nuclear umbrella of protection against possible threat from the East.

Nevertheless many Europeans now feel that the price they paid for this relatively short-lived "Pax Americana" was never clearly spelled out. There are deep-rooted feelings in Europe that American pressure for liberalization of the world has led to the hasty and disorderly decolonization programs that the United States insisted on in return for its assistance. There are some who go so far as to suggest that the United States undertook to break up the colonial system not so much because of its humanistic considerations but rather because it wanted to eliminate future European competition, cartels, and potential economic powers that were unquestionably linked to its sources of raw materials in various Third World countries.

If this were the intention of some American business circles it failed in the long run, because the two old enemies—Japan and Germany—are today more powerful than they have ever been and are successfully challenging the United States—even in its own markets.

But whereas the postwar rise of Japan and Germany took place under the security umbrella of the United States the effectiveness of this arrangement is now being questioned by Europeans and Americans themselves. As a result of the defeat in Vietnam, indecision in Angola and Ethiopia, the helplessness in Iran, and the aftermath of the Soviet invasion of Afghanistan other Western industrialized countries are beginning to perceive the United States as unable or unwilling to stand up to Soviet challenges and protect even its own vital interests, let alone those of its allies. All this means an increasing threat to Western Europeans, and pressures are building up for Western Europeans to develop their own security arrangements outside those of American guarantees. Because of this and because they are much more aware of their own vulnerability to the disruption of strategic and critical raw materials supplies, western European countries are tempted to take matters into their own hands.

There are some political speculators and observers who suggest that the revolution in Iran may have been conceived by Western European countries—and particularly France—to wrest the control of that vital region away from the United States. Education and asylum received in France by present Iranian leaders such as Bani Sadr, Ghotbzadeh, and Ayatollah Khomeini himself, immediately preceding the revolution, seems to give some credence to those theories. All this points to a certain loss of credibility in the United States as an effective and crucial NATO member that can be relied on to guarantee strategic materials supplies to its allies.

EXPOSED FLANKS OF THE NATO ALLIANCE

The security of western Europe and the Western world rests on the strength of NATO, also known as the "Atlantic Alliance." The treaty includes 15 member nations—Belgium, Canada, Denmark, France, Germany, Greece, Iceland, Italy, Luxembourg, the Netherlands, Norway, Portugal, Turkey, the United Kingdom, and the United States. The political stability of member countries in turn depends on economic well-being, reasonable employment, and tolerable inflation levels, and the American strategic guarantees in the form of its nuclear deterrent.

However NATO commands are responsible for the defense of Europe as far south as the Mediterranean Sea and Turkey and in the West from Portugal across the Atlantic Ocean as far south as the Tropic of Cancer, which runs between Key West in Florida and Havana in Cuba.

Under the circumstances any Soviet action outside those limits are not of any concern or responsibility of NATO. It is clear to see that Cuba, Angola, Afghanistan, or Ethiopia are clearly outside NATO's defense perimeter as are all the important OPEC countries in the Persian Gulf. Similarly all of southern Africa, Australia, Latin America, and Japan are also outside NATO's jurisdiction; yet western Europe, the main region NATO must defend, is critically dependent on most of its strategic materials from those areas.

This situation also creates a diplomatic opportunity for Soviet bloc countries that can exploit it by providing selective economic and particularly military assistance in the form of weapons and training to those Third World countries that are in opposition to any extension of the NATO concept to defend its critical raw materials supply areas.

This weakness of NATO and fears that it is being outflanked by Soviet-backed actions outside NATO areas of responsibility led to the creation in 1955 of the Central Treaty Organization (CENTO), designed to create a complementary defensive grouping against the Soviet Union in the northern sector of the Middle East. The organization included Turkey, the United Kingdom, the United States—all NATO members—Iran, Pakistan, and Iraq. Originally known as the "Baghdad Pact" CENTO's effectiveness is questionable because Iraq, Iran, and Pakistan have since left the organization.

More meaningful groupings in the Pacific and Asia are the countries that agreed to the ANZUS pact and the Southeast Asia Treaty Organization (SEATO), which agreed to the Southeast Asia Collective Defense Treaty. The ANZUS pact is a security treaty between the United States, Australia, and New Zealand. SEATO includes Australia, France, New Zealand, the Philippines, Thailand, the United Kingdom, and the United States.

Nevertheless these peripheral arrangements are now seriously questioned, particularly by western European nations that observed the impotence of the United States in the case of Cuba, Iran, Angola, Ethiopia, and Afghanistan and are increasingly concerned about the value of the NATO alliance which may be further rendered ineffective by Soviet-backed penetration of strategic areas outside the primary NATO responsibility.

These concerns of NATO allies in Europe are understood by more conservative and less liberal forces in the United States whose objective now is to expand NATO's sphere of responsibility to include those vital areas on which NATO member countries depend most for their energy resources and raw materials supplies. The concepts that are now emerging are striving toward the formation of a Trioceanic Alliance to include such vital areas and powers of the future as Brazil, South Africa, Japan, Australia, and the old NATO countries in a new global alliance spanning both hemispheres.

The role of China in such a new constellation has not been defined as yet, but since Afghanistan the chances of considering China as a potential associate member have clearly increased. China's geopolitical location and its relatively large self-sufficiency level makes it a valuable potential member of such a grouping. China has the unique quality of being able to present a realistic threat of the "second front" that the Soviet Union and even czarist Russia always dreaded.

There is little question that the need for a more effective defense organization to replace NATO is growing every day in view of the increasing threat to NATO's strategic resources outside its current sphere of operations. What remains to be seen is to what degree individual countries in vital supply areas will feel threatened themselves before they will join such an organization. The strategic materials end-user on the other hand must keep in mind these strategic considerations when relying on or investing in sources of critical materials in some of these countries.

REFERENCES

Batelle Institute, "World Minerals and Energy Resources," *Batelle Monograph*, No. 6, December 1974.

Behrmann, Neil, "Strategic Metals," *Barron's Weekly*, 5 February 1979.

Faure, Patric-Rene, "Natural Resources: France, Counts Its Blessings," *France Information*, French Embassy Information Center, New York.

International Institute for Strategic Studies, *The Military Balance 1978–1979*, London 1979.

Keyes, William F., Roman V. Sondermayer, and Joseph B. Huvos, *Mineral Industry of Western Europe*, U.S. Bureau of Mines, Washington, D.C., October 1977.

"Percentage of U.S. Consumption Met by Imports," *Readers Digest*, May 1974, p. 162.

"Proportion of U.S. Consumption Met by Imports," *U.S. News & World Report*, 12 November 1979, p. 75.

Reilly, Ann M., "More Trade, Less Politics," *Dun's Review*, January 1979.

"Strategic Metals, Critical Choices," *Time Magazine*, 21 January 1980, p. 64.

Szuprowicz, Bohdan O., "Strategic Materials Supercartel," *International Essays for Business Decision Makers,* Vol. 4, Center for International Business, Dallas, 1979.

"Understanding the Flow of World Trade," *U.S. News & World Report,* 7 May 1978.

U.S. Bureau of Mines, *Far East and South Asia,* MP-1 Mineral Perspectives, U.S. Department of the Interior, Washington, D.C., May 1977.

U.S. Department of Commerce, *U.S. Foreign Trade Annual 1970–1976,* Washington, D.C., April 1977.

U.S. Department of the Navy, *"U.S. Life Lines,"* Office of the Chief of Naval Operations, Washington, D.C., January 1978.

U.S. Department of State, *Treaties in Force,* Washington, D.C., January 1979.

U.S. Senate, Committee on Foreign Relations, *Western Investment in Communist Countries,* U.S. Government Printing Office, Washington, D.C.

Yuan-li, Wu, *Raw Materials Supply in a Multipolar World,* Crane, Russak, and Company, New York, 1973.

CHAPTER
FOUR

Soviet Bloc's Apparent
Materials Self-Sufficiency

The Soviet Union is at present the most self-sufficient economy in the world with regard to energy and raw materials. On a comparative basis it leads the world as the largest producer of at least 13 important minerals, including oil, is the second largest producer of another seven important materials such as natural gas, copper, and gold, and is the third largest producer of coal, bauxite, and uranium (see Table 2.1 in Chapter 2).

In addition the whole energy, minerals, and metals production industries are centrally controlled by the politburo of the Communist party of the Soviet Union through a series of state-controlled ministries. Production proceeds according to five-year and one-year plans that have the force of law and carry mandatory obligations. Long-term plans of 10 and 20 years are also used to provide perspectives for future economic and political objectives.

This unique combination of abundant resources and centralized production control provides the Soviet Union with important advantages that can be exploited in its international policy. Supplies of energy and raw materials to east European countries, Cuba, Mongolia, and Vietnam allow the Soviet Union to keep these countries within its sphere of influence. At the same time ample supplies of domestic resources allow the Soviet Union to seek political opportunities among the countries of the Third World to expand Soviet influence and power at minimum risk and at the same time to reduce the power of the United States, western Europe, and Japan—all of which must depend on supplies of their critical materials from the Third World.

RESOURCES OF THE SOVIET UNION

The Soviet Union is a leading producer of practically all the important minerals in the world and accounts for a very large share of the world's mineral production. It produces at least 10 percent of the global output of over 30 important minerals and metals. It dominates the world's output, producing one-fifth or more of such materials as oil, natural gas, coal, lignite, asbestos, beryllium, cadmium, chromium, diamonds, gold, iron ore, magnesium, manganese, molybdenum, nickel, platinum, phosphates, potash, steel, titanium, tungsten, uranium, and vanadium (see Table 4.1).

The Soviet minerals position is further strengthened by the fact that in most instances the country also has very large reserves of those same minerals. However, in about 10 important materials the Soviet's share of world production is larger than its estimated share of world reserves. These materials include some very important metals and minerals, including high-grade bauxites, chromium, copper, diamonds, fluorspar, nickel, phosphates, tin, and zinc. It is impossible to assess when Soviet reserves of these minerals will be depleted to a point that the Soviet Union will have to become an important importer of these minerals.

Since the Soviet Union is the second largest economy in the world its consumption of all these materials is very high. But the Soviet Union is also a large exporter of minerals to the world. Oil, minerals, and metals are the leading Soviet exports, representing about 50 percent of the total official value of Soviet exports. Because of such a large demand and export position the Soviet Union is a significant factor in the mineral economy of the whole world.

Minerals development is considered to be the basis of industrial growth and holds a key place in Soviet economic planning. Because minerals production is centrally controlled to support political or economic objectives, the costs of production are not a prime factor in the establishment of selling prices for minerals either on the domestic or international markets. Many minerals enterprises are considered uneconomic by Western standards. This only proves the point that the Soviet Union does and will use its significant position in this industry to attain political and economic objectives or to influence its foreign policy.

There are conflicting views about the real state of Soviet minerals self-sufficiency. Some sovietologists believe that the Soviet Union is truly self-sufficient in most minerals and metals and exercises its dominant position to extend political control over the countries of eastern Europe which must import most of their energy and strategic materials to keep their industries going.

Other observers hold the view that the Soviet Union in fact experiences domestic shortages of all minerals that it exports because this is a major way to earn foreign exchange to pay for imports of machinery, technology, and grains. Since most of Soviet minerals trade is conducted with COMECON countries that can hardly offer equipment or technology that does not already exist in the Soviet Union it is more likely that the Soviet Union is in fact self-sufficient and produces a surplus. Such disputes are almost impossible to settle with actual data because a Soviet decree going back to 1956

Table 4.1   Soviet Minerals Position Relative to the World

Commodity	Share of World Production (percentage)	Reserves Position and Comments
Aluminum	12	Second largest producer in the world
Antimony	11	7% of world reserves
Asbestos	46	25% of world reserves
Barite	7	Imports from North Korea, Bulgaria
Bauxite	6	Limited reserves of high-grade ore
Beryllium	60	One of the largest in the world
Bismuth	1	
Cadmium	17	Largest world producer
Chromium	26	Only 1% of world reserves
Columbium	na	6% of world reserves
Coal	20	Largest in the world
Cobalt	5	20% of world reserves
Copper	11	9% of world reserves
Diamond, gems	18	
Diamond, industrial	25	4% of world reserves
Fluorspar	11	4% reserves, some imports
Gold	19	21% of world reserves
Iron ore	27	31% of world's high-grade reserves
Lead	14	13% of world reserves
Lignite	19	Very large reserves
Magnesium	46	Largest magnesite producer
Manganese	34	45% of world reserves
Mercury	18	Small imports
Molybdenum	10	20% of world reserves
Natural gas	21	Largest in the world
Nickel	19	7% of world reserves
Oil	18	Fourth largest reserves in the world
Phosphates	22	4% of world reserves
Platinum	46	13% of world reserves
Potash	36	
Steel	22	Largest producer in the world
Silver	14	36% reserves in communist world
Sulfur	16	
Tin	13	6% of world reserves
Titanium	63	16% of world reserves
Tungsten	21	19% of world reserves
Uranium	28	13% of world reserves
Vanadium	20	75% of world reserves
Zinc	12	8% of world reserves

Source. U.S. Bureau of Mines, National Foreign Assessment Center, American Metal Market, Metal Progress.

classifies data on nonferrous, precious, and rare metals and some minerals as state secrets.

EAST EUROPE'S MINERALS POSITION

Compared with the Soviet Union eastern Europe produces only about 20 minerals of significance, but even collectively all those countries account for a relatively smaller share of the total world production than the corresponding share of the Soviet Union in most of the same materials. The Soviet Union also produces many more materials not available in eastern Europe.

Eastern Europe accounts for more than 10 percent of the global output of only four materials—chromite, lignite, potash, and sulfur. Poland and Romania are the two countries most endowed with minerals, each having a significant production of eight important minerals. Even so all countries have serious deficiencies of various alloy metals and more exotic minerals that they must import from the Soviet Union (see Table 4.2).

The most abundant mineral in eastern Europe, found in practically all countries of the area, is lignite. It is an alternative source of energy and plays an important role in the economies of East Germany, Czechoslovakia, and Poland, where it supplements coal as an alternative fuel. Despite increasing use of oil east Europe and even the Soviet Union are still very large consumers of coal in the production of their energy requirements.

Romania is the only country with significant domestic oil and natural gas resources. The rest of the region is almost entirely dependent on the Soviet Union to supplement their energy needs with imports of oil, natural gas, and even coal. Considering the need to maintain and operate relatively large military establishments that must have oil for mobility east Europe is strategically dependent on oil from the Soviet Union.

Relative to its industrialization and population eastern Europe is deficient in minerals resources and could not sustain production and employment levels in its industries without continuing imports of practically all the industrial materials. Most of the imports come from the Soviet Union, but in several materials these must be supplemented by additional imports from the rest of the world. These include primarily iron ore, oil, tin, and steel products such as large diameter steel pipe.

However taken as a bloc jointly with the Soviet Union eastern Europe's production, combined with corresponding Soviet production, represents a very substantial share of the world's output of those materials, ranging from as much as 70 percent of world lignite down to over 10 percent of the world's supply of molybdenum. In many instances these production shares are not very far from the Soviet bloc's consumption levels, which illustrate the result of its attempts to achieve planned self-sufficiency in industrial supplies. There is little question that eastern European economies, with their

Table 4.2 East Europe's Minerals Position as Percentage of World Production[a]

Material	Albania	Bulgaria	Czecho-slovakia	German Democratic Republic	Hungary	Poland	Romania	Total East Europe (percentage)
Aluminum	–	–	+	+	1.0	+	2.0	3.0
Bauxite	–	–	–	–	4.6	–	1.3	5.9
Cadmium	–	1.0	–	+	–	2.3	0.6	3.9
Chromite	10.0	–	–	–	–	–	–	10.0
Coal	–	+	1.0	+	+	7.0	+	8.0
Copper	+	+	+	+	+	3.3	+	3.5
Gold	–	–	–	–	–	–	0.1	0.1
Iron ore	+	+	+	–	+	+	+	+
Lead	–	3.0	+	–	–	2.0	1.2	6.2
Lignite	+	3.0	10.0	29.0	2.0	5.0	2.0	51.0
Molybdenum	–	0.2	–	–	–	–	–	0.2
Manganese	–	–	–	–	1.0	–	+	1.0
Mercury	–	–	2.5	–	–	–	–	2.5
Natural gas	+	+	+	–	+	+	2.0	2.0
Nickel	–	–	–	0.3	–	0.4	–	0.7
Oil	+	+	+	+	+	+	1.0	1.0
Phosphate	+	+	+	–	–	+	–	+
Potash	–	–	–	12.0	–	–	–	12.0
Steel	–	+	2.0	1.0	1.0	2.0	2.0	8.0
Sulfur	–	–	–	–	–	13.0	–	13.0
Uranium	–	–	some	+	+	–	–	some
Zinc	–	1.0	+	–	–	4.0	–	5.0

Source. U.S. Bureau of Mines, National Foreign Assessment Center, American Metal Market, and other data compiled by 21st Century Research.

[a] (–): means no production of this material. (+): means negligible production, usually less than 0.5% of the world output.

large literate populations and trained work forces, and the Soviet Union, with its vast mineral resources and raw materials, form a group of complementary economies that will probably continue to develop jointly for at least the rest of this century (see Table 4.3).

The relative minerals position of eastern Europe and the Soviet Union and their geographical proximity to each other create natural conditions for economic integration such as is being attempted within the COMECON organization. The opportunities for both sides in this cooperation are not unlike those existing between Canada and the United States.

An analysis of eastern Europe's energy and minerals position also explains why it is extremely difficult for the West to think of splitting those countries from the Soviet sphere. Such cannot be done successfully unless considerable

Table 4.3   Comparison of East European and Soviet Shares of the World's Minerals Production as Percentage of Global Output

Commonly Produced Minerals	Soviet Share of World Production	East Europe's Share of World Production	Combined Soviet and East Europe Shares
Aluminum	12	3	15
Bauxite	6	6	12
Cadmium	17	4	21
Chromium	26	10	36
Coal	20	8	28
Copper	11	3.5	14
Gold	19	0.1	19
Iron ore	27	neg	27
Lead	14	6	20
Lignite	19	51	70
Manganese	34	1	35
Mercury	18	2.5	20
Molybdenum	10	neg	10
Natural gas	21	2	23
Nickel	19	7[a]	26
Oil	18	1	19
Phosphates	22	neg	22
Potash	36	12	48
Steel	22	8	30
Sulfur	16	13	29
Uranium	28	2[b]	30
Zinc	12	5	17

Source.   Based on tables developed previously in this chapter.

[a] Includes estimate for Cuban share of the world's nickel production.

[b] Estimate of author.

supplies of energy and raw materials are made available from the Third World in which the United States is now beginning to compete more seriously with western Europe and Japan.

THE COMECON ORGANIZATION

In 1949 the Soviet Union and the east European countries formed the Councal for Mutual Economic Assistance (COMECON or CMEA), with the objective of assisting each other in economic development and coordinating economic planning within the Soviet bloc. Original members included the Soviet Union, Albania, Bulgaria, Czechoslovakia, Hungary, Poland, and Romania. East Germany joined in 1950; Albania withdrew in 1961; Mongolia became a member in 1962; Cuba, in 1972; and Vietnam, in 1978. Finland, Iraq, and Yugoslavia are associate members, and Angola, Ethiopia, and Laos have observer status.

The COMECON organization is sometimes described as the Soviet answer to the Marshall Plan. It now seems to be much more than that and is developing various long-range cooperation programs similar to those among member nations of the European Community (Common Market).

The COMECON objective is to implement a long-range complex program for socialist integration of member state economies. This policy is administered through a series of committees, permanent commissions, and industrial organizations as well as joint research and development programs. The industrial organizations coordinate the development of specific industries throughout the Soviet bloc and now exist in ferrous metallurgy, bearings, nuclear power and instrumentation, electric power distribution, chemicals and chemical fibers, textiles, computers, and transportation of freight (see Table 4.4).

The COMECON organization is little known and understood in the free world, and its objectives and achievements are often belittled as unimportant or doomed to failure within the inefficient communist bureaucracies. Nevertheless it is an important influence on the foreign trade of COMECON countries, 60 percent of which is conducted through state monopolies within the COMECON membership. This trade has been doubling every five years since 1955 and by 1975 reached a level of 70 billion rubles, equivalent to about $100 billion or the total foreign trade of the United States during the late 1970s.

Much criticism of COMECON and its policies in recent years also stems from the fact that COMECON member countries have been trading more with the West during the second half of the 1970s. This is interpreted by wishful thinkers as being the result of COMECON failures and preferences of east European countries for Western products. It is also conveniently forgotten that much of these trade increases are more often than not due to

Table 4.4 COMECON Committees, Permanent Commissions, Industrial Organizations, and Joint Research and Development Programs, Including Their Dates of Founding in Chronological Order

Committees	Cooperative Planning Cooperation in Material and Technical Supplies Scientific and Technical Cooperation
Permanent commissions	Agriculture, Coal Industry, Construction, Currency and Finance, Electric Power, Ferrous Metallurgy, Economics, Scientific and Technical Research, Foreign Trade, Geology, Peaceful Uses of Atomic Energy, Standardization, Transportation, Electric and Postal Communications

Industrial organizations	1952 Office of Maritime Freight Rationalization
	1962 Central Electric Power Grid Administration (MIR)
	1963 Freight Transportation Cooperation (OPW)
	1964 Iron and Steel Cooperation (INTERMETALL)
	     Anti-friction Bearings Industry Cooperation (OSPP)
	     International Bank for Economic Cooperation (IBEC)
	1969 Center for Scientific and Technical Information (MTsNTI)
	     Joint Computer Industry Development (RIAD)
	1970 Joint Shipping Services Organization (INSA)
	     Joint Space Research Program (INTERKOSMOS)
	     Chemical Industry Cooperation (INTERKHIM)
	     International Investment Bank (IIB)
	1972 Joint Instrumentation and Measurement Apparatus Programs (INTERETALONPRIBOR)
	     Nuclear Equipment Production (INTERATOMINSTRUMENT)
	1973 Nuclear Power Development (INTERATOMENERGO)
	     Electric Power Technology Joint Research and Development (INTERELEKTRO)
	     Textile Industry Cooperation (INTERTEXTILMASH)
	     Coordination of Seaport Facilities (INTERPORT)
	     Photochemical Industry Cooperation (ASSOFOTO)
	1974 Chemical Fibers Industry Production Coordination (INTERKHIMVOLOKNO)

Source. Compiled by 21st Century Research from various government and media reports, 1978, 1979.

liberal credit and joint venture arrangements rather than competitive market forces and were planned by those COMECON organizations as a method of speeding up industrialization, using Western credits and high technology. The resulting problems created in western Europe by the sudden glut of COMECON synthetic fiber imports produced in Western-built modern chemical and petrochemical plants is a good case in point of Western naivete.

Whatever the shortcomings and inefficiencies of COMECON and its constituent bodies it must be borne in mind that this organization has survived and expanded for the last 30 years and will obviously incorporate new areas of international "cooperation" in the future.

As the new Third World countries such as Cuba, Vietnam, Angola, Ethiopia, and perhaps Afghanistan, Libya, Zambia, Zimbabwe, or Peru are induced to join COMECON as a result of political or economic pressures other organizations may come into existence to coordinate the production and exports of minerals and metals under the control of such member countries.

Specialized international minerals organizations of COMECON, when they come into being, could become a minerals production and trade supermonopoly of the world if they control a big enough share of minerals resources. This would be likely since all COMECON organizations are groupings of representative state monopolies of each member country.

In each COMECON member state there exists one or more ministries that control the exploration, production, allocation, and trade of all energy and mineral resources. These ministries are important state monopolies that influence the development of other industries dependent on supplies of critical materials from those state cartels. In the cases of more industrialized COMECON countries such as Bulgaria, East Germany, Poland, the Soviet Union, and even Cuba and Romania special ministries control materials supplies on a national basis. In other centrally planned economies this function is probably performed by a department of the State Planning Commission or similar national planning body (see Table 4.5).

It is also worth noting that there is now a new State Committee for Material Reserves in the Soviet Union that was elevated to this ministerial status only in 1978. This could mean that the Soviet Union is concerned with the availability of some strategic materials within COMECON as a result of the domestic depletion of resources or increasing costs of production and rapidly growing demand. It may also mean that the Soviet Union is preparing to implement more political leverage, using top-level strategic stockpiling or reserves control within and without the Soviet Union. Interpretations of such developments differ, depending on political convictions of many analysts and in this case could actually mean that the Soviets are pursuing both objectives at the same time.

The inescapable fact remains that COMECON provides a framework however imperfect to implement swiftly international planning and production programs in mining and metal processing if specific opportunities come into view. What is more as a supranational mechanism COMECON can readily accommodate existing quasi-state monopolies of many Third World countries already in operation.

The individual ministries in each COMECON country are in fact state-operated monopolies in control of all activities within their industries as well

Table 4.5   Ministries of COMECON Member Countries Concerned with the Central Control of Energy and Minerals Resources

Country	Ministries
Albania[a]	Ministry of Industry and Mines
Angola[b]	Ministry of Industry and Power Ministry of Petroleum
Bulgaria	Ministry of Metallurgy and Mineral Resources Ministry of Supply and State Reserves
Cuba	Ministry of Steelworking Industry State Committee for Material and Technical Supply
Czechoslovakia	Ministry of Fuels and Power Ministry of Metallurgy and Heavy Industry
Ethiopia[b]	Ministry of Mines, Energy and Water Resources
East Germany	Ministry of Geology Ministry for Materials Management Ministry for Ore Mining, Metallurgy, and Potash
Hungary	Ministry of Metallurgy and Machine Industry
Mongolia	Ministry of Fuel and Power Industry Ministry of Geology and Mining Industry
Poland	Ministry of Materials Management Ministry of Metallurgy Ministry of Mining
Romania	Ministry of Metallurgical Industry Ministry of Mines, Petroleum, and Geology Ministry of Tech-Material Supply and Control of Fixed Assets
Soviet Union	Ministry of Coal Industry Ministry of Ferrous Metallurgy Ministry of Gas Industry Ministry of Geology Ministry of Non-ferrous Metallurgy Ministry of Petroleum Industry State Committee for Material Reserves State Committee for Material and Technical Supply (GOSSNAB)
Vietnam	Ministry of Engineering and Metals

Source.   National Foreign Assessment Center, *Chiefs of State and Cabinet Members of Foreign Governments,* January 1980.
[a] Left COMECON in 1961.
[b] Observer status at COMECON at present, potential member.

as foreign and domestic trade. The superposition of an international organization coordinating the policies and activities of such state monopolies are in fact supermonopolies or supercartels promoted and operated by the governments of those countries. Depending on specific political objectives of the Soviet bloc such organizations can be used to pursue trade and development policies with the Third World and other trading partners designed to support those objectives without regard to the free market forces.

ROLE OF CUBA, VIETNAM, MONGOLIA, ANGOLA, AND AFGHANISTAN

The integration of Third World countries such as Cuba, Mongolia, Vietnam, Angola, Ethiopia, Laos, and others into the Soviet bloc's trade and economic development patterns plays an important role as an element of Soviet struggle against capitalism and Chinese interests in the Third World. Such overall objectives have never been abandoned by the Soviet bloc even at the height of détente.

The fact that such countries as Cuba, Angola, and Vietnam are located far away from the Soviet periphery and yet continue to develop within the Soviet orbit has an important effect on other Third World countries that may be looking for alternative solutions to their current economic and financial problems. The Soviet Union also demonstrates effective use of its growing navy and merchant marine to project the image that it is now a global and far-reaching power.

One means to exploit such Third World connections is the availability of Soviet military assistance and equipment. This has been demonstrably done in Cuba, Angola, Vietnam, Ethiopia, and Afghanistan. Many Third World countries that are turned down by "liberal" Western governments insisting on democratization are able to obtain unlimited supplies of arms and assistance from Soviet bloc countries in the name of "liberation wars."

Mongolia is a special case, primarily intended to provide a buffer state between the Soviet Union and China. Interestingly this country is not important as a minerals supplier, although it exports fluorspar, but it may hold considerable potential.

However there is also an autonomous region of Inner Mongolia in China contiguous to the Mongolian People's Republic that is a COMECON member state. This special role of Mongolia is reflected in Soviet Mongolian trade which shows almost an annual $500-million deficit that the Soviets are clearly meeting in the form of payment credits and foreign aid.

Afghanistan seems to have followed a similar pattern in recent years and now with overt Soviet occupation of that country it will most likely become another fully grown communist buffer state. There is the possibility of carving out a pro-Soviet Baluchistan, using the ethnic Baluchi populations of

Iran, Afghanistan, and Pakistan. This would give the Soviets the long-dreamed of Indian Ocean ports with direct access to Soviet central Asia through Afghanistan. Strategically it makes a lot of sense for the Soviets to pursue such an objective. They may yet get away with it because neither Afghanistan nor Baluchistan otherwise present any direct threat to Western resources or strategic materials supplies.

The Soviets may have been encouraged to invade Afghanistan—and later may attempt to "liberate" Baluchistan—because of their successes in Cuba, Angola, and Ethiopia in previous years. All these countries are relatively minor strategic minerals suppliers to the Western world; therefore their loss only inconveniences a few corporations; supplies from them can readily be replaced from alternative sources. On the other hand even though the Soviets pay a high price in foreign aid they gain strategic footholds in new regions of the world, new markets for their products, and bases for their navy and military forces.

EFFECT OF POTENTIAL ENERGY SHORTAGES IN THE 1980s

Since 1978 there have been repeated reports that the Soviet Union may be facing energy shortages during the mid-1980s and could be forced to become an importer of oil from the Middle East or other Third World oil-producing countries. These predictions are based on the fact that growth in the production of oil, natural gas, and coal has been slowing down in recent years, although it must be understood that the actual amount of energy produced continues to increase and the growth of hydroelectric and nuclear power has been increasing sharply. Nevertheless the industrial demand will continue to require faster energy growth than in recent years, and high energy-consuming industries such as iron and steel and minerals processing may create severe problems for the Soviet economy if the country's output is curtailed.

In the production of oil most of the older oil fields in the Soviet Union have shown a decline in output, and the huge West Siberian Samotlor oil field that accounts for 25 percent of the national oil output was believed to be peaking out in 1978. High rates of depletion, requirements for more investment in expensive equipment for deeper drilling, and failure to meet massive drilling and infrastructure schedules to open up new oil fields in remote and difficult terrain are believed to be the main causes of Soviet oil production slowdowns.

Soviet leadership will have to choose between importing substantial amounts of oil from noncommunist countries, reducing oil exports to eastern Europe and other COMECON members, and introducing a system of rationing for domestic end-users.

Because Soviet oil exports to the capitalist countries account for almost 50 percent of hard currency earnings this also creates a need to develop new ways of earning hard currencies should political considerations require that exports to COMECON members be maintained. Such prospects, it is believed, are what drives the Soviet Union to seek new alliances with radical oil-producing countries such as Libya. A Soviet-dominant position in non-oil minerals may be another way in which the Soviets will attempt to develop new ways of generating hard currencies by organizing producers cartels under their control.

Much is being said about the possibility that the Soviet Union will continue to export its oil for the hard currencies it needs but will increase the domestic production and consumption of natural gas—of which it has the largest reserves in the world. However, the rich gas regions are located in Tyumen Oblast in a remote and northern part of Western Siberia and require immense investment. Already the Soviets have organized a consortium of COMECON countries to build the famed Orenburg pipeline, but the gas production in more accessible regions peaked in 1977.

In the case of coal many deposits in European Russia are nearing exhaustion, and more remote mines must be put into operation. This poses an additional problem for the railroad transportation system that is strained to capacity and already has the highest utilization rate in the world.

Because of those looming energy shortages Soviet planners are developing nuclear power as the most promising source of energy in the European part of the country and among COMECON countries. At least three COMECON organizations are in operation, designed to coordinate the development of this industry in the Soviet bloc.

NUCLEAR POWER PROGRAMS IN THE SOVIET BLOC

Interestingly in 1973, the year when the OPEC oil cartel quadrupled the oil prices, COMECON countries organized their Nuclear Power Development (INTERATOMENERGO) group that is designed to coordinate and promote the development of nuclear power within the Soviet bloc. Contrary to Western experience there is negligible domestic opposition to nuclear power on the grounds of safety, and COMECON media are also careful not to relay Western concerns about nuclear power to their audiences in the Soviet bloc.

Because of potential shortages of energy, one of the key links keeping eastern Europe firmly within the Soviet orbit, COMECON countries have undertaken to develop nuclear power as the most promising energy source for eastern Europe and western Russia. Current plans call for the development of 150,000 megawatts of nuclear-generating capacity by 1990 almost 10 times the present capacity. This is a target that would bring the Soviet bloc capacity up to the projected nuclear-generating capacity of the United

States by that year. COMECON plans are to generate 25 percent of electricity from nuclear power by 1990 compared with only 4 percent in 1980.

What such a massive nuclear power development program implies is a rapidly growing and huge demand for nuclear fuels and uranium as well as other critical materials that are necessary for the production of nuclear reactors and operating equipment. The Soviet Union and Czechoslovakia are the major suppliers of uranium in the Soviet bloc, but it is not known precisely how extensive those reserves really are. Western estimates put Soviet uranium production at up to 28 percent of the world's total and combined COMECON reserves at about 30 percent.

Other sovietologists believe that COMECON's reserves are considerably smaller and to a large extent are preempted to support the Soviet nuclear weapons program that includes nuclear warheads on strategic missiles and tactical weapons, nuclear-powered submarines, ships, and satellites. As a result it is believed that the COMECON nuclear power program may have to depend on imports of uranium or nuclear fuels from Third World sources to keep up its momentum.

Because uranium and nuclear fuels are such a strategic material and significant nuclear power development programs are under way in western Europe, North America, Japan, and various other countries future COMECON demand for uranium may greatly increase the competition for available supplies. Depending on how serious COMECON's energy shortages will be in the future and how extensive their uranium resources turn out to be, this situation poses a threat of political and military action by the Soviet Union that is designed to secure adequate supplies of uranium resources.

The most promising uranium sources from the Soviet point of view are in Namibia. That country now contains the largest uranium mine in the world and is a politically unstable Third World country under the control of South Africa. The South West Africa People's Organization (SWAPO) liberation movement operating from Marxist Angola seeks to establish immediate independence in Namibia presumably under socialist rule. Under these circumstances the Soviet-Cuban presence in Angola becomes much more significant and will undoubtedly be an important factor in the future of that region.

SOVIET MATERIALS SUPPLY ORGANIZATIONS

Minerals production and supply in the Soviet Union are controlled by over 100 agencies of state grouped within at least 15 specialized committees, commissions, ministries, and departments. Ultimate control is exercised by the Central Committee of the Communist Party through its Heavy Industry Department that contains geology, oil, coal, ferrous, and nonferrous metallurgy sections.

The State Planning Committee (GOSPLAN) and the State Committee for Science and Technology (GKNT) are involved in defining the investment and technological limits for the Soviet minerals industries and are particularly influential bodies. These committees also operate through specialized departments corresponding to those of the five major minerals industry sectors of the Central Committee. Production targets and investment allocations developed by GOSPLAN are approved by the politburo of the Communist party of the Soviet Union before implementation can take place (see Table 4.6).

There is also a State Committee for Material Reserves that was elevated to this top ministerial status only in 1978 and a State Commission for Stockpiling Useful Minerals, the specific functions of which are unknown. The names of these organizations suggest that they exist to provide both central control mechanisms of the state controlling the stockpiling and exploitation policies pursuant to political objectives of the Soviet government. Undoubtedly these high-level control organizations play an important role in developing policies pertaining to foreign trade and assistance programs that are extended to Third World countries.

The State Committee for Material and Technical Supply (GOSSNAB) is a top-level materials and equipment supply and distribution agency with its counterparts in Soviet republics and lower administrative levels. GOSSNAB controls the availability of materials through a series of specialized administrations pertaining to specific resources similar to those of the Central Committee and the State Planning Committee. This is the third parallel bureaucracy concerned with materials resources of the Soviet Union.

The ministries of the Council of Ministers of the Soviet Union are all specialized organizations responsible for the production of specific materials and equipment for their extraction and processing. They can be regarded as the fourth minerals bureaucracy, although the ministries are subservient to the planning and political bodies of the Soviet hierarchy. Within the Ministry of Foreign Trade there is also a fifth minerals bureaucracy consisting of specialized foreign trade organizations that are basically import and export trade monopolies in specific minerals resources. These organizations buy and sell oil, minerals, and metals according to specific guidelines of the current five-year plan.

It is important to realize the extent of centralization and political control of the Soviet minerals production and supply apparatus. Because the Soviet apparatus operates as a huge state monopoly it has significant advantages vis-à-vis individual Western corporations or other governments without a similar system of controls. The Soviet apparatus can be particularly effective in making immediate decisions to supply military equipment, and economic aid or to engage in barter deals, depending on the political expediency of the moment.

Table 4.6   Major Soviet Central Organizations Concerned with Materials Planning, Production, Stockpiling, and Supply

Central Committee of the Communist Party of USSR Heavy Industry Department	Geology Sector Petroleum Industry Sector Coal Industry Sector Ferrous Metallurgy Sector Non-ferrous Metallurgy Sector
State Planning Committee (GOSPLAN)	Materials Balances Department Fuel and Petroleum Balances and Distribution Plans Petroleum and Gas Industry Department Geology and Mineral Resources Department Ferrous Metallurgy Department Non-ferrous Metallurgy Department
State Committee for Science and Technology (GKNT)	Mineral Resources Directorate Metallurgy Directorate
State Committee for Material and Technical Supply (GOSSNAB)	State Inspectorate for the Surveillance of Use of Materials Reserves SOYUZGLAVNEFT (oil) SOYUZGLAVUGOL (coal) SOYUZGLAVTSVETMET (nonferrous metals) SOYUZGLAVKHIM (rubber and chemicals) SOYUZGLAVPODSHIPNIK (bearings) and many other administrations
State Committee for Materials Reserves	Precise organization unknown Was upgraded to the committee ministerial status only in July 1978
State Commission for Stockpiling Useful Minerals	No details are available of the function or administrations of this organization
Ministries	Geology Petroleum Industry Construction of Petroleum and Gas Industry Enterprises Petroleum Refining and Petrochemical Industry Coal Industry Gas Industry Non-ferrous Metallurgy Defense Industry (not Ministry of Defense) Foreign Trade

Source.   National Foreign Assessment Center, November 1979.

GROWTH OF SOVIET NAVY AND MERCHANT MARINE

The Soviet navy and its merchant fleet are both the largest in the world, having grown rapidly since 1962. Many analysts believe that Soviet naval buildup was motivated by the humiliation that Russian leaders suffered when the United States warships confronted Soviet ships that were carrying missiles to Havana during the Cuban crisis. Whatever the reason it is clear that the Soviet Union possesses a formidable capacity to disrupt shipping anywhere in the world but simultaneously has a huge capacity to conduct its own shipping, using the Soviet merchant marine.

The Soviet concept of sea power includes coordinated and intensive use of its merchant and naval resources in support of state policies. During the last 30 years the Soviet merchant fleet has grown from an insignificant size to become the largest in the world in numbers of ships, although it is still sixth largest in terms of deadweight (carrying) capacity. Soviet ocean-going cargo fleet includes over 1700 ships aggregating over 16 million deadweight tons, whereas the U.S. merchant marine has slightly over 500 ships under 16 million deadweight tons and ranks sixth in number of ships and carrying capacity in the world. However Liberia, Panama, Japan, Greece, the United Kingdom, and Norway are operating very large merchant fleets, and many of the ships in those registries are owned by U.S. interests.

It is interesting to note that although most nations have reduced their passenger-carrying fleets the Soviets continue to expand theirs and now have a greater number of passenger ships than the rest of the world combined. This gives the Soviets a merchant fleet that can perform varied commercial missions and satisfy military logistics effectively and efficiently. Rather than building supertankers, container ships, liquid gas tankers, and bulk carriers the Soviets concentrated to improve the designs of large sophisticated cargo ships and small multipurpose tankers and stressed the development of high-speed Roll On/Roll Off (RO/RO) combination vessels that give them considerable versatility.

Over 20 RO/RO ships are in service that can unload cargos via large ramps. These ships can easily transport all types of military hardware without the necessity of sophisticated port facilities and can be very useful in Third World countries.

The Soviet merchant marine is regarded to be an effective tool in extending Soviet influence and neutralizing Western activities in strategic areas. The use of the Soviet merchant fleet in support of Soviet policies in Africa, the Middle East, and the Indian Ocean has contributed to the political acceptance of Soviet presence in those areas.

The Soviet merchant fleet is presently operating in over 60 trade routes calling at over 120 countries throughout the world. It continues to develop as a multimission merchant marine that can compete economically in international markets and provide effective support to achieve Soviet political, military, and economic objectives.

SOVIET TRADING SUBSIDIARIES IN THE WORLD

Coupled with the expansion of Soviet political influence in Third World countries and the growth of the Soviet merchant marine was the explosion during the 1970s of foreign-based Soviet firms to promote Soviet products and services. From a mere 28 such firms at the end of 1970 the number grew to 84 by the end of 1976. The activities of those firms are mostly concentrated in shipping and fishing, banking and insurance, and marketing and leasing of Soviet products.

Most Soviet firms are small and include Western partners, but Soviet authorities usually control 50 percent or more of the equity. Soviet parent organizations of the firms are normally appropriate foreign trade organizations of the Ministry of Foreign Trade. In the case of shipping and fishing firms they are controlled by the Soviet Ministry of Maritime Fleet (MORFLOT). Soviet-owned banks and insurance companies are wholly owned by Soviet State Bank (GOSBANK) or Vneshtorgbank in Moscow or have a majority share by Ingosstrakh, the Soviet foreign insurance organization.

Of most significance to Soviet foreign trade in minerals and critical materials are the 22 Soviet shipping firms located on the Atlantic and Pacific coasts of North America, in western Europe, and in North and Southeast Asia. In specific countries these firms exist in Australia, Austria, Belgium, Canada, Finland, France, West Germany, Italy, Japan, the Netherlands, Spain, Sweden, the United Kingdom, the United States, the Philippines, and Singapore (see Table 4.7).

Jointly owned shipping firms represent the largest proportion of all Soviet firms in the West and are a measure of the importance of this activity in Soviet global policies. These firms assist Soviet shipping worldwide by cutting the costs of commissions and fees associated with Soviet activities in foreign ports. They also direct customers to the 16 steamship companies under the control of MORFLOT. The most active of those companies in the Soviet Union are the Far Eastern Steamship Company of Vladivostok, Baltic of Leningrad, Black Sea of Odessa, and the Arctic of Murmansk.

It is common practice for Soviet shipping firms to offer lower rates than Western competitors and not to join shipping conferences that set rates on all cargoes on a given route. As a result Soviet shipping firms have been able to offer rates 20 percent and more under the established rate structures. Some Western competitors believe that in the long run Soviet policy is to gain control of world shipping by exploiting its low-cost railway land bridge between Japan and Europe in combination with its large and far-reaching merchant marine.

Table 4.7   Soviet Shipping and Related Firms in the West

Date First Established	Country and City	Name of Firm
1967	Singapore	Singapore-Soviet Shipping Company
1969	Japan, Tokyo	United Orient Shipping Agency Co., Ltd.
1970	Belgium, Antwerp	Transworld Marine Agency
1971	Spain, Barcelona	Sovhispan
1972	Netherlands, Rotterdam	Transworld Marine Agency
1974	Germany, Hamburg	Ueberseeshiffahrtsagentur Transnautic GmbH
	France, Paris	Sagmar, SA
	Australia, Sydney	Opal Maritime Agency, Ltd.
	Philippines, Manila	Fil-Sov Shipping Company
1975	Canada, Vancouver	Morflot Freight Liners, Ltd.
1976	Austria, Vienna	Asotra
	Italy, Genoa	Dolphin Agenzia Maritima
	Australia	Fresco Australia Line
	Spain, Madrid	Intramar
	United States, Clark, N.J.	Morflot American Shipping Inc.
	Sweden, Stockholm	Scansov Transport AB
	Mozambique	Soviet-Mozambique Fishing Company
	Italy	Sovitalmare
	Italy, Leghorn	Sovitpesca
	Germany, Koln	Wesotra Spedition und Transport
	United Kingdom, London	Anglo-Soviet Shipping Company Ltd.
	Finland	Saimaa Lines Ltd.
	United States, New York City	Sovfracht (USA) Inc.

Source. Central Intelligence Agency, *Soviet Commercial Operations in the West,* ER 77-10486, September 1977.

SOVIET BLOC'S FOREIGN AID POLICIES

The Soviet Union maintains extensive military and economic programs with over 80 Third World countries in the world. During the 1956–1978 period the Soviets delivered over $25 billion in military equipment whereas eastern European countries accounted for another $2.6 billion. The Soviet bloc's military commitments are best illustrated by the number of military personnel in specific countries (see Table 4.8).

The largest military program recipients, excluding Soviet invasion of Afghanistan, were the countries in the Middle East, where the Soviet Union sells its military hardware for hard currency, often exploiting Western re-

Table 4.8 Soviet, East European, and Cuban
Military Personnel in Third World Countries
during 1978

Country	Soviet and East European Personnel	Cuban Personnel
Afghanistan[a]	90,000	—
Angola	1,300	19,000
Ethiopia	1,400	16,500
Syria	2,580	—
Libya	1,750	200
Iraq	1,200	150
Algeria	1,000	15
South Yemen	550	1,000
Mozambique	230	800
Mali	180	—
North Yemen	155	—
India	150	—
Peru	150	—
Guinea	100	200
Guinea-Bissau	65	140
Equatorial Guinea	40	150
Morocco	10	—
Guyana	—	10

Source. National Foreign Assessment Center, September 1979.
[a] Includes Soviet troops that invaded Afghanistan in 1979.

luctance to provide arms to countries in that troubled region. However there was a time when the Soviet Union was willing to barter arms in return for commodities, although it is no longer following that policy with Arab countries such as Libya, Algeria, or Iraq that are rich in petrodollars.

During the 1954–1978 period the Soviet Union also extended $17 billion in economic credits and grants to Third World countries of which slightly over $7.5 billion has been drawn. Eastern European countries extended over $9 billion during the same period of time and about $3.3 billion of that amount has been used up.

In 1978 the Soviet Union renewed increasing foreign aid extensions, and two Western-oriented countries Morocco and Turkey received Soviet commitments that are among the largest ever extended by the Soviet Union to any Third World country.

Both military and economic assistance of the Soviet bloc has been heavily concentrated in the Arab countries of the Middle East. Syria, Libya, Iraq,

Algeria, Iran, Morocco, South and North Yemen, Tunisia, and recently even Jordan have been receiving Soviet foreign aid credits and grants. Clearly the resources of the oil countries are much on the Soviet Union's mind, and approaches have even been made to Saudi Arabia to establish diplomatic relations.

In Africa the countries of Angola, Ethiopia, Mozambique, Mali, Guinea, Guinea-Bissau, Equatorial Guinea, Ghana, Tanzania, Sierra Leone, and Madagascar also have been receiving Soviet economic aid. In many instances the policy with these relatively poor countries is to propose major industrial projects in return for repayment in the form of commodities or future production of the plants that are being built with Soviet aid.

The COMECON organization advocates long-term agreements with Third World producers and cooperation with developing countries to establish mining and processing plants as the most practical way to satisfy those long-term agreements. Large quantities of nonferrous metals, minerals, and tropical agricultural commodities are to be committed to Soviet bloc end-users in return for development assistance. Soviet promoters offer technical assistance in the form of geological surveys and have already engaged in mineral reserves studies in 30 countries and actually explored for oil in 15 of them. New sources of oil, iron ore, and bauxite or aluminum are believed to be of prime interest to Soviet planners.

REFERENCES

Central Intelligence Agency, *Nuclear Energy*, ER 77–10468, August 1977.

Central Intelligence Agency, *Soviet Commercial Operations in the West*, ER 77–10486, September 1977.

Fine, Daniel I., "The Soviets' New Foothold in Central Africa," *Business Week*, 10 March 1980, p. 59.

Fullerton, John, "The Strategic Power of Soviet Shipping," *Defense and Foreign Affairs Digest*, June 1978.

"International Organizations," *Europa Yearbook*, 1979, p. 161.

Morgenthaler, Eric, "Soviet Bloc Is Pushing Nuclear-Power Plants Even as U.S. Pulls Back," *Wall Street Journal*, January 1980, p. 1.

National Foreign Assessment Center, *Communist Aid Activities in Non-Communist Less Developed Countries 1978*, ER 79–10412U, September 1979.

National Foreign Assessment Center, *Directory of Soviet Officials: Volume I: National Organizations*, CR 79–16593, November 1979.

National Foreign Assessment Center, *The World Oil Market in the Years Ahead*, ER 79–10327U, August 1979.

"Potezne Zrodlo Energii," *Czerwony Sztandar*, 4 November 1976, Vilnius, Lithuanian SSR, USSR (in Polish).

"Russia Turns to Nuclear Power as Oil Strains Show," *Economist*, 26 May 1979, p. 105.

"Russia's Drive to Surpass U.S. in Sea Power," *U.S. News & World Report*, 6 March 1978, p. 27.

"Soviets Go Atomaya Energiya," *Time,* 30 October 1978.

Strishkov, V. V., "Mineral Industries of the U.S.S.R.," *Mining Annual Review,* London 1978.

Szuprowicz, Bohdan O., "Russian Drive to Control Africa's Strategic Minerals," *Bulletin,* 15 May 1979.

Szuprowicz, Bohdan O., "Soviet Squeeze on Strategic Materials," *Datamation,* October 1978.

U.S. Bureau of Mines, "Mineral Industries of Eastern Europe and the U.S.S.R.," MP-5 Mineral Perspectives, May 1978.

U.S. Department of Commerce, *Merchant Fleets of the World,* Washington, D.C., December 1977.

U.S. Department of the Navy, *Understanding Soviet Naval Developments,* Office of the Chief of Naval Operations, Washington, D.C., 1978.

U.S. House of Representatives, Report of the Committee on International Relations, "The Soviet Union and the Third World: A Watershed in Great Power Policy?" U.S. Government Printing Office, Washington, D.C., May 1977.

CHAPTER
FIVE

Strategic Importance of Southern Africa

In comparison with other areas of the world the southern African subcontinent from the Cape of Good Hope to the Congo basin in Zaire probably contains more known reserves of numerous strategic minerals than any other part of the world. The Republic of South Africa alone has often been labeled the "Saudi Arabia of non-oil minerals."

These reserves include gold, diamonds, platinum, chromium, cobalt, manganese, uranium, copper, tantalum, rhodium, palladium, ruthenium, vanadium, germanium, beryllium, antimony, and lesser quantities of many other minerals that are vital to the modern economy. The only missing resource in the region is oil, but there is an abundance of coal and uranium more than adequate to make the region self-sufficient in energy.

The subcontinent south of the equator contains about 20 political entities, ranging from island nations like the Comoros, Mauritius, and Reunion to populous and large countries like Zaire and South Africa. About 125 million people, predominantly black African tribes with relatively low average literacy rates, live in the area. The ruling governments range from military regimes and people's republics to more democratic multiparty states and a monarchy.

For many years strategic minerals from southern Africa were the lifeblood of western European economies. In recent years the United States has become also increasingly dependent on minerals supplies from that region. At the same time decolonization, racial issues, civil strife, revolutions, and wars, along with Soviet, Cuban, east European, and even Chinese penetration into the area have combined to destabilize the subcontinent.

The coming to power of Marxist-Leninist regimes in Angola and Mozambique in 1975 is regarded by South Africa as the first "event" of the Third World War that must be considered as a significant victory for the Soviet bloc. From that same point of view rebel invasions of the copper and cobalt-rich Shaba province of Zaire in 1977 and 1978 is probably viewed as a successful counteraction by the West to further aggression. It now remains to be seen how the South Africans will judge the emergence of Robert Mugabe as Marxist prime minister of Zimbabwe, the second most important strategic materials supplier in that region.

It is important to realize that the United States and the West are so preoccupied with the OPEC cartel and the Middle East conflicts that little attention is paid to southern Africa. The racial policies of South Africa are a further constraint on more open involvement, particularly of the Anglo-Saxon world, with its vociferous liberal constituencies.

Among the Western countries only France appears to brave world opinion and dares to act openly in Africa in defense of its own interests. But French action and intervention are primarily confined to the ex-French and ex-Belgian colonies, where it is effectively assisting governments in power to counteract Soviet and Libyan ambitions in Africa. Both Libya and Nigeria are two emerging African OPEC powers, primarily based on surplus revenues from the sales of their oil to the consuming nations of the West. Whether France has been acting strictly on its own account or on behalf of western Europe is not yet clear, but it is a clear signal to the Anglo-Saxon world that complacent attitudes to Third World developments will not be tolerated by the other threatened industrialized countries.

Yet there are increasing numbers of observers who are calling for much more attention to be given to the southern African subcontinent because of its predominant position as a strategic materials supplier. There is oil in many countries other than OPEC countries, and alternatives such as natural gas, coal, nuclear power, and other forms of energy will play an increasing role in all economies. Most of the non-oil minerals of southern Africa also exist in other parts of the world, but nowhere except the Soviet Union are their deposits and reserves so large and significant as in the southern African subcontinent.

In addition South Africa and even Zimbabwe are agriculturally rich countries able to produce food surpluses to feed the whole subcontinent. This is an important factor in the geopolitics of the area. It also means that any economic sanctions invoked against a country like South Africa would have very limited results. Any nation that can feed itself and has the resources of South Africa is bound to develop into a regional superpower.

This is certainly the potential of southern Africa, and one of the ambitions of South Africa has been the formation of a regional constellation of strategic materials-producing countries, including Zimbabwe, Mozambique, Angola, Zambia, Namibia, and Botswana. The polarization of the region on racial grounds, uncertainty of Western support and investment, emergence of Marxist-Leninist regimes, and Soviet-Cuban penetration in the area have combined to prevent the formation of such a political grouping. However, it must be kept in mind by the Western end-users that whoever finally comes to control the subcontinent will probably want to drive toward such a regional economic integration of the area.

RESOURCES OF "HIGH AFRICA"

The countries of "High Africa," as the mineral-rich southern African area is sometimes known, are a veritable treasurehouse of mineral commodities, many of which are found in other parts of the Western world, only in inadequate quantities. The backbone of High Africa are the mineral deposits of the Kaapvaal region of South Africa and the Great Dyke chromium-asbestos district in Zimbabwe. In fact there are over 40 major mineral districts located throughout the southern African plateau. The plateau ranges from the Cape of Good Hope to the Congo river valley of Zaire and gives the southern African subcontinent the appearance similar to that of a huge heel of a shoe (see Figure 5.1).

Geologists are beginning to discover the reasons why High Africa is so well endowed with so many valuable minerals. The conclusions so far point to the fact that this subcontinent attained geological stability before other geological nuclei could form elsewhere in the world, with the possible exception of similar formations in the Soviet Union. Basically such early geological formations were particularly favorable to concentrations of native elements or oxides that now make up the rich ore deposits of High Africa. Thus the uniqueness of the region results from its age and alternative sources of such rich minerals deposits may be very hard or almost impossible to find anywhere else in the world.

As a result of those unique geological formations the reserves of High Africa of some of the most strategic materials are by far the largest in the world. This is particularly true in the case of such minerals and metals as chromium, platinum metals, diamonds, manganese, gold, fluorspar, columbium, tantalum, uranium, and mica (see Table 5.1).

On the other hand even though High Africa reserves of other strategic minerals are among the largest in the world those of the Soviet Union are larger still. Estimated reserves of antimony, asbestos, cobalt, coal, beryllium, silver, iron ore, titanium, lead, tin, and germanium are believed to be more extensive in the Soviet Union. In some cases conflicting estimates exist as, for example, in the case of vanadium in which some sources estimate that the Soviet Union possesses 75 percent of the world's reserves and other sources believe that High Africa accounts for 64 percent of the world's total. There are also discrepancies with regard to reserves of asbestos in the two regions (see Table 4.1 in Chapter 4).

The question of reserves is extremely difficult to settle when comparisons are made between various countries that may use differing yardsticks to measure their reserves. Comparisons with Soviet bloc countries are particularly uncertain because of a relatively low volume of data available about their minerals industries. Even among the developed and Third World countries, comparisons of reserves are often in question. Much depends on whether

Figure 5.1 "High Africa" region showing unique concentration of major mineral districts in the subcontinent.

economic or subeconomic reserves are included. Even within identified deposits reserves are classified as measured, indicated, or inferred, depending on the degree of exploration that has taken place. Changing prices and technology can drastically affect the magnitude of recoverable reserves in a very short time.

The magnitude of High Africa reserves is also paralleled by the predominant position of the subcontinent as a producer of strategic materials. In this concern there is a rough comparison between the role played by the Soviet Union as a supplier of all the strategic materials to its COMECON clients and that of High Africa as the major purveyor of strategic materials to the free market economies.

Table 5.1 Estimated Reserves of Major Minerals and Metals in Africa South of the Equator as Percentage of Global Reserves

Minerals	Percentage in High Africa	Countries with Major Mineral Deposits
Chromium	95	South Africa, Zimbabwe, Madagascar
Platinum metals	86	South Africa
Diamonds	83	Zaire, Botswana, South Africa, Namibia, Angola
Vanadium	64	South Africa
Vermiculite	60	South Africa
Manganese	53	South Africa, Gabon
Gold	50	South Africa, Zimbabwe
Fluorspar	50	South Africa
Columbium/tantalum	38	Zaire, Mozambique, Zimbabwe
Uranium	27	South Africa, Namibia, Gabon
Asbestos	25	Zimbabwe, South Africa, Swaziland
Mica	25	Madagascar
Cobalt	17	Zaire, Zambia
Copper	13	Zaire, Zambia, South Africa
Nickel	10	South Africa
Zinc	10	Namibia, South Africa
Graphite	10	Madagascar
Phosphate	8	South Africa
Gypsum	7	Angola, South Africa
Silver	6	Namibia, South Africa
Coal	5	Mozambique, Zimbabwe, South Africa, Swaziland
Arsenic	5	Namibia
Beryllium	5	Mozambique, Zambia, Angola, Rwanda
Iron ore	5	Angola, South Africa
Titanium	5	South Africa
Antimony	4	South Africa
Lead	4	South Africa
Tin	4	Zaire, Burundi, South Africa
Cadmium	2	Namibia, Zaire
Germanium	2	Zaire

Source. Compiled by 21st Century Research from various documents and reports, including the U.S. Bureau of Mines and statistical yearbooks. These estimates are indicative of the state of reserves during the 1975–1978 period, and it must be pointed out that such data change with time.

High Africa produces 50 percent or more of the total world output of about 10 of the most strategic minerals. These include such critical platinum metals as rhodium, ruthenium, and platinum itself, although the Soviet Union leads in the production of palladium. High Africa is also the top producer of gold, diamonds, vanadium, chromium, germanium, and cobalt. It is well to remember here too that the OPEC oil cartel controls only about 52 percent of the world's oil production, whereas another 26 percent or so is under the control of Soviet state monopolies (see Figure 5.2).

There is also significant production in High Africa countries of manganese, beryllium, antimony, copper, and tantalum of which the region provides between 10 and 30 percent of the global output. Other metals and minerals are also produced but are of relatively lesser importance because their deposits in High Africa are not particularly rich and their occurrence in other parts of the world is relatively common.

EFFECTS OF STRATEGIC MATERIALS OVERHANG

This unique concentration of very large minerals reserves and production creates a huge overhang of economically exploitable mineral deposits in High Africa countries that does not exist anywhere else in the world. The existence of such a huge overhang directly affects the decisions of Western corporations and financial circles pertaining to new investment in the exploration and development of mineral resources in other countries.

What this means is that private interests that could be searching for alternative sources of minerals are reluctant to invest in new mining ventures to produce minerals and metals in which High Africa countries enjoy such an overwhelming supply position unless special incentives and concessions are available. Yet if the production of High Africa is disrupted by political action or attempts to form a multimineral cartel, security interests of the West might dictate the development of alternative sources of these minerals.

Such new mining ventures would require enormous investments in exploration and equipment and would probably take several years to bring production in these enterprises to significant levels. This could only be achieved if the scarcity of the strategic materials drove the prices to considerably higher levels or if Western governments became major partners, underwriting some of the investment and guaranteeing profitability of those new ventures.

Even then the High Africa strategic materials overhang would remain a constant threat to world minerals markets in which they possessed such a dominant position. Even after lengthy supplies disruptions or production curtailments whoever controlled High Africa resources could create havoc in free world markets by sudden resumption of production and increased supplies of strategic minerals that would put the new mining ventures liter-

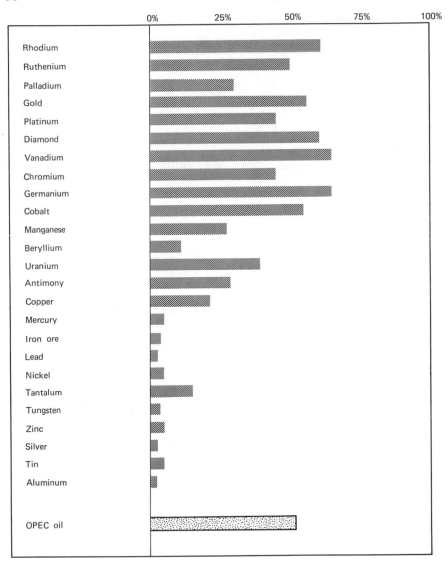

Figure 5.2 "High Africa" strategic minerals and metals production as percentage of global supply.

ally out of business in a very short time. The control already exercised by South Africa over gold, platinum, and diamond supplies is a good example, although it is impossible to show that the overhang in those metals and minerals is in fact responsible for relatively limited production elsewhere in the world outside the Soviet bloc.

The overhang factor would not have an effect if the High Africa mining regions were permanently put out of commission, but such an occurrence is not practical unless "dirty" nuclear explosions are used to contaminate key mining areas and make them inaccessible to humans for many years into the future. This is one reason, aside from the more common nonproliferation arguments, why there is so much concern about the acquisition of nuclear weapons or even nuclear reactors by African countries such as South Africa or Zaire.

The end-users of strategic materials are usually unaware of these considerations, leaving the questions of supplies to enterprises that specialize in the exploration, mining, and processing of minerals. However the developing situation in High Africa countries today contains many dangerous elements that may lead to serious supply disruptions and price escalations such as were experienced by cobalt users in 1978 and 1979.

FOREIGN INVESTMENT IN SOUTH AFRICA

A combination of factors, including those huge and rich mineral reserves, relatively cheap labor, and the threat of the minerals overhang, contribute to the direction of the foreign investment process in High Africa in general and in South Africa in particular. Basically these factors force Western capital sources to consider investment in South Africa minerals development before looking at alternative opportunities in other parts of the world.

At the same time the unique political and social fabric of South Africa—most often denounced because of its apartheid policies—and the concerted attacks on this system by black African states, Soviet bloc countries, and democratic governments and institutions constitute a deterrent acting to seriously curtail foreign investment in that country.

Underlying this situation is the fact that South Africa is basically a Third World country despite its relatively industrialized state in Africa as a whole. South Africa's GNP of about $50 billion in 1980 makes it the largest economy in Africa, but its per capita GNP of over $1600 per year puts it in the developing countries' league, along with Algeria, Brazil, Turkey, or Mexico. In European terms South Africa's GNP is comparable to that of Romania or Yugoslavia, but its population is larger than that of those two countries.

As a result South Africa has only limited potential to generate domestic investment funds to develop its huge mining industry and infrastructure, but unlike other developing countries South Africa receives no foreign aid. Instead it must depend on corporate and private investment from Western industrialized countries and industries that realize the strategic importance of South African minerals. However, the dramatic escalation in the price of gold, platinum, and diamonds in recent years benefited South Africa tremendously, setting off a new domestic investment boom.

The bulk of foreign investment in South Africa comes from western Europe, particularly the United Kingdom, France, and West Germany. The European Community accounts for at least 57 percent of a total direct foreign investment of about $10 billion. The United States has a relatively smaller stake in the country, amounting to 17 percent of this total, mostly represented by the assets of almost 350 American companies operating in South Africa. A good part of the remainder is probably represented by Japanese, Canadian, Australian, and other interests.

There has been continuing controversy about trade and investment in South Africa by Western countries, mostly promoted by liberal and church institutions of the Anglo-Saxon world. Soviet bloc countries and the United Nations membership also denounce South Africa's social policies and demand the imposition of sanctions further limiting investment and trade with South Africa. In theory economic pressures are believed to speed up social change in that country, but there is also the danger of violence and revolution, because such pressures will primarily affect the black and poor sectors of the population.

The more liberal South African point of view, often supported by black South African leadership, is to encourage further Western investment and trade in South Africa that is seen as an effective tool of social reform which may prevent violent change.

Since 1975, however, the South African government also concentrated on the development of domestic defense, electronics, motor vehicles, and chemicals industry sectors to reduce import dependence on foreign sources of technology and to escape any future sanctions. Thus even the threat of sanctions and the imposition of a limited embargo against the sale of equipment destined to South African military and police forces only had the effect of intensifying domestic industry development and reducing the export markets for American manufacturers.

The current investment boom supported by the high prices of gold and mineral exports continues to develop import substitution industries but provides much greater investment funds for the expansion of the mining and energy sectors as well as the country's infrastructure. In effect South Africa is becoming a more self-sufficient economy with a greater ability to make its own decisions about its future.

GROWTH OF SOUTH AFRICAN MINERALS PROCESSING INDUSTRIES

During the 1980s South Africa is planning to embark on the largest mining industry expansion in its history, coupled with the development of end-user and consumer goods industries—all of which is becoming possible as a result of increasing revenues derived from the sales of gold and foreign investment. This effort is expected to increase even further South Africa's already significant minerals processing industries and lay to rest any attempts by Angola, Zambia, and Zaire to establish a competitive minerals processing base in High Africa countries outside the jurisdiction of South Africa.

The expansion of gold and uranium mining and processing are leading this growth program. This is so because these are the metals that produce the lion's share of South Africa's export revenues. Western Europe, which is rapidly developing its nuclear power industries, is already dependent on South Africa for about 50 percent of its uranium needs. If this growth continues and uranium prices maintain their current or higher levels it will displace even gold as South Africa's largest revenue-producing commodity in the future.

The mining and processing of diamonds, coal, and other metals such as chromium, copper, nickel, vanadium, platinum, tin, lead, and zinc are also included in the new expansion plans. By early 1980 up to 40 foreign enterprises had already been attracted to the renewed upsurge in exploration in South Africa.

On the other hand South African sources claim that the country already has a sophisticated exploration industry in place which is as advanced as that of any other country in the world. Remote sensing, geochemistry, and geophysical techniques make prospecting a very efficient business in South Africa.

The lack of domestic oil resources but an abundance of coal and uranium directed South Africa's attention to the development of synthetic fuels from coal and nuclear power that includes uranium enrichment capabilities. As a result South Africa's SASOL, a government-owned corporation, is already considered a world leader in synthetic fuels production. SASOL supplies less than 10 percent of South Africa's oil needs at present but is expected to provide more than 50 percent of the demand in a few years, and over $7 billion is being spent on SASOL expansion between 1980 and 1984.

The abundance of coal also provides a source of feedstocks to the chemical industry that includes such projects as the production of methanol to further increase domestic liquid fuels supplies. Over $600 million is slated for new investment in this project by the AECI organization. In a joint venture with SENTACHEM, the company is also developing another synthetic fuels plant valued at $750 million to produce ethanol from corn and sugar as an additive to gas and diesel fuel that may replace another 25 percent of South Africa's oil imports by 1985. Synthetic rubber, polyethylene, nylon, and plastics are also produced and even exported by South Africa's coal-based petrochemicals industry.

Coal-fired and nuclear power generating stations are being expanded at a planned cost of over $13 billion through 1990, with unknown additional investment being scheduled for the development of a uranium enrichment plant. This is an important program on which further expansion of the mining industry depends because it is a large consumer of energy without which its planned growth would be impossible. This is also an important reason why other countries in the region could not offer alternative opportunities for developing minerals processing industries in competition with South Africa.

Clearly South Africa is developing an infrastructure that is taking it rapidly down the path of industrialization and is departing from the more standard development model of other Third World countries. It has all the requirements, once its energy base is completely secure, to become a dominant manufacturing and exporting country not only in Africa but also in the southern hemisphere.

IMPORTANCE OF NAMIBIA

Namibia, known for many years as South West Africa, became South Africa's mandate territory as a result of the Treaty of Versailles that disposed of this German colony at the conclusion of World War I. By the end of World War II in 1946 South Africa applied to the United Nations, proposing to incorporate the territory as one of its provinces, but this was rejected by the General Assembly. After a period of closer administration of Namibia under South African laws South Africa finally agreed in principle to leave the territory and allow it to become independent.

At present the question of Namibian independence has not been finally resolved in terms of the new power structure to control the territory. A Marxist-oriented SWAPO liberation movement is in operation in Namibia and neighboring Angola and Zambia. It continues to present the danger of a future confrontation that may end up in an occupation of Namibia by South Africa, while SWAPO calls for the assistance of Cuban troops, Soviet weapons, and advisers from Angola.

It is now believed that the Soviet price for assisting SWAPO militarily to win control of Namibia is the nationalization of Namibia's mining industry, the mainstay of an expanding economy. Namibia now accounts for 6 percent of the world's uranium production and the new uranium mine developed by the Rio-Tinto Zinc Corporation at Rossing is described as the largest uranium mine in the world. In addition Namibia is a significant producer of diamonds and gems, copper, lead, vanadium, tungsten, zinc, cadmium, arsenic, and salt and a minor producer of other metals. Namibia's uranium resources could be a major attraction to COMECON countries to secure nuclear fuel sources for their expanding nuclear power programs.

ZIMBABWE RESOURCES

Following South Africa and Zaire, Zimbabwe is probably the most important country in the High Africa region with regard to mineral resources. It dominates the area in high-grade chromium and asbestos reserves and is believed to possess 10 percent of the global reserves of those minerals. It is also a significant producer of coal, gold, tantalum, columbium, and lithium. There is also some production of copper, nickel, and platinum.

In 1965 Rhodesia declared Unilateral Declaration of Independence under Ian Smith that continued until 1979 when bishop Abel Muzorewa emerged as the first black leader of Zimbabwe. Muzorewa's rule was short-lived and ended in a new election that brought Marxist Robert Mugabe to power in February 1980.

During the Ian Smith rule the United Nations imposed a trade embargo on Rhodesia, and guerrilla warfare erupted between Rhodesian forces and the Patriotic Front liberation movements. The Zimbabwe African People's Union (ZAPU), led by Joshua Nkomo, who later became Home Affairs Minister in Mugabe's cabinet, was mostly based in Zambia. Zimbabwe African National Union (ZANU) led by Robert Mugabe was operating mainly from bases in Mozambique.

The two movements draw their support from two different tribal groups within Rhodesia. ZAPU is strongest among the Ndebele-speaking peoples, and ZANU is predominant among the Shona-speaking tribes. The present black leadership under Robert Mugabe appears to be a temporary coalition of those two movements and the remaining political groupings within the country.

Prior to the Unilateral Declaration of Independence Rhodesia had achieved a state of economic development surpassed only by South Africa in that region. Rhodesia's GNP reached $1 billion by 1965 and although it decreased after the United Nations sanctions were imposed it reached $1.5 billion by 1971 and stood at $3.3 billion by 1978. Agriculture suffered the most, but the manufacturing sector increased as a result of the creation of import substitution industries.

The minerals industry has prospered despite trade embargoes, and substantial progress was achieved in the local processing of minerals before export. Because the United States was heavily dependent on Rhodesian chromium imports the Byrd Amendment was passed in the U.S. Congress in 1971 permitting the importation of strategic materials from Rhodesia despite the trade embargo. Although this action is not believed to have contributed significantly to Rhodesia's economy at the time, it underscores the vulnerability of the United States in its foreign policy as a result of its growing import dependence on foreign sources of strategic materials.

Since 1965 Rhodesia has not published any trade statistics, although it continued to export asbestos, coal, copper, chromium, pig iron, ferrochrome, and even electric power to neighboring Zambia. Rhodesia in fact became the only country besides the People's Republic of China not to publish foreign trade statistics, but it demonstrated—albeit at a price—the futility of economic sanctions against a determined nation. It is also believed that chromium exports found their way to China during that period and that some Rhodesian chrome was sold to the Soviet Union which in turn re-exported it to other countries, including the United States at a considerably higher price than that paid in Rhodesia.

ZAMBIA'S MINERAL RESOURCES

Zambia was formerly Northern Rhodesia that became the first British terri-tory to become a republic immediately on attaining independence in 1964. It is now a "one party participatory democracy" based on a constitution promulgated in 1973.

Zambia's economy is dominated by copper production and exports, of which it is believed to possess 7 percent of the world's reserves and enor-mous resources. It is the fourth largest copper producer in the world after the United States, the Soviet Union, and Chile.

Copper accounts for 50 percent of Zambia's GNP, over 90 percent of its exports, and one-third to one-half of government revenues. As a result the Zambian economy is extremely sensitive to the world's copper demand and prices. In addition as a landlocked economy Zambia is constantly concerned about the transportation lines for its minerals to the ports of Angola, Tanza-nia, Mozambique, and South Africa. Since 1971 the Zambian government has been acquiring controlling interest in copper mining from foreign firms under a steady policy of "zambianization" of all industries.

Zambia is also the fourth largest producer of cobalt in the world and be-came an important African source of the metal after the Shaba rebel inva-sion of cobalt-producing areas in Zaire. It is believed to have about 2 per-cent of the world's cobalt resources.

Zambia also produces silver, lead, zinc, relatively poor-quality coal, and smaller quantities of gold, manganese, beryllium, cadmium, selenium, tin, gypsum, limestone, and mica. There are also known deposits of nickel and iron ore and uranium, and it is generally conceded that the true minerals po-tential of Zambia is still far from being realized.

CRUCIAL ROLE OF ZAIRE IN COBALT SUPPLIES

Zaire is probably the second most important minerals-producing country bordering on the northern reaches of High Africa with its copper-rich Shaba province and diamond-bearing Kasai region. Zaire is estimated to contain 48 percent of the world's industrial diamonds reserves, 26 percent of colum-bium-tantalite reserves, 15 percent of the world's cobalt, 4 percent of cop-per, 2 percent of tin and germanium, and 1 percent of the cadmium reserves.

Among other known resources are gold, bauxite, iron ore, manganese, and coal and 13 percent of the global hydroelectric potential. There is also some production and exports of oil in the country, and it is believed to have one of the largest agricultural potentials in all of Africa.

Zaire is by far the largest cobalt producer in the world, this being a by-product of the production of copper in the Shaba province. About 41 percent of the cobalt produced in the world in the late 1970s comes from Zaire. Because cobalt is among the most strategic materials in the world Zaire is constantly the target of various political forces that see great leverage in the ability to control such an overwhelming supply of the world's cobalt supply in a single country.

Since independence in 1960 Zaire was the scene of mutinies, rebellions, secessions, invasions, and Western military intervention. The most recent invasion that disrupted the supply of cobalt from Zaire occurred in 1978 when former Katangan gendarmes based in Angola invaded the Shaba province for the second year in a row and took over the important mining center of Kolwezi where some of the largest copper and cobalt mines are located.

France took the lead in providing military assistance to Zairean armed forces by flying in 1000 Foreign Legion paratroopers and 1750 Belgian soldiers who repelled the invaders and established a Pan-African peace-keeping force in Zaire. It is widely believed that these invasions have been inspired by the Soviet Union and that Cuban military advisers from neighboring Angola took part in their execution, while Zambia allowed the passage of rebel forces through its territory. Many observers believe that strikes against the Shaba mining regions will continue as more pro-Soviet or Marxist countries bordering Zaire consolidate their power in the region.

Despite its Western orientation and interest in attracting private investment, Zaire is also pursuing a policy of "zairianization" in various industries and claims to be a nonaligned nation promoting the interests of developing countries. As such Zaire is one of five full members of CIPEC and in 1978 agreed jointly with Zambia and Peru to reduce copper production by 15 percent in an attempt to raise depressed world copper prices at the time.

ANGOLA AND MOZAMBIQUE

In comparison with South Africa, Namibia, Zimbabwe, Zambia, and Zaire the two ex-Portuguese territories of Angola and Mozambique are relatively minor producers of minerals in general and of strategic minerals in particular. Of the two Angola is more important because it controls up to 9 percent of the world's diamonds reserves. Otherwise it has 1 percent of the world's beryllium and iron ore reserves, and the Cabinda region produces oil and natural gas. Angola's oil production is approximately equal to South Africa's annual imports, and since it is the only significant source of oil in the region this makes Angola strategically important in High Africa as well.

Mozambique is believed to possess about 10 percent of the world's reserves of columbite-tantalite, but it contributes only about 1 percent as a producer of these minerals. Mozambique also produces bauxite, beryllium, coal, copper, lithium, mica, and other minerals but in no case does it account for production levels larger than 1 percent of the global output. As a result Mozambique is relatively unimportant in the world's minerals supply system as a source, and the disruption of all supplies from Mozambique would be of no consequence in world markets. However, together with Angola, Mozambique controls the nearest ports for exports of minerals from landlocked minerals-mining regions of Zaire, Zambia, and Zimbabwe. During the 1970s access to those ports has been disrupted by military action or by political decree, and this contributed to the cost of the production of minerals in those areas. Nevertheless, although delayed and more costly, exports continued through the TAZARA railroad and the South African transportation networks.

Although Angola and Mozambique are relatively unimportant as minerals producers both countries are believed to be considerably underexplored as yet. The minerals potential of Angola is believed to be immense because of the country's location in relation to other mineral-rich areas of High Africa. Until complete geological surveys are made it is impossible to assess whether Angola is simply rich or extremely wealthy as a source of minerals. Mozambique is relatively poorly endowed as a low-lying country on the eastern fringe of High Africa, but its minerals industry is underdeveloped and its mineral potential vastly underexplored.

The present strategic importance of Angola and Mozambique, aside from the availability of the nearest ports, centers on the fact that both countries are run by Marxist-Leninist regimes that took power after Portugal decided to grant independence to the two territories in 1974. Although the Popular Movement for the Liberation of Angola (MPLA) claimed victory over rival factions it was able to do so with the support of Soviet, east European, and Cuban military aid and troops. At present another faction National Union for Total Independence of Angola (UNITA) under the leadership of Jonas Savimbi continues guerilla warfare inside Angola; and Cuban, Soviet, and east European troops now present in the country are believed to be over 20,000 in number.

Mozambique, although also a Marxist state, is less militant than Angola and is eager to accept assistance from the Soviet bloc, the Western world, South Africa, and even China. Traditionally Mozambique has been linked economically to South Africa, serving as another outlet for minerals from the Johannesburg and Swaziland areas and providing significant numbers of laborers for South African mines and industries.

SIGNIFICANCE OF OTHER SOUTHERN AFRICAN COUNTRIES

Of the remaining southern African countries around the strategic High Africa region only Botswana and Gabon are of significance to the world's minerals industry at present. Many areas, however, remain unexplored and are relatively inaccessible because of a lack of the appropriate infrastructure.

Botswana, which borders on South Africa and Namibia, is believed to contain about 10 percent of the world's diamonds reserves, and recently copper and nickel deposits have been discovered in the country. There are also indications of large deposits of low-grade coal, but Botswana is a relatively sparsely populated landlocked country highly dependent on South Africa for mining technology, capital financing, transportation lines, and energy. The lack of physical infrastructure and inadequate exploration of the country are the major obstacles to further minerals industry development.

Gabon is not strictly a High Africa country, but it is strategically located in adjoining central Africa and has significant oil, uranium, and manganese resources. It is estimated to possess about 5 percent of the world's uranium reserves and a similar amount of manganese reserves. However, both these minerals are abundant in South Africa and Namibia, and Gabon's importance in the area is primarily as another source of oil.

Swaziland is a small landlocked state between South Africa and Mozambique and has iron ore, asbestos, and coal resources that it exports. Although it is estimated to possess 5 percent of the world's asbestos reserves, neighboring Zimbabwe and South Africa account for 20 percent of the total, thereby diminishing Swaziland's importance.

Lesotho, also an enclave within the South Africa Customs Union, is similarly positioned to Swaziland and has only limited resources of diamonds and coal. Practically all output of those countries is likely to be absorbed by the nearest South Africa consumers.

Malawi, landlocked between Zambia, Mozambique, and Tanzania, is of no significance to the world's minerals industry. There are some bauxite deposits and minerals that contain strontium and niobium, but Malawi is basically an agricultural country and is trading and cooperating with South Africa in several commodities. Because of this unique relationship Malawi could be a target of attack and takeover by the more militant surrounding Marxist or socialist black African states.

The Congo is a country of no mineral resources, located immediately north of Zaire. However the Congo is important politically in the area because it is another little-known Marxist people's republic and could present a convenient basing region if more concerted attacks are mounted against Zaire from all sides.

Rwanda on the east border of Zaire has beryllium and tungsten reserves estimated at about 1 percent each of the world's total. It is too insignificant as a minerals producer to play any role in the regional mineral industry.

Madagascar, a large island nation in the Indian Ocean, has some chromium, mica, and graphite. The Comoros Islands, off Madagascar's north west coast, is an Islamic republic that also unilaterally declared its independence from France in 1975. Reunion, an island on the east of Madagascar, is still a French possession but has two politically active communist parties.

REFERENCES

Baumhagger, G., G. M. E. Leistner, J. P. Breitengross, and K. Schliephake, "Southern African Community of Interests, a South African Viewpoint," Institut für Afrika-Kunde, Hamburg, 1976.

"Japan's Two South African Ports," *Economist,* 25 February 1978, p. 80.

Jensen, Michael C., "The American Corporate Presence in South Africa," *New York Times,* 4 December 1977.

"Largest Mining Expansion in History Foreseen for South Africa in 1980's," *Engineering & Mining Journal,* February 1980, p. 39.

Leistner, G. M. E., "*Economic Relations among Southern African States,*" Unpublished Paper, Africa Institute of South Africa, Pretoria, 1978.

Nickel, Herman, "The Case of Doing Business in South Africa," *Fortune,* 19 June 1978, p. 60.

Oryehov, B., "Zair-Obyekt Agressyi Stran NATO," *Pravda,* 23 May 1978.

Rubinstein, Alvin Z., "Soviet Policy in the Third World in Perspective," *Military Review,* Vol. 58, No. 7, July 1978.

Rukeyser, Louis, "South African Investment Should Not Be Banned," *Human Events,* 1979.

"Sanctions End Reopens Rhodesian Ore to U.S.," *Purchasing,* 14 February 1980, p. 18B3.

"South Africa's Investment Boom," *Economist,* 8 March 1980.

United Nations, "Activities of Transnational Corporations in Southern Africa," Economic and Social Council, Publication E/C 10/39, 16 March 1978, New York.

U.S. House of Representatives, Report to the Committee on International Relations, "The Soviet Union and the Third World: A Watershed in Great Power Policy?" U.S. Government Printing Office, Washington, D.C., 1977.

"Why France 'Adopted' Black Africa," *U.S. News & World Report,* 31 March 1980, p. 53.

van Rensburg, W. C. J., and D. A. Pretorius, *South Africa's Strategic Minerals,* Valiant Publishers, Johannesburg, 1977.

SIX

Chinese Minerals Position

China is one of the largest undeveloped areas of the world believed to possess huge mineral resources and a significant minerals production. Nevertheless at present China is not yet completely self-sufficient and must import some strategic materials such as chromium, cobalt, nickel, aluminum, copper, iron ore, and steel. However China is self-sufficient in most other minerals and energy, and this makes China a potential superpower of the future.

Because of its huge population, large armed forces, and continuing confrontation with the Soviet Union, China is looked on as a potential military ally of the West in any East-West conflict of the future. Thus the continuing development of China and its resources is of interest to both China and the West, but the possibility of political instability and a preemptive Soviet action puts a damper on significant investment in China. On the other hand China is a poor and developing country, lacking the necessary infrastructure, capital, and technology to tap all its natural resources on its own. Yet without such a development it is not likely to present a credible military deterrent against the Soviet Union.

At present China has embarked on a program of "four modernizations," designed to develop its agriculture, industry, science and technology, and military power to the ranks of the leading powers in the world by the year 2000. Within this modernization effort the development of the country's materials and minerals technology is regarded to be of paramount importance and is among the top development priorities.

SINO-SOVIET COOPERATION PERIOD

Following the establishment of the People's Republic of China in 1949 the Soviet Union extended significant economic and military assistance to China. This took the form of the design and construction of almost 300 major basic plants and exports of machinery and technology. At the peak of this cooperation as many as 10,000 Soviet technicians were working in China, and teams of other experts from East Germany, Czechoslovakia, and Poland also assisted with specific projects.

At the time Chinese mineral resources other than coal were poorly developed. Nevertheless China was from the start assured of an adequate energy base because coal is plentiful throughout the country. In fact China is believed to possess the third largest coal reserves in the world after the Soviet Union and the United States.

China imported several strategic materials from the Soviet Union to start its industrialization program, including oil, petroleum products, nickel, chromium, cobalt, and other metals required to develop a modern steel industry and machine building industries.

Soviet assistance also included the transfer of technology to assist China in developing its military-industrial complex to equip and maintain what has now become the largest standing army in the world. The Soviets provided licenses to build several models of jet fighters and helicopters, tanks, armored personnel carriers, artillery, trucks, locomotives, electronic components and computers, radios, telecommunications equipment, power-generating machinery, and numerous machine tools.

Origins of China's Nuclear Programs

Chinese nuclear industry also originated from Soviet assistance in training nuclear scientists in Russia and in developing China's uranium enrichment plant at Lanzhou in the Gansu province. There are some indications that in 1957 in a secret agreement the Soviet Union promised to provide China with a prototype nuclear bomb and details of its manufacture, and in 1958 China purchased its first nuclear reactor from the Soviet Union.

The Soviet Union repudiated the secret agreement to transfer nuclear bomb technology to China in 1959 but prior Soviet assistance stimulated further Chinese investment in the nuclear industry and nuclear weapons program, particularly because China possesses adequate uranium resources. Some observers suggest that the Soviets changed their mind about giving China nuclear bomb technology after Mao Tse-tung expressed an opinion that the use of nuclear weapons could be justified by a quick victory of world socialism. Apparently the majority of leaders attending the First International Meeting of the Communist Parties in the fall of 1957 in Moscow overwhelmingly rejected this idea.

It now seems that the Sino-Soviet cooperation also began to drift apart during those years when Mao Tse-tung also proposed to Stalin the abolition of the Sino-Soviet border and creation of a huge Euroasian communist state that would have no equal in the world. Geopolitically this is not an unreasonable suggestion that was apparently made in the name of building and strengthening world socialism.

Practically, however, because there are four times as many Chinese as Soviet citizens and Soviet per capita GNP is about 10 times higher than that of China such an event would have been tantamount to the absorption of the Soviet peoples into the Chinese economy. Stalin shuddered at the idea, and the two countries began to move apart quite rapidly in the next few years. Nevertheless between 1949 and 1957 China's GNP has grown on the average a remarkable 11 percent annually, and massive technological assistance poured in from the Soviet Union and eastern Europe, both in the civilian and military sectors of the economy.

CAUSES OF THE SINO-SOVIET RIFT

Communist sinologists today are apt to claim that the Chinese leaders were not satisfied at that time with the amount of economic and technical aid received from the Soviet Union and eastern Europe. The Chinese also indicate sometimes that the Soviets insisted on becoming involved in China's economic planning to steer it primarily to their benefit, whereas China began to entertain the "Grand Plan" ideas of overtaking even the United States economically by the end of the century.

The Sino-Soviet break became inevitable when China began demanding increasing levels of assistance that would be proportional to the accelerating growth rate of China's economy and claimed that it was the responsibility of the Soviet bloc to provide the largest possible assistance to an underdeveloped fraternal socialist country to bring its low level of economic development more in line with the other members of the communist world.

Because of China's size such action would have quickly bled the other Soviet bloc economies white and subordinate them to the endless requirements and demands of China. It may never be revealed what cooperation promises were made by the Soviet Union and other COMECON countries in the first place, but it appears that when China called their bluff the Sino-Soviet rift became a reality.

DEVELOPMENT OF THE ALBANIAN CONNECTION

At the time of the Sino-Soviet break China was importing several strategic materials from the Soviet Union. Chief among those was Soviet oil that during the 1950s accounted for as much as 11 percent of Chinese imports. Albania and Romania, two relatively minor oil producers in the Soviet bloc, were also small suppliers of oil to China. In effect China was as dependent on Soviet oil as the other eastern European countries, although it was not overtly dependent on the Soviet's total energy supplies because of relatively large coal production and reserves in China.

The discovery of large oil deposits in China in 1960 and rapidly growing domestic production since then may have been a significant factor that allowed China to sever its close economic ties with the Soviet Union when more basic economic and doctrinal issues came into play. Although until 1965 China continued to be an importer of oil its self-sufficiency was only a question of time, and it reached that point in that year. From then on China could risk being cut off from oil supplies by the Soviet Union because it had a predominantly coal-based economy and any temporary oil shortages until domestic production fully meets the demand could always be met by Albanian or Romanian supplies.

The reader may well wonder why such arrangements were necessary when there were obvious and plentiful oil sources closer to China in the Persian Gulf or Indonesia. What is relatively little known is the fact that China at that time was under a Western trade embargo as a result of its earlier role in the Korean conflict.

Individual Third World countries, for instance, Ceylon, did in some cases disregard the China trade embargo, but this was at the risk of losing Western foreign aid and economic assistance from the United States and its allies in Europe. In the case of Ceylon, now Sri Lanka, the country after achieving its independence was on the brink of economic disaster and continued to export natural rubber to China. In return for this support in meeting one of its most strategic import requirements China extended to Sri Lanka a long-term rice-for-rubber barter trade agreement that saw Sri Lanka through many lean years during the fifties and sixties despite the withdrawal of Western assistance and financial aid.

Besides oil and technology China also imported other strategic materials from the Soviet Union during the 1950s. These included chromium, cobalt, nickel, and ferroalloys that were vital to China's growing steel industry, only recently established as the "backbone" of its developing economy with considerable Soviet assistance.

After the Sino-Soviet rift took place the Soviets reduced and eventually stopped shipments of chromium and ferroalloys to China, thereby creating significant shortages. Chromite became extremely scarce in China and magnesia-alumina bricks were widely substituted for refractory chromite in metallurgy. Chinese metal end-users were also affected in various ways. For example, the expanding railway rolling stock production came to a standstill because railway wheels made of certain resistant alloys were all previously imported from the Soviet Union. When these imports stopped China realized that it needed some strategic materials inputs to produce useful railway wheels and a search was begun for new independent sources of all the missing ingredients.

It was then that Albania became the principal chromite supplier to China, and between 1963 and 1974 as much as two-thirds of Chinese chromium requirements came from Albania. In addition Albania produces oil, copper, and nickel and could provide at least partially some of the strategic materials required by China. Albania actually occupies an important place among world minerals suppliers because it is the third largest chromite producer in the world after the Soviet Union and South Africa. Even Zimbabwe, a major chromite supplier to the West does not produce as much, although its reserves are very much larger than those of Albania and the Soviet Union.

Albania and Romania are unique among communist countries, because, besides China, they are the only other two practically self-sufficient countries in energy resources. All the other east European countries and Cuba must depend on the Soviet Union for their energy and raw materials supplies to keep their economies running. Perhaps this is one good reason why Albania and Romania have been able to take a more independent stance than the other countries in the Soviet bloc and still have been able to maintain a fairly close relation with China despite the Sino-Soviet break.

Nevertheless the "Albanian Connection" did not come cheap to China, which had to undertake to meet Albania's perennial trade deficit after its break with the Soviet Union. China, itself an impoverished country under embargoes from the Soviet bloc and the West simultaneously, extended foreign aid to Albania that by the mid-1970s was estimated to have amounted to $800 to $900 million during the preceding decade.

Chinese involvement in Albania became quite significant, and Albania became a major trade partner of China. A special Sino-Albanian Shipping Line was formed to provide a direct transportation link between the two countries for the movement of ores and equipment. In addition China equipped the Albanian armed forces with tanks, guns, Chinese-built MIGs, naval units and patrol boats, and even four submarines. The Chinese also assisted in the construction of the Elbasan Metallurgical Complex to produce steel, nickel, and cobalt. The plant's planned ferronickel capacity was 800,000 tons per year by 1980.

Sino-Albanian cooperation also included assistance in the expansion of nickeliferrous iron ore mine at Gur-i-Kuq, while a chromium concentrator and a ferrochrome plant were built with Chinese help at Burrell. Chinese assistance also extended into other technologies, and in 1975 China even transferred its know-how to design and build a chinese computer at the Tirana University in Albania.

Perhaps the best proof that all this effort was spent to relieve China's strategic materials problems is the fact that China committed resources to build huge electric power generating plants in Albania. Even today China itself is extremely short of electric power and Chinese citizens must obtain special permission to purchase light bulbs larger than 25 watts. Yet in 1974 a huge 250-megawatt Mao Tse-tung hydroelectric power plant was completed in Albania, and another 500-megawatt power plant was begun at Fierze to provide electricity to process Albanian ores.

Albania was clearly of extreme strategic importance to China during the 1960s and early 1970s. But because of Albania's relatively vulnerable geographic location, its poverty, political insignificance, and relatively limited minerals reserves despite high production levels, China clearly could not rely on Albania as a strategic materials supplier in the long run as its domestic industrialization grows rapidly and strategic materials consumption looms larger in the future.

There was always the threat that after the death of Tito in Yugoslavia Albania would become entangled in a conflict with that country which includes a minority of almost one million ethnic Albanians in its province of Kosovo. Under such circumstances there is always the possibility of Soviet intervention, and once again a danger surfaces to China's newly found sources of its most strategic materials. It is probably with this realization that China began to diversity its strategic materials sources by extending foreign aid to African countries and building the famed TAZARA railroad from Tanzania on the Indian Ocean coast to the heart of Zambia's mineral country, where it connects with Rhodesian and South African railway networks.

CHINA'S STRATEGIC MATERIALS DEFICIENCIES

Whereas China's minerals potential is considered very good China is not as yet completely self-sufficient in all the critical materials to run a modern economy, particularly with such a large and self-contained military establishment. In this regard China has to provide equipment and supplies for the largest army in the world, the second largest navy in number of vessels, and the third largest air force as far as the deployment of aircraft is concerned.

Although China's strategic materials import dependence is considerably smaller than that of western Europe or the United States it continues to have serious deficiencies of critical materials such as chromium, cobalt, platinum metals, nickel, diamonds, and magnesium—judging by the high levels of imports of these commodities compared with the probable demand for these materials. China also imports relatively large quantities of natural rubber, aluminum, copper, vanadium, iron ore, steel and steel products, and sulfur, although considerable production and reserves of those materials exist within the country.

Approximately 30 percent of China's imports by value in 1978 consisted of iron and steel and nonferrous metals, and this percentage has been slowly increasing during recent years. This fact is a surprise to many people who believe that China is well endowed with minerals and is a famous metals exporter.

Actually China's trade deficit in these commodities was over $3 billion in 1978. By far the largest share of this deficit is due to very heavy imports of iron and steel, but there was a trade deficit of at least $220 million in nonferrous metals and another $70 million in metalliferous ores.

This misconception about China's favorable current minerals position derives from the fact that China is one of the largest producers in the world of several important metals, including antimony, mercury, tin, and tungsten (see Table 6.1). Nevertheless China's exports of those nonferrous metals and ores yield a mere $200 million annually, and this is more than offset by almost $500 million in imports of other nonferrous metals and ores.

The Chinese leadership is well aware of this problem and is taking concrete steps to make the country more self-sufficient in the future. This necessitates considerable investment in exploration and new plant construction in China as well as expansion of electric power generation. Because its investment capital is limited, China is seeking foreign assistance in developing both iron and steel and nonferrous metals sectors. Japan and West Germany are the two countries most heavily involved in this activity at the present time.

THE FOUR MODERNIZATIONS

China's awareness of its strategic materials vulnerability becomes apparent on examination of its modernization policies that were first announced in 1978 following the death of Mao Tse-tung and the ending of domestic political turmoil better known as the "Gang of Four" disruptions. At that time China announced a national development program known as the "Four Modernizations" that was to include the modernization of agriculture, industry, science and technology, and the military establishment.

The objectives of this policy are to mobilize China's population and capital resources to develop its economy to a level that will compare favorably with the advanced economies of the world. This is an awesome task when measured on a per capita basis because of China's huge population that will be well over one billion people by the year 2000. It is now believed that the broad objectives of the modernization policies are to develop China's economy to a point where it will be comparable in size to the economies of the United States, the Soviet Union, or Japan but which on a per capita basis will resemble more the consumption levels that existed in Brazil or Taiwan in the late 1970s.

The first steps to implement these modernization policies were a series of development programs for the period 1978–1985 that turn out to be good indicators of China's development priorities. In 1978 these programs were widely promoted immediately preceding diplomatic recognition of China by the United States. There was considerable excitement among American, Japanese, and European financial and business circles because many of the projects announced by China held the promise of lucrative contracts and large potential sales.

After an initial round of negotiations and contract awards the Chinese re-

Table 6.1 China's Minerals and Metals Position

Major Material	Share of the World's Output (percentage)	Reserves Positions and Comments
Aluminum	1.5	Moderate, large imports up to 50%
Anthracite	11.0	Adequate domestic supplies
Antimony	15.0	Surplus capacity, exports
Asbestos	4.0	Moderate reserves
Barite	5.0	Huge good-quality deposits
Cadmium	2.0	Unknown
Chromium	neg	Some deposits discovered
Coal	17.0	Huge reserves, growing exports
Cobalt	neg	Some deposits, large imports
Copper	2.0	Moderate, large imports up to 30%
Fluorspar	7.0	Huge reserves, large exports
Gallium	na	Some exports
Gold	0.1	Small, unknown reserves
Graphite	6.0	Large poor-quality reserves
Iron ore	5.0	Large low quality reserves, some imports
Lead	2.0	Small, some imports
Manganese	3.0	Large reserves, exports
Magnesium	7.0	Huge reserves, imports meet demand
Mercury	10.0	Huge and excellent quality
Mica	1–2.0	Large poor quality, some exports
Molybdenum	4.0	Huge excellent quality, exports
Natural gas	1.0	Large
Nickel	neg	Large imports necessary
Oil	2.0	Moderate, about 10% exported
Phosphates	3.0	Medium reserves, some imports
Platinum	small	Unknown reserves, imports
Steel ingot	4.0	Imports continue at 15% demand
Sulfur	1.0	Large, some imports
Tantalum	na	Medium reserves, some imports
Titanium	na	Large, some imports
Tin	14.0	Large, largest metal export
Tungsten	20.0	Huge, second largest export metal
Uranium	na	Adequate
Zinc	2.0	Moderate, some imports

Source. Compiled by 21st Century Research from U.S. Bureau of Mines data and other Department of the Interior publications.

assessed many of their planned objectives and in early 1979 attacked Vietnam. This action in its turn initiated a Western reassessment of the stability of Chinese markets and of political risks involved in doing business with China.

The reassessment of China's development programs shifted emphasis from heavy industry to agriculture and light industries. Nevertheless basic priorities to develop energy resources, raw materials, and communications remain as major objectives of the plan. Relatively little is known about China's military modernization program, but some objectives are apparent when China's 1978–1985 Science and Technology Plan is examined in some detail.

MILITARY MODERNIZATION REQUIREMENTS

China's military-industrial complex is one of the largest in the world, and annual military spending is estimated at around 10 percent of China's GNP. This would suggest a total of about $45 billion in 1978, comparable in size to worldwide sales of such enterprises as Ford Motor Company or Texaco.

Following the reassessment of the industrial development programs and the relatively unsatisfactory action in Vietnam it is now believed that China is also going to put more emphasis on the modernization of its armed forces than was formerly thought likely. This is particularly true since the Soviet blitzkrieg invasion of Afghanistan that also had the effect of focusing Western attention on China as a potential ally that could present a deterrent against further Soviet expansion.

At present despite very large armed forces estimated to number 4.5 million China remains rather vulnerable to a Soviet preemptive attack. China's huge army is primarily a defensive force, and much of its equipment is rather obsolete by world standards and particularly with respect to Soviet materiel. As a result China would not be able to prevent a limited Soviet incursion, although it is generally agreed that it could wage the so-called People's War for a very long time if large portions of China were occupied.

Deng Xiaoping, the vice premier of the state council, himself in 1979 pointed out that if the Soviets decided to invade China there would be nothing that China could do about it. Since the early 1970s Chinese policy has been to work toward the establishment of an anti-Soviet entente to include western Europe, Japan, and the United States.

No formal agreements have been reached as yet nor are any expected in the near future, but Soviet initiatives in Afghanistan and previous Soviet expansionist action in places like Angola, Ethiopia, and Yemen during the 1970s have cumulatively given a new impetus to such concepts. This is already evident in Western approvals of sales and transfers of some military and "dual-use" technology to potential civilian and military use in China.

The Soviet strategists appear to have decided that such a course of events is also very likely in the future.

China's credibility as a potential ally depends on its ability to deter the Soviet Union from a preventive strike against its northern provinces bordering on the Soviet Union and Mongolia. This is the most likely Soviet threat, sometimes known as the "Kuropatkin Line" from the name of the Soviet commander during the Russian-Japanese War who outlined the limits of an effective Russian penetration of that part of the world for strategic purposes. This line extends from the Xinjiang province in the west of China through Inner Mongolia to the North Korean border. Such an incursion would give the Soviets control of much of China's oil, coal, iron and steel, and aluminum production capacity (see Figure 6.1). It would also have a crippling effect on China's military establishment because a large number of machine building enterprises, including aircraft plants, shipbuilding yards, electric power equipment factories, and steel plants are concentrated in that region.

To improve its strategic posture China is trying to develop alternative sources of oil and critical materials in central and southern China—areas less vulnerable to a preemptive Soviet invasion by conventional means. The strategy is of course not of much value if a nuclear attack were launched against China. This diversification policy may also be designed to induce Western interests to invest more time and resources in the exploration of China's minerals and offshore oil resources because the probability of political risk is diminished even in the case of Soviet invasion of northern provinces of China.

On the other hand there always remains the question of political stability within China. From past history it is clear that considerable groups within China believe in closer cooperation with the Soviet Union. The economies of the Soviet Union and China are particularly complementary along the long Sino-Soviet border and will become even more so as the industrialization of China takes place.

Soviet oil production is expected to level off during the 1980s, and industrial labor is beginning to be in short supply. Western China's largely untapped oil reserves and those in Manchuria could more than adequately supply increasing demands for oil in Soviet central Asia and the Far East—both geographically very close to the large Chinese oil fields.

Chinese labor, increasingly unemployed or underemployed, could also find useful and well-paid employment in numerous Soviet factories or agricultural establishments, particularly as the Soviet economy is expected to experience increasing labor shortages during the 1980s. It seems inevitable that the continued growth of those two large and contingent economies must develop into a situation not unlike that along the U.S.–Mexican border unless preventive action is taken.

Figure 6.1 Major Chinese minerals-producing areas. Source. U.S. Bureau of Mines, Department of the Interior, 1977.

INDUSTRIAL DEVELOPMENT PLAN

It is clear from the original 1978–1985 Industrial Development Plan announced by China in 1978 that investment in energy and raw materials development projects accounted for over 50 percent of all the major projects in the plan. When reassessment of the plan was made in 1979 some of the large iron and steel projects requiring foreign know-how and technology had been postponed or cancelled. Nevertheless the plan is worth analyzing in its original state because it is probably a good indication of China's strategic materials requirements and production plans in the future.

Energy projects accounted for 48 of a total 120 major projects, which is understandable considering China's continuing shortages of electric power. This development is basic if large ferrous and nonferrous plants are to be built because such industries are voracious consumers of energy (see Table 6.2).

The heavy emphasis given to transportation projects underscores another basic problem in China's development programs. Much of the country is rural and undeveloped with very poor communication networks of single track railways and unpaved roads. This means that initially many minerals development projects require massive investments in infrastructure to gain access to promising areas and later to transport extracted minerals to refining centers and end-user enterprises.

Table 6.2   Major Projects of the 1978–1985 Industrial Development Plan of China before Reassessment

Project Breakdown	Number of Projects	
Major energy projects		48
Electric power stations	30	
Oil and gas fields	10	
Major coal mines	8	
Major minerals development projects		19
Large iron and steel projects	10	
Major nonferrous projects	9	
Major transportation projects		30
New trunk railways	10	
Major railway improvement projects	8	
Key station modernization projects	7	
Harbor and port expansion projects	5	
Other major projects and new plants		23
Total		120

This situation poses a problem to Western enterprises that have considered getting involved in developing Chinese resources. These businesses must negotiate contracts and agreements that will assure profitability of such investments. They are not in a position to undertake the infrastructural development that is required to implement many of those projects. On the other hand the Chinese authorities operate basically with very limited capital and budgets and must distribute these throughout the country and to various industries. This results in policies of priorities and shortages and is not conducive to the most rapid development of any particular sector.

At the same time the concepts of foreign financing and management are alien to the Chinese who operate a centrally planned communist economy and basically do not allow foreign ownership or control of their resources or industries. The newly developed joint-venture laws despite expectations will probably prove to be as restrictive and cumbersome to Western potential partners as those that surfaced in eastern European countries during the 1970s.

The picture that now emerges is one of developing lines of credit for purchases of whole plants or equipment by China extended by major Western commercial banks and others supported by the governments of lending countries. Because the terms of these credits carry interest provisions that are considerably lower than those prevailing in business in the early 1980s these arrangements are being increasingly looked on as foreign aid extensions to China. China in effect is not in a position to pay for its planned development programs, and this fact, coupled with it being a closed communist society threatened by a powerful neighbor, does not make it the most attractive investment region for Western entrepreneurs despite expectations of large mineral deposits.

STRATEGIC MATERIALS DEVELOPMENT PRIORITIES

Whereas China's industrial development plans call for the construction of specific plants and mines and the associated infrastructure within the short term the lesser-known 1978–1985 Science and Technology Development Plan indicates research and development objectives and programs that are being undertaken to provide longer-term solutions to Chinese energy and materials supplies. Although the industrial development programs have been cut there is little indication that the science and technology plans suffered a similar fate. On the other hand many programs of this plan appear to have military modernization potential, and for this reason the plan may have been left untouched despite reassessments that took place in the industrial programs.

The overall objective of the 1978–1985 Science and Technology Development Plan is to allow China to reach world levels of the 1970s in key science and technology disciplines by 1985 and to generally narrow the gap to about 10 years in comparison with the most advanced countries of the West.

This plan consists of 108 projects that have not been explicitly defined in a variety of areas. Nevertheless eight priority areas have been singled out and are defined by the Chinese to represent important pace-setting technologies for them that have a bearing on the overall situation.

These priorities include agriculture, energy resources, materials, electronic computers, lasers, space sciences, high-energy physics, and genetic engineering. It is fairly clear on closer analysis of the specific objectives within these priorities announced by China that much of this research and development activity is designed to enhance national security and provide a basis for modernization of the military establishment. The priorities concerned with energy resources and materials are of particular significance to China's strategic materials position.

Energy Resources Development Priorities

The main premise of energy resources research and development programs is to change China's energy patterns by developing alternative energy resources and improving the use of existing supplies of oil, natural gas, and coal. Coal in fact remains the predominant energy source in China, accounting for 68 percent of all the energy produced. Oil provides another 20 percent and is a major export commodity, providing almost $1 billion in hard currency earnings every year. Oil is also mainly produced in the northern parts of China, which are dangerously close to Soviet borders. Any loss of those provinces not only strikes a blow to China's industrialization but also seriously affects its foreign trade (see Table 6.3).

Chinese planners would probably like to export more of their oil now that OPEC countries continue to raise prices and keep their output under con-

Table 6.3   China's Energy Supply Pattern in 1977

Primary Energy Source	Percentage of Supply
Coal	68
Oil	20
Natural gas	11
Hydroelectric	1

Source. National Foreign Assessment Center, *China: Economic Indicators,* December 1978.

trol. But domestic demand for oil in China is also increasing rapidly primarily because of an estimated 11 percent growth rate of Chinese industry. As a result the Chinese leaders are committed to increase oil production in China and already indicated that they would like to see 10 more oil fields as large as the Taching oil field in Manchuria which produces about 40 percent of over 100 million tons of oil produced in China every year.

Whether this will happen remains to be seen and will require very significant new investment in exploration and drilling capacity. Chinese leaders are also hedging their bets by calling for the development of practically all conceivable energy alternatives in China. The 1978–1985 Science and Technology Plan calls for speeding up nuclear power plant construction and stepping up research on controlled thermonuclear fusion research. Considerable emphasis is also given to lasers, with one intent being to develop lasers for isotope separation purposes. This process is being developed by all advanced countries as a more promising uranium enrichment method. Since China maintains a nuclear weapons program it faces large expenditures of electric power in uranium enrichment by gaseous diffusion that is currently in use. New and more efficient ways of doing this would in effect provide nuclear fuels and nuclear weapons at lower cost and provide more alternative power sources for industrial plants in more strategically safe regions of southern China that are relatively distant from energy sources.

In addition the plan calls for the development of more conventional energy alternatives such as geothermal, solar, tidal, and wind power. A new program of construction of several large hydroelectric power plants is already in progress under the provisions of the industrial development program.

Even so the plans call for the development of yet other alternatives, including bone coal, shale oil, marsh gas, and biogas. This is a shrewd decision because many of the large new power centers under development will primarily be needed to provide energy for minerals processing or new industrial plants. At the same time increasing requirements of rural China, which includes 70 percent of the country's population, will often have to be taken care of by local authorities using local resources. This policy will also save on the costs of distribution and equipment that in a large country like China are not insignificant. The strategic value of such rural alternatives is also obvious in case of a military conflict that could lead to the destruction of large central power plants.

This diversification of energy sources is probably conceived with just such strategic objectives in mind because they provide a large measure of strategic self-sufficiency. If major oil fields and coal mines in northern China were taken over by the Soviets or destroyed this program would provide some means for the rest of the country to continue in operation while remaining oil and coal reserves are used in critical industries. It will be many years before offshore areas in southern China start yielding significant amounts of oil that could compensate for any loss of its northern oil fields.

Non-Oil Minerals Development Priorities

The 1978–1985 Science and Technology Development Plan considers materials priority to be of "paramount importance to the all round modernization" of China. The development of natural resources and recycling are given serious consideration as are the technology of mining, dressing, and processing ores. Special attention is to be given to the production of "special purpose" materials, structural materials, and compound materials required by the military industries (see Table 6.4).

Iron and steel remain the key elements in China's modernization, but work is to proceed on a breakthrough in new technologies of intensified mining and hematite beneficiation that presumably would allow China to use more of its large deposits of relatively low-grade iron ores. Whether China succeeds in solving iron ore beneficiation problems may have a significant bearing on future iron ore trade in the world. If China continues its rapid industrialization and its imports of iron ore rise significantly this could

Table 6.4   Major Materials Development Programs in China

Material	Recent Imports Dependence	Planned Development
Iron ore and steel	15% +	High-grade ore location Intensified mining methods Hematite beneficiation
Aluminum	50% −	Reach world level in refining techniques, intensify exploration efforts
Copper	30% +	Reach world levels in refining Intensify exploration
Titanium	None	Become one of top world producers
Vanadium	50% −	Become one of top world producers
Nickel	95%	Reach world refining levels
Cobalt	100%	Reach world refining levels
Rare earths metals	None	Reach world refining levels
Special compounds	Unknown	Required for military uses
Plastics	Medium	Modernize production
Synthetic rubber	Low	Modernize techniques
Synthetic fibers	High	Modernize production

Source.   Based on the report of Fang I to the National Science Conference held in Beijing, China, 18 March 1978, Foreign Broadcasts Information Service (FBIS), 29 March 1978, p. E1.

create short-term shortages and accelerate the formation of an iron ore exporters cartel. Some estimates predict that China may be importing as much as 30 million tons of high-grade iron ore within 10 years. At present major suppliers of iron ore to China are Australia, North Korea, and Brazil, whereas India is also beginning to develop a trading relationship in this commodity.

In basic metals such as copper and aluminum China possesses considerable reserves, but its exploration and refining techniques are inadequate, resulting in costly imports of large quantities of those metals. The plans call for intensified exploration for those metals for reaching world levels in refining techniques. When that happens and China stops importing those metals this could lead to some market instability, depending on how big an importer China will become in the future that in turn depends on the country's ability to continue the rapid rate of industrialization of recent decades.

Perhaps the most intriguing is China's commitment to become one of the largest producers in the world of titanium and vanadium. Titanium is a very strategic material because its primary use is in the production of jet engines, supersonic aircraft, space vehicles, rockets, and submarines. The Soviet Union, the United States and Japan are the three significant producers of titanium sponge metal. The two superpowers use it primarily in the production of their respective military and civilian aircraft and other military equipment.

The fact that China proposes to become one of the leading producers of titanium clearly indicates that it proposes to continue to maintain and modernize its large air force and aircraft production. China's air force is now the third largest in the world and numbers about 5500 fighters, bombers, helicopters, and transports, mostly of obsolete Soviet-based designs. More recently China developed two supersonic jet fighters of its own design that may be entering large-scale production.

In addition Chinese armed forces are lacking in logistics and mobility because of poor transportation facilities. It is now believed that a large jet transport is being developed by the Chinese aircraft industry to correct that deficiency. The space program also requires a variety of strategic materials for the construction of rockets, satellites, and orbiting space laboratories—all of which are being planned by China within its science and technology development program.

China's plans to become one of world's largest vanadium producers is a new development, perhaps partially designed to substitute for the country's chromium deficiency. Vanadium's chief use is as an alloying metal for high-strength steels used in large diameter pipe, construction steel, transportation equipment, and machine tools. Vanadium also has more strategic uses in titanium-based alloys in aircraft and as fuel cladding in fast breeder nuclear reactors.

Plans to reach world refining levels in nickel and cobalt suggest that China will be a large importer of those materials and metal ores rather than refined products as in previous years. Although recent reports on geological exploration of southeastern China indicate that area's potential for numerous minerals, including nickel and cobalt, China will probably have to depend on increasing imports of those metals for the foreseeable future.

GROWTH OF MINERALS PROCESSING INDUSTRIES

Whereas China's leaders always stressed the production of steel as the "key link" of industrialization, the production of nonferrous metals has been extremely uneven. Priorities in other sectors, particularly oil exploration and production, preempted limited investment resources. Political disruptions such as the Cultural Revolution and the "Gang of Four" period are also blamed for lagging development of this industry. In some metals production levels have not regained their peaks reached during the height of the Sino-Soviet cooperation during the 1950s.

Processing facilities in China fall into two broad categories. Large national-level plants produce metals for top-priority applications and the military establishment and are controlled by the Ministry of Metallurgical Industry. Although these incorporate the most advanced technology in China they are still relatively small and obsolete by global standards. Local plants that produce inferior-quality materials depend to a high degree on labor available in the area in which they are located. These are small and unsophisticated facilities whose output is unsuitable for applications that require high-quality specifications.

Production stagnated in China during the 1970s, and the output of aluminum and copper failed to keep up with rising domestic requirements, resulting in large imports of those materials. Large reserves of manganese, molybdenum, and zinc are not being exploited as yet to any degree of significance in world markets.

Although the output of aluminum is inadequate to meet the demand, production has grown sharply during the 1970s, practically doubling between 1970 and 1976. It is believed that China is planning to reach aluminum production capacity of about 1 million tons annually by 1990. At present only the United States, Canada, Japan, and the Soviet Union refine more than 1 million tons of aluminum per year.

The modernization of China's nonferrous industry is now badly needed to correct the lag created by the lack of sufficient progress in the industry during the last decade. The technology used in many cases is largely of Soviet origin and mostly 20 to 30 years out of date. This results in very high production costs and poor quality of output and creates a situation where imports of many metals are relatively cheaper than the cost of domestic production.

There are indications that since 1978 China is speeding up its nonferrous industry development to match the growth experienced by other sectors of its industries. Chinese leaders even stated that China was determined to surpass the United States in nonferrous metals production by the end of the century. This is not entirely impossible, considering the increasing import dependence of the United States and the still unexplored resources of much of China.

Much of the growth and modernization of minerals processing industries will take place with the participation of Western enterprises that can bring up-to-date technology to the exploration, mining, and refining processes. Imports of Western technology in this industry began in the early 1970s with Japanese, West German, Canadian, and American firms in the lead.

CHINA METALS AND MINERALS TRADE

Contrary to some popular beliefs China's foreign trade is not very large and in 1978 totaled about $20 billion. On a comparative basis this is not larger than the foreign trade of countries like Austria or Denmark. Japan is by far the largest single trading partner of China and in 1979 provided 28 percent of China's imports and took 22 percent of its exports. Hong Kong is the second largest trading partner, primarily as a large export market for Chinese goods absorbing 22 percent of the total exports in 1979. West Germany, the third largest trading nation with China, provided 10 percent of China's imports but took only 3 percent of its exports. The United States ranked fourth, supplying 9 percent of Chinese imports, a lot of it in the form of wheat and other grains, and accounted for only 5 percent of Chinese exports in 1979.

Chinese trade is usually balanced, although in 1979 it showed a trade deficit of about $420 million, resulting from rapid increases in imports in two previous years. Chinese foreign trade has never amounted to more than 5 percent of China's GNP. China's imports of about $10 billion in 1978 account for only a little over 2 percent of that total, which is another measure of China's relatively high self-sufficiency. On the other hand those overall figures obscure the actual importance of some of this trade that becomes more apparent when a more detailed analysis of traded commodities is made.

Trade in minerals, metals, and other critical materials accounts for 26 percent of the total. On the export side 17 percent of the value of Chinese export goods is represented by minerals and metals, with oil and petroleum products being the most important. However, China's import dependence is clearly shown by its import side, where 35 percent of all the imports represent such critical materials as iron and steel, aluminum, copper, nickel, chromium, cobalt, natural rubber, and other materials. Iron and steel alone is by far the largest single import commodity in Chinese trade and ac-

Table 6.5   Import and Export of Minerals and Strategic Materials in Chinese Foreign Trade during 1978[a]

Commodity	Exports	Imports
Iron and steel	155	2,885
Nonferrous metals	110	330
Metal ores	80	150
Coal	120	—
Oil	985	—
Oil products	235	55
Natural rubber	—	170
Total trade	9,895	10,315
Total materials	1,685	3,590
Percentage of total trade	17%	35%

Source.   National Foreign Assessment Center, *China: International Trade Quarterly Review,* ER CIT 80–001, January 1980.
[a] All figures are in millions of U.S. dollars unless otherwise stated.

counted for almost 28 percent of total imports to China in 1978 (see Table 6.5).

In the case of iron and steel China continues to import high-grade iron ores to "sweeten" its own low-grade ores and improve smelting efficiency. Experts believe that the construction of very large capacity modern steel plants on the coast of China means that China will continue high-grade iron ore imports in the future at an increasing rate as its industrialization programs expand. Within 10 years China may be consuming up to 30 million tons of imported ores. Before its steel capacity is further increased China will also continue to be one of the largest importers of steel products such as steel pipe and sheet that cannot be produced in sufficient quantities in China.

China's aluminum resources appear quite large, but imports are expected to continue at relatively high levels for two reasons. Chinese bauxites are not the highest-grade ores, and aluminum refining consumes very large quantities of electricity that is chronically in very short supply in China. Imports of aluminum at depressed world prices are a good way to stockpile and save electricity at the same time.

Iron and steel, aluminum, copper, and nickel are the most costly imports of China because of the large volumes of ores and metals involved. Chromium, cobalt, and platinum on the other hand are more critical because only minor deposits exist in China. Natural rubber is also costly as an import, but China needs only partial imports to meet its demand and possesses some territories in southern China such as the Hainan Island, where natural rubber cultivation may be expanded on land presently used for other crops such as rice that also earn foreign exchange for China.

The most important trend in Chinese minerals and metals trade has been diversification of China's sources of supply of the 15 or so critical materials the country must import every year and an attempt to contract for plants and technology to substitute domestic production for imports whenever possible. This is why China will continue to expand its relationships with Japan, West Germany, and the United Kingdom—the leading nations in minerals exploration and metals refining technology. Contracts signed between those countries and China suggest that some of the arrangements may also provide future supplies of minerals and ores to the participating nations for processing in Europe and Japan.

In general China's critical materials suppliers are also Japan and western Europe, which of course process imported ores from the Third World. It seems to be in China's interest to continue developing its domestic resources to improve its strategic materials self-sufficiency and eliminate the high vulnerability that dependence on such foreign sources creates (see Table 6.6).

Table 6.6   Major Suppliers of Some Critical Materials to China

Material	Major Countries Supplying China
Iron and steel	Japan, West Germany, Australia, Belgium, France, Italy, Netherlands, United Kingdom, Yugoslavia, Romania, Soviet Union
Aluminum	Canada, Japan, West Germany, France, United States, Italy, Australia, Norway
Copper	Chile, Peru, Canada, Japan, United Kingdom, Yugoslavia, Zambia, Philippines
Nickel	Canada, Albania, Cuba, Soviet Union, France, Netherlands, West Germany
Chromium	Albania, Iran, Pakistan, Turkey, Sudan, and probably southern African countries
Cobalt	Soviet Union, Belgium, Africa
Platinum	France, United Kingdom, West Germany
Lead	Peru, Canada, North Korea, Burma
Zinc	Peru
Natural rubber	Singapore, Thailand, Malaysia, Sri Lanka

Source.   National Foreign Assessment Center, *China: The Non-ferrous Metals Industry in the 1970's,* ER 78–10104U, May 1978.

CHINESE ADVENTURES IN AFRICA

One of the most intriguing episodes in Chinese foreign policy and foreign trade in recent years has been its involvement in Third World regions and particularly in African countries. After the Sino-Soviet split in 1960 China lost its secure sources of many strategic materials in the Soviet Union or perhaps decided to embark on a policy of diversification to escape dependence on Soviet sources and any problems that Soviet embargoes could pose.

The trade embargo maintained against China at that time under American leadership did not allow China simply to switch to alternative sources in the West or Third World countries without paying some sort of a political price. Albania, which was outside the western sphere, was a useful stopgap solution, but China must have realized that Albania's resources are limited and its strategic location highly vulnerable to Soviet-backed initiatives in the Balkans.

The alternatives were in the Third World, where Japan and western Europe were getting their strategic materials, but here the resources in question were uniquely concentrated in southern African countries dominated by white-minority governments in Rhodesia and South Africa. Decolonization, wars of liberation, revolutions, and Soviet support of several emerging black African regimes complicated the problem of access to African resources.

China's solution to its strategic materials problems was ingenious and not yet clearly understood in the West. This was a time when the West and the Soviet Union were competing for influence in the new African countries by extending military and economic aid, providing technicians, and training Third World nationals in their countries.

China at the time was itself a developing country that only just experienced the withdrawal of Soviet economic assistance with some devastating effects on its economy. Despite its weak economy China nevertheless managed to explode its first nuclear bomb in 1964, and during the same year premier Chou En-lai toured several African states belittling Soviet foreign aid, explaining that it was costly and carried dangerous conditions.

It appeared that China was competing with the Soviet Union for political influence among the newly emerging nations of black Africa. Actually China did not have the resources to do so and more likely than not it was developing links to nations which controlled strategic resources that were vital to the development of Chinese economy and particularly its rapidly growing military industries. It may well be that China even promoted the concepts, advanced by many Western media at the time, that it was engaged in spreading the Maoist revolution in the Third World to divert attention from its real objectives.

China realized that without Soviet sources of strategic materials and lacking the capital and technology to develop its own potential it had to gain access to alternative sources in the Third World that supplied most of the needs of Japan, western Europe, and partly even the United States. Sooner or later this meant dealing with southern African states, but when China first traded with that area in 1963 it was immediately attacked by the Soviet media as a traitor to the black African socialist cause. Clearly direct trade was not the way, and China then embarked on its policy of extending foreign aid to various Third World countries.

By 1978 over $2.6 billion in foreign aid was extended by China to almost 30 African countries, but the largest share went to Tanzania and Zambia for the construction of the famed TAZARA railroad linking the Indian Ocean port of Dar es Salaam on the east coast of Africa to the mining heartland of Zambia almost 1100 miles to the southwest. There the TAZARA railroad naturally connects with other railroads of neighboring High Africa countries. High Africa is the area that is a major exporter of copper, cobalt, chromium, diamonds, platinum, gold, and practically all other minerals that China has to import.

At the peak of construction activity as many as 16,000 Chinese technicians were employed on this project. Up to 15,000 are believed to have been China's People's Liberation Army (PLA) Railroad Engineering Corps and Signal Corps personnel. In addition China equipped Tanzanian armed forces with tanks, guns, patrol boats, hydrofoil craft, and Chinese-built MIG jet fighter planes. Over 1000 Tanzanian military personnel have been trained in China, and by 1978 an estimated 1000 Chinese technicians still remained in Tanzania.

Zambia was the second largest recipient of Chinese foreign aid in Africa, and although only 50 Zambian military personnel were trained in China in 1978 there were an estimated 5500 Chinese technicians still working in that country on the completion and extension of the TAZARA railroad and other projects. Zaire also benefited from Chinese largesse with 75 military personnel trained in China and over $100 million in economic aid extensions.

Chinese involvement in this part of Africa during the mid-1970s raises an intriguing question about whether it provoked the Soviet Union into sending Cuban forces to Angola during the 1975 crisis. At the time China and the West were backing the National Front for the Liberation of Angola (FNLA), one of three liberation movements in Angola, while the Soviet Union, eastern Europe, and Cuba provided swift and decisive assistance to MPLA, a Marxist organization that quickly won the struggle and continues in power today with the assistance of over 20,000 Cuban soldiers and at least 8500 technicians.

Although South Africa did make an effort to enter the Angola struggle by supporting UNITA and there was a half-hearted attempt mounted by the Central Intelligence Agency (CIA), the mood of the United States following the Vietnam defeat and the Watergate affair was not conducive to support overseas adventures of that type. This clearly must have played a decisive role in making up the minds of Soviet strategists to recommend swift and effective action, using Cuban surrogates that resulted in victory in Angola.

Although some American politicians understood the import of the Angola debacle it was extremely difficult to demonstrate any threat to vital American interests in that country, which has been a minor producer and supplier of minerals. The importance of Angola lies rather in its huge future potential and its strategic location alongside such important strategic materials suppliers as Namibia, Botswana, Rhodesia, Zambia, and Zaire. As the Shaba province rebel invasions later proved in 1977 and 1978 Angola provided a convenient staging area for that action which led to global cobalt shortages.

Chinese leaders appear to have understood the importance of the struggle for Angola because they made the effort to support one of the liberation groups and developed a nucleus of a Chinese military contingent in Zaire, where a Chinese general and about 200 military specialists were training FNLA guerrillas. Clearly China was sending a message to the West that it was willing to support opposition against Soviet penetration of this vital area which was indeed more important to Chinese interests.

China must have experienced terrible frustration and disappointment when the United States and western European countries chose not to become involved in the Angola crisis and left the victory to the Soviet-Cuban–backed MPLA forces headed by Aghostino Neto.

It may be argued that from the Soviet point of view it was the West that actually looked the other way, allowing China to penetrate deep into High Africa by building the TAZARA railroad. To the Soviet strategists in the Kremlin the Chinese were the Cubans of NATO being maneuvered into position to assist anti-Soviet liberation movements to take power in Angola.

The Soviets knew very well that the Chinese presence in that part of Africa resulted from their own strategic materials embargo against China in the 1960s. The Chinese made a very large investment in building the TAZARA railroad to escape potential Soviet dependence in the future. They also had large numbers of Chinese personnel in Zambia and Tanzania—all of which added up to powerful incentives to actively oppose any Soviet-backed penetration and potential threat to their newly built critical "African Connection."

The 16,000 Chinese of the PLA Railroad Engineering Corps paramilitary technicians and labor and the military advisers in Zaire formed a nucleus of a very powerful armed force in that region. Such a force could have been decisive in the struggle for Angola if only the West decided to provide the weapons, supplies, and logistics. The Soviets probably could not risk that to happen, and perhaps it is not by accident that the Soviets arranged for a similar number of Cubans to be transported to Angola by air and provided them with armaments and supplies by immediate use of the Soviets' own merchant marine. The first round in the battle for southern Africa was lost by the West despite extremely favorable conditions to keep it under control.

The emergence of Robert Mugabe as prime minister of Zimbabwe now allows China to deal openly with that country as a supplier of chromium. However in Tanzania and Zambia Chinese influence seems to be on the wane since the completion of the TAZARA railroad, and both countries have been more receptive to Soviet and even Cuban assistance in recent years, perhaps as a result of the failure of the West to support China and present a more determined stance against Soviet expansion.

The most recent setback suffered by China in its African policy was the rejection of its offer of arms and military training for Zambia in return for secure cobalt supplies. President Kenneth Kaunda, so far regarded as a staunch pro-Western leader, accepted a Soviet counteroffer valued at $85 million that is believed to be a barter deal of MIGs and other Soviet arms in return for cobalt. This took the West by surprise, coming so soon after the Soviet invasion of Afghanistan.

CHINESE FOREIGN AID PROGRAMS

China is the only developing country in the world that extends both economic and military assistance to other developing countries within and without the communist sphere. Since 1956 China extended almost $5 billion in foreign aid, not counting special assistance to North Korea and North Vietnam during military action in those countries. Chinese foreign aid extensions reached a peak between 1970 and 1973 when well over $500 million was offered every year. Since then Chinese foreign aid extensions have tapered off and in 1978 amounted to $185 million, but China also concluded military assistance agreements with several countries valued at another $90 million.

Since the 1950s Chinese foreign aid has been offered to about 60 different countries, but by far the largest proportion was granted to African states, accounting for almost 50 percent of all Chinese foreign aid.

Although it is believed that China allocates its foreign aid primarily based on its perception of competing Soviet influences an analysis of foreign aid recipient countries also shows that most are existing or potential suppliers of strategic or raw materials that China has to import from abroad because of inadequate domestic supplies. Besides exporters of chromium, cobalt, copper, and aluminum other countries receiving Chinese aid are also important suppliers of sugar, cotton, phosphates, iron ore, and diamonds—all of which are commodities that must be imported by China to some degree (see Table 6.7).

Chinese foreign aid is mostly extended in the form of interest-free loans for the construction of projects or purchase of Chinese products. It often provides for repayment over a period of at least 10 years, with a 10-year grace period before repayments have to start. During the first decade up to

Table 6.7 Major Recipients of Chinese Foreign Aid and Their Potential as Suppliers of Import Commodities to China

Country	Total Extensions, 1956–1978 (millions of U.S. dollars)	Number of Chinese Technicians, 1978	Actual or Potential Major Chinese Imports
Albania	$ 800+	na	Chromium, nickel, cobalt
Pakistan	598	na	Cotton
Tanzania	362	1,000	Copper, diamonds
Zambia	331	5,500	Cobalt, copper (chromium)
Romania	300+	na	Petroleum know-how
Sri Lanka	222	325	Natural rubber
Nepal	183	280	Sugar, timber, jute
Somalia[a]	155	3,000	
Egypt	134	25	Phosphates, cotton
North Yemen	130	300	Cotton
Zaire	103	na	Cobalt, copper, diamonds
Ethiopia	102	250	Sugar, oil seeds
Mali	100	550	Cotton
Tunisia	97	85	Phosphates, oil
Algeria	92	300	Iron ore, petroleum
Kampuchea	92	na	Natural rubber
Madagascar	89	na	Chromium, sugar
Mauretania	87	300	Iron ore, copper
Burma	84	125	Sugar, lead
Guinea	83	300	Bauxite, alumina
Sudan	82	650	Chromium, cotton
South Yemen	79	450	Cotton
Afghanistan	76	125	Cotton
Congo	75	na	Oil, timber
Bangladesh	74	150	Jute
Cameroon	71	na	Natural rubber, aluminum
Chile	65	na	Copper, iron ore
Syria	61	25	Cotton
Senegal	60	na	Phosphates
Niger	52	na	Uranium
Togo	45	na	Phosphates
Ghana	42	80	Bauxite, aluminum, gold, diamonds
Peru	42	10	Copper, silver, lead, zinc
Sierra Leone	41	na	Diamonds
Morocco	35	na	Phosphate

Source. Compiled by 21st Century Research, 1980.

[a] Was major ship registry for China.

20 percent of Chinese foreign aid was also extended in the form of grants. One additional advantage of Chinese aid to the recipient country is that it often includes long-term financing to cover the local costs of projects.

From the point of view of minerals end-users the Chinese foreign aid extensions are of some interest because the terms of these agreements often provide for repayment in commodity exports or, on mutual agreement, in domestic or convertible currencies.

Most of those foreign aid programs were extended and accepted during the early 1970s, and if grace periods are taken into account repayments should begin during the first half of the 1980s. Specific terms of those repayments are unknown, but if these are made in the form of strategic materials some of the countries may find themselves in a position of having to ship relatively large quantities of their output to China. This may turn out to be an additional factor contributing to future shortages of some of the strategic materials, particularly in central African countries that received the largest foreign aid extensions from China. Another unknown are China's arrangements made with Robert Mugabe who visited Beijing as a leader of the liberation movement of Rhodesia a few years before he became the leader of Zimbabwe, which has the most critical materials required by China.

REFERENCES

CIA Research Aid, "China's Minerals and Metals Position in the World Market, ER 76–10150, Washington, D.C., March 1976.

Copper, John F., "China's Foreign Aid in 1977," *Current Scene*, Vol. 16, Nos. 8 and 9, August–September 1978.

Fine, Daniel I., "The Soviets' New Foothold in Central Africa," *Business Week*, 10 March 1980, p. 59.

"Minerals for China's Modernization," *China Reconstructs*, June 1979, p. 39.

National Foreign Assessment Center, "China: The Nonferrous Metals Industry in the 1970's," ER 78–10104U, Washington, D.C., May 1978.

National Foreign Assessment Center, "China: The Steel Industry in the 1970's and 1980's," ER 79–10245, Washington, D.C., May 1979.

P. C. Lucke and Associates, "China Metals Study," New York, 1979.

PRC: Already a Major Minerals Producer, Its Growth Has Just Begun," *Mining Engineering*, Vol. 28, No. 7, 10 February 1976.

Szuprowicz, Bohdan O., and Maria R. Szuprowicz, *Doing Business with the People's Republic of China*, John Wiley & Sons, New York, 1978.

U.S. Bureau of Mines, "Far East and South Asia," Department of the Interior, Washington, D.C., 1977.

Wang, K. P., "Mineral Industries of China," U.S. Bureau of Mines, Washington, D.C., 1979.

CHAPTER
SEVEN

Strategic Materials
Supercartel

The strategic materials predominance of High Africa, growing import dependence of the West, and Soviet-Cuban expansion into the region are three major factors that are converging in southern Africa. If the Western world is not to be caught up in a massive squeeze on its vital non-oil minerals supplies in the future that could become much more serious in its effects than the OPEC cartel, considerably more attention must be paid now to the developments in that area.

The "correlation of forces," to use a favorite Soviet phrase, that is shaping up is such that it favors additional Soviet initiatives in High Africa, whereas the West is preoccupied with the threat to the Middle East oil supplies and its attention is otherwise diverted by such events as terrorism in Iran, the Soviet invasion of Afghanistan, and mounting inflation in its domestic economies.

Events could be leading up to the formation of a bloc of black Marxist Soviet-controlled African states isolating South Africa and designed to engineer a takeover of that country by Marxist forces. The West may suddenly find itself on the sidelines in a confrontation in which it will be damned if it does and damned if it does not act decisively to support South Africa in whatever initiatives that country decides to undertake to wrest control of the vital High Africa region from Soviet bloc domination or to make a desperate stand for its own survival as an independent entity.

A WORST-CASE SCENARIO

If the Soviet Union has not abandoned its long-term objective of spreading communism throughout the world it will soon have the opportunity of the century to start putting it into effect by engaging in a resources war in which it enjoys all the advantages. All that is necessary is to gain control of the key

High Africa countries that produce and supply most of the free world's strategic materials. This is especially possible because the Soviet Union itself possesses the only alternative sources of most of the same strategic materials that are comparable in size to those of High Africa.

In fact whoever can gain collective control of the key High Africa countries will be in a position to form a strategic materials supercartel whose effects could dwarf the impact of the OPEC oil cartel. Such a development would be extremely serious to the security and economic well-being of NATO countries, Japan, and even China.

By "liberating" one by one High Africa countries into a subcontinent of Marxist people's republics and bringing each into the COMECON trade and economic development system the Soviet bloc has a potential mechanism in place to put the concept of a strategic materials supercartel into reality. Control of Soviet bloc and High Africa minerals production and supply means the control of over 50 percent of the global output of about 15 of the most strategic materials in the world. This would give the Soviets sufficient leverage to demand political and economic concessions that would be otherwise unwarranted by the free market forces (see Figure 7.1).

Once in control of such a strategic materials supercartel the Soviets could achieve their objectives by relatively simple manipulation of strategic materials supplies to specific countries in the West that critically depend on those imports. Here the choice of opportunities truly boggles the mind. These could range from selective supplies allocation of a single critical material to specific countries operating in the form of a restrictive cartel to a complete embargo on the supplies of all strategic materials to one or more countries unless political demands are acquiesced.

The problems associated with the formation of such a strategic materials supercartel are not trivial and would require considerable investment, diplomacy, centralized political and economic policy, and time. Although the Soviet Union has the capabilities on all counts many sovietologists express considerable doubts that the Soviets would be able to organize such an international structure. Be that as it may, the "correlation of forces" in High Africa at present is so favorable to the Soviet Union that this could be the necessary incentive to make a special effort because the stakes are so incredibly high.

It is not inconceivable, for example, that having obtained control of the production of most of the world's strategic materials the Soviet Union could demand unilateral nuclear disarmament. The alternatives then available to NATO and the West would be an immediate nuclear attack of the Soviet Union, a regional nuclear war for control of High Africa, or unconditional surrender to Soviet dictates and unilateral disarmament. Only the first alternative could effectively remove the Soviet threat if the West were prepared to start a nuclear war and have the necessary equipment, personnel, and defenses to survive a Soviet retaliation.

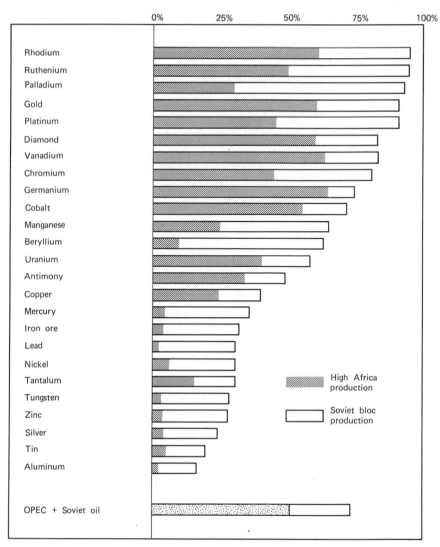

Figure 7.1 High Africa and Soviet bloc strategic minerals and metals production as percentage of global supply.

CHINA UNDER SOVIET AND WESTERN EMBARGOES

The devastating effects of the denial of supplies of strategic materials such as chromium, nickel, cobalt, platinum, and oil to a country without its own exploitable reserves was dramatically demonstrated in the case of China immediately following the Sino-Soviet rift of 1961. Almost 100 percent of China's rapidly growing demand for those materials were imported from the

Soviet Union at the time because China's own reserves of these materials were negligible or nonexistent.

The sudden withdrawal of Soviet economic assistance to China, the recall of 10,000 Soviet technicians, and the abandonment of new plants under construction has been widely publicized. But probably more serious to the Chinese economy was the Soviet decision to cut back shipments of chromium, nickel, cobalt, and even oil on which China was then almost completely dependent on the Soviet Union.

The Soviet strategic materials embargo dealt a crippling blow to China's emerging industrialization program and was designed to bring that country to its knees. This embargo was all the more effective because at the time trade with China was also embargoed by the United States. Third World countries with alternative sources of strategic materials required by China would be risking the loss of Western foreign aid if they traded with China. This Soviet embargo demonstrates how effectively the Soviet Union can exploit its dominant strategic materials position, coupled with a favorable international "correlation of forces."

In desperation China began even trading with South Africa. There are records of some transactions between those countries in the early 1960s. But almost immediately Chinese trade initiatives in South Africa were attacked and condemned by the Soviet media as a betrayal of the cause of black African states, and China withdrew from further direct transactions.

It was then that the Chinese developed their "Albanian Connection" but the Chinese leaders obviously realized that Albania can only be regarded as a temporary and politically unstable supplier of strategic materials and concentrated on finding alternative sources that unfortunately were mostly limited to High Africa countries, particularly Rhodesia, Zaire, and South Africa. Chou En-lai himself visited several countries in Africa during 1964, ostensibly extending Chinese foreign aid to newly emerging black African countries, but a major objective was to arrange for new sources of strategic materials in Africa.

This relatively little-known Sino-Soviet resources war was probably the most significant Soviet action involving the use of central political power to manipulate its dominant position as a strategic materials supplier. However, there are also other instances when the Soviet Union engaged in commodity manipulation for political reasons. During the 1950s the Soviet Union took advantage of shortages in the West and agreed with other COMECON countries to export such critical materials as chromium, asbestos, timber, and coal from Poland, only in exchange for strategic goods and equipment from the West that were crucial to the development of its own industries.

In some lesser minerals manipulation actions the Soviets have also been known to have dumped tin on world markets in the late 1950s, causing the collapse of the prices of that metal. Even through the 1960s they also exported oil and titanium at 40 and 20 percent below market prices, respectively. More recent they have suddenly withdrawn platinum from world markets, causing an abrupt escalation of prices of that metal to historic heights.

It is precisely because the Soviet Union is almost self-sufficient in strategic materials that it can engage in these actions and plan to use the possible control of major foreign sources for its political ends. The Soviets are risking very little by such activity, and there is practically nothing that Western powers can do to retaliate that could have any adverse effect on the Soviet economy. The Soviets appear to be very much aware of their strategic superiority in this regard, and there is little question that much attention is given to this subject in the Soviet Union. Discussions of problems of the supplies of capitalist metals markets are appearing quite regularly in Soviet trade and technical publications, whereas practically nothing is known officially about corresponding Soviet markets.

SINO-SOVIET CONFLICT IN AFRICA

It appeared to outside observers during the 1960s that when the Western powers were granting independence to their African colonies the Soviet Union was on the prowl backing various Marxist movements in the hopes of gaining influence among newly emerging black African states. When China also entered the arena and began extending foreign aid to African countries it was generally assumed that this was done to counteract the Soviet influence by exporting Maoist revolution to Third World countries. It seems that China with its "People's Diplomacy" happily assisted in maintaining such views that were also widely disseminated by the Western media at the time.

This helped to divert the world's attention from the real purpose of the mission: to establish a means of access to the rich supplies of chromium, cobalt, platinum, vanadium, gold, diamonds, and many other strategic materials available in the High Africa region that China had to import in increasing amounts.

China's ingenious solution to the access problem was to offer extensive economic and military aid to many black African countries, including Zaire, Zambia, Tanzania, and Mozambique. What was unique about this approach was the fact that China is still a developing nation itself in need of economic assistance, yet it embarked on a program of foreign aid extensions that in one or two years during the early 1970s reached about $1-billion levels, surpassing even the corresponding extensions of the Soviet Union in Africa. Clearly China decided to pay a price for vital access to the strategic materials it needed, and this method effectively counteracted any Soviet accusations of acting against the interests of black Africa.

The bulk of China's foreign aid went to Zambia and Tanzania for the construction of the 1100-mile long TAZARA railroad linking the Indian Ocean port of Dar es Salaam in Tanzania with the mining heartland of Zambia. There the railroad links with the cobalt-rich Shaba province of Zaire and with Rhodesian and South African railway networks that provide access to other strategic materials also required by China. The railroad was built at an estimated cost of over $400 million through virgin east African territory, using massive Chinese labor teams and equipment imported from China (see Figure 7.2).

At the time of the Angola crisis in 1975 the TAZARA railroad was in its final stages of construction in neighboring Zambia and Tanzania. There were

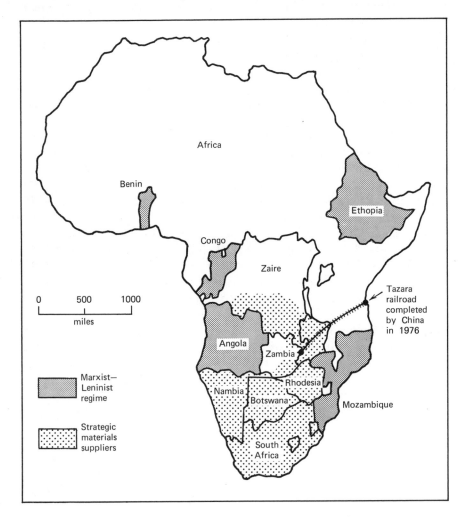

Figure 7.2 Chinese TAZARA railroad and Marxist regimes in High Africa.

about 16,000 PLA Railroad Engineering Corps workers actually building the railroad and literally "living off the land" in line with Chinese self-sufficiency policies.

It is not unreasonable to suppose that the introduction of about 16,000 Cubans by the Soviet Union into Angola at that time was at least partly prompted by this relatively large Chinese presence in neighboring Zambia, with even more Chinese "technicians" in Tanzania. It was no secret that China and Zaire jointly supported the FNLA liberation movement in Angola led by Holden Roberto. In Zaire a Chinese general and a military mission was established to train anti-Soviet liberation forces for Angola, and Chinese river fleet experts presented president Mobutu Sese Seko of Zaire with plans to strengthen Zaire's riverborne defense forces.

In 1976 Zaire agreed to import 20 Chinese T-62 tanks, and Chinese jet fighters were already in service in Sudan and Tanzania as a result of previous military and economic aid programs. In all by 1978 significant Chinese foreign aid was extended to over 20 African countries, but by far the largest amounts went to Zambia and Tanzania for the construction of the TAZARA railroad.

These Chinese must have been genuinely concerned about Soviet-Cuban penetration into Angola that must have looked to them as a possible threat to their huge investment in developing costly access to the strategic materials of High Africa via the TAZARA railroad. On the other hand they probably expected that the United States, western Europe, and South Africa, whose vital interests were clearly also threatened, would not allow Soviet penetration in Angola and Mozambique. It now looks as if the Chinese may have been ready to fight against Soviet-Cuban infiltration of Angola, but seeing only half-hearted support of the cause by the Western world they withdrew from further involvement in the Angola conflict.

On the other hand the Soviets may have also decided to act resolutely by sending about 16,000 Cuban troops to Angola. The Soviets' decision may have been influenced by the large Chinese presence in the High Africa region whom they could view as a potential force "invited" by the West by virtue of not being prevented from building the TAZARA railroad. Even though those were railroad workers it is believed that most were under Chinese military discipline of the PLA Railroad Engineering Corps, a major railroad building organization having performed well in China and Vietnam.

The Soviets, once committed to capturing Angola and Mozambique for Marxist regimes, could not risk the possibility of unilateral reaction by the Chinese and opposing liberation movements even if they were convinced that Western powers would not be able to organize sufficient resistance. They knew that it was the previous Soviet strategic materials sanctions against China that forced the Chinese to the huge expenditures of resources in building the TAZARA railroad which helped to break the Soviet embargo.

As a result Soviet-Cuban adventures in the High Africa region should be regarded at least in good part as an extension of the Sino-Soviet dispute. If the Soviets succeed in capturing control of key High Africa countries in the future they will not only be striking a blow against Western industrialized world but against China as well. This fact further enhances the incentives that the Soviet Union may have to exploit this opportunity. This fact also creates the common interest between the Western world and China and is at the roots of Deng Xiaoping's philosophy for presenting a common front to the Soviet threat.

The permission granted by Zambia more recently to allow Cubans to train Rhodesian guerrillas and the coming to power of Robert Mugabe in Zimbabwe creates a new set of political factors that China now must consider in its African policies. These developments clearly favor the Soviet Union in terms of High Africa stakes. The Chinese counteroffer to supply Zambia with military equipment and training was rejected in 1979, whereas Soviet "MIG diplomacy" triumphed again when Zambia and the Soviet Union signed a barter deal worth $85 million to provide Soviet MIG fighters and other weapons in return for Zambian cobalt.

SOVIET TECHNOLOGY FOR AFRICAN COMMODITIES

The threats of cartels in non-oil commodities are not normally considered as grave in their consequences as that of the OPEC oil cartel. There is a considerable amount of disbelief in many quarters that cartelization of any commodities other than oil will prove successful for any length of time.

Since 1973 various organizations in the West studied cartel possibilities in key non-oil commodities in connection with the issues of the North-South Dialogue and the proposals for "buffer stocks" in Third World countries. The conclusions of most of these research efforts were somewhat similar and suggested that for most materials cartel possibilities were either low or economically unattractive. Although the findings confirmed the existence of some cartel and quasi-cartel organizations in the form of state trading monopolies or government-industry consortia their overall effect on supplies of strategic materials was not considered likely to ever approach anything like that of OPEC.

However most studies analyze cartel potential on a single commodity basis, concentrating primarily on the economic aspects rather than the use for political manipulation. It is only when a multimineral non-oil cartel is taken into acccount that the tremendous potential of a political force becomes apparent. There are, however, very few areas where an effective cartel of such type could be organized. The Soviet Union as a whole is one such multimineral state cartel. High Africa as a region is probably the only other area in the world that has such potential. Jointly the Soviet bloc and High Africa would present a most formidable supercartel potential as outlined earlier in this chapter.

On the other hand there are neumerous reasons being advanced by commodity and trade analysts why the cartelization of High Africa minerals could not succeed. Key arguments center on the fact that individual African supplier countries must export their minerals to survive and obtain foreign exchange for imports of food, equipment, and technology to run their economies.

But if the High Africa countries are taken over one by one by pro-Soviet Marxist regimes they could also become members of the Soviet bloc COMECON community in which Angola has an observer status. Once this is accomplished the specialized state minerals monopolies could be readily brought under central control of an appropriate COMECON organization that would in effect become a strategic materials supercartel.

The Soviet Union has already been able to establish quite extensive commercial footholds in many African countries, and under COMECON barter-type arrangements could considerably expand this trade and at the same time eliminate Western suppliers and competitors. Soviet aircraft, for example, have been exported to such African countries as Angola, the Congo, Ethiopia, Mozambique, Nigeria, Somalia, Ghana, Guinea, Mali, Libya, and the Sudan. The recent MIGs-and-arms-for-cobalt deal with Zambia is only the latest of these transactions. There is also no question that the Soviets are willing and able to provide expeditiously military equipment, including jet fighters, helicopters, ships, tanks, small arms, and ammunition. Both the Soviet Union and east European countries also produce power equipment, trucks, mining and construction machinery, rolling stock, and electronics that could be bartered in return for High Africa commodities which do not necessarily have to be its minerals. These may include various agricultural products, tropical fruits, and textiles.

The Soviet bloc is a huge unsaturated market for agricultural products, tropical produce, textiles, and similar consumer goods that can be produced in all African countries but for which the Western markets are relatively soft because of massive supplies from Latin American and Asian countries. Since trade between COMECON countries is conducted by means of annual trade and payment agreements the hard currency problems of poor African countries can be eliminated by centralized planning within the COMECON framework.

Because the Soviet Union is also a dominant producer of the same strategic minerals as those from High Africa and centrally controls its own output it is in a position to establish the buffer stocks of minerals that the Third World countries are demanding. In this regard the Soviets have a tremendous advantage over the Western world. In effect they would not have to round up any international financing for this purpose once COMECON controls High Africa minerals production centers. All that would be needed is a curtailment of Soviet domestic production of specific minerals in effect creating buffer stocks in the ground under direct Soviet control. At the same time High Africa production could be centrally adjusted to maintain appropriate output levels to supplement the Soviet bloc's demand and create a surplus for the controlled allocation of strategic materials exports to Western end-user countries according to political expediency. Needless to say prices to Western customers would be set according to what the markets could bear, taking full advantage of the overhang potential to keep Western exploration and development to a minimum.

The Soviet bloc–High Africa trade interchanges would then consist of a series of barter agreements in which arms, technology, industrial machinery, and transportation equipment would be exchanged for minerals and consumer goods under centralized COMECON control. The West would lose control of access not only to its most critical strategic materials but also to practically all markets for its industrial and transportation products.

There are some who argue that most countries if given the choice prefer Western to Soviet goods. There is little question that this is so, but with increasing inflation, the costs of energy, and foreign trade deficits many of those countries are constantly negotiating various loans and foreign aid grants to keep their economies afloat. Under such circumstances liberation movements are bound to flourish, creating endless opportunities for Marxist-type government takeovers. These in turn could gain popular support by promising to cartelize minerals and commodities to exact higher prices from the end-user nations.

PROSPECTS FOR COMECON SUPERCARTEL FORMATION

Potentially the elements for the formation of a strategic materials supercartel in High Africa are in place, but at present the political fragmentation of the area is such that only strict dictatorships implementing well-coordinated policies could bring this about. Whereas the Soviet economy has many aspects of such centralized discipline the Marxist states in High Africa, such as Angola or Mozambique, are far from sufficiently organized to be immediately effective.

Initially the objective in High Africa would have to be the establishment of pro-Soviet Marxist regimes in as many countries in the region as possible and the formation of a solid front-line alliance in preparation for the final assault on "fortress South Africa." Some impetus also comes from the Organization of African Unity, the United Nations UNCTAD proposals characterized by the New International Economic Order concepts that include the buffer stocks and international commodity agreements. Clearly the overall objectives of the so-called Group of 77 promoting the NIEO principles are rather conducive to the formation of an international framework, making a strategic materials supercartel more likely in High Africa in the future.

Marxist regimes in Angola and Mozambique appear to have come into being as a result of decisive Soviet-Cuban support to the liberation movements of their choice. Whether the Soviet planners conceived of the larger role that those countries could play in the formation of a strategic materials supercartel is hard to determine. But it is clear now that the relatively easy victory and the growing capabilities of Soviet logistics establishment is opening up new possibilities to Soviet strategists.

Victory in Angola in particular must have proved to the Soviet hawks that a "blue waters strategy" has become a reality for the Soviet navy and merchant marine. It also showed that Soviet long-range aircraft deployment forces are capable of supporting a mission even in a strange and remote country like Angola.

The Soviets must have analyzed the situation rather well after Portugal granted early independence to Angola and Mozambique and realized that although these countries form an integral part of the southern African subcontinent, both play a relatively minor role as strategic materials suppliers to nations in the West. The choice of providing all-out assistance with the help of Cuban troops was especially shrewd at the time. If similar moves were made against other countries in High Africa the Soviets correctly assumed that Western powers would have responded much more vigorously, because in terms of immediate minerals supply importance, much more would have been at stake. In the case of Angola and Mozambique economic losses were already suffered by Portugal whose political direction at the time was somewhat uncertain.

The election of Robert Mugabe in 1980 as Marxist prime minister of Zimbabwe is a new development that has ominous similarities to the election of Allende in Chile. It now remains to be seen how the policies of the new government will shape the country's future, but there is little question that Zimbabwe's direction will be much more important than that of Angola and Mozambique.

It is well to remember that a well-established relationship exists between Mugabe and Beijing. Mugabe visited China while leading his ZANU guerrillas in Mozambique during the mid-1970s before winning in the 1980 Zimbabwe elections. There are also many indications that despite previous UN sanctions against Rhodesia that have been lifted recently China obtained considerable amounts of chromium shipped through Zambia and the TAZARA railroad. Thus Mugabe's "China Connection" gives Zimbabwe a special coloration in the present scheme of things in High Africa.

But although this may favor the cause of anti-Soviet forces it also creates a reaction in other quarters. Zambia's recent rejection of Chinese military assistance and acceptance of Soviet MIGs for a cobalt deal clearly indicates that the Sino-Soviet conflict may be simmering in that region for a long time to come.

Much will depend on the stability of Mugabe's regime in Zimbabwe, but the present "correlation of forces" among the front-line states immediately north of South Africa is clearly not conducive to any longer-range political or economic stability. The situation still favors Soviet policies overwhelmingly, and Western resolution and decisive action vis-à-vis further Soviet-backed initiatives will determine the outcome of any policies for a Soviet-controlled strategic materials supercartel in High Africa.

SOUTHERN AFRICAN FEDERATION CONCEPTS

The threat of a COMECON strategic materials supercartel is only one possible outcome for the future of High Africa. South Africa has long been known to have its own plans to organize a federation of strategic minerals-producing countries in that region. Except for its apartheid policies it is otherwise extremely well placed to undertake such a program, since it is by far the most powerful economy in Africa and dominates the southern African subcontinent in many ways.

Western inability to formulate and put into effect a coherent joint policy toward South Africa based on the vital interests of the United States, western Europe, and Japan is not only playing into the hands of the Russians but also must be extremely frustrating to South Africa. Some of the developments in South Africa clearly indicate that it cannot and will not idly await further developments because its own survival is at stake.

Such international developments as the Islamic Revolution in Iran that resulted in the cutoff of South Africa's oil supplies and threats of further sanctions against South Africa have been pushing that country toward unilateral decisions that may yet cost the West its relatively free access to High Africa minerals it has so far enjoyed. If, for example, South Africa acted in concert with Zimbabwe to cartelize only the supplies of chromium this would be a severe blow to all Western industrialized chromium-economy nations.

In fact South Africa has the potential to undertake the organization of a federation of strategic materials-producing countries throughout High Africa with some chances of success. Further Soviet penetration or threats in Angola, Zaire, Zambia, Namibia, and Mozambique and perhaps attempts to destabilize the new Mugabe regime in Zimbabwe may cause South Africa to take further unilateral preventive action to protect its future.

There is therefore the potential for two alternative strategic materials supercartels developing in High Africa, resulting from the lack of Western attention in that region. Besides the possibility of a Soviet-controlled group of Marxist states the alternative could turn out to be a South African initiative designed to remove the Soviet supercartel threat by attempting to create one under its own control.

As the dominating minerals processing and marketing country in High Africa, South Africa can also offer extremely attractive incentives to all the other minerals-producing countries under the conditions of cartelization. It is already also well experienced in central "market stabilization" of supplies and prices of materials such as gold, diamonds, and platinum.

South Africa is in fact the only regional power capable of taking effective action to prevent Soviet control of High Africa. However the country's social policies have provided the Soviets with a means to alienate South Africa from much Western support and turn the world's opinion against it. Many well-meaning Western politicians and liberal reformists are in fact playing into the Soviet hands probably unaware of the real issues that are at stake.

PROSPECTS FOR SOUTH AFRICAN SUPERCARTEL

A strategic materials supercartel controlled by South Africa would differ from a COMECON supercartel in size and scope, but the supercartel's effect on the West could be equally devastating. It would not have the immediate benefit of Soviet resources and their buffer stocks potential nor the international centrally controlled organizations to implement it. This means that the supercartel would have to depend on investment from within and without High Africa to come into being, because all southern African countries are Third World states with relatively low per capita incomes and insufficient domestic capital formation rates.

Any attempt to create such an organization by diplomatic means is out of the question at present, except within the smaller group of South Africa, Botswana, Namibia, Swaziland, Lesotho, and the new homeland states of Transkei, Venda, and Bophuthatswana not recognized internationally that form the South African Customs Union. Otherwise the apartheid policies make it not acceptable to the remaining black African states in the region. Although some social and labor changes are now under way in South Africa it is unlikely that anything but a radical change in government to a black-majority rule would satisfy the surrounding black African states. This in turn is unlikely to happen very soon through constitutional means, and as a result racial tensions are mounting in South Africa, and many observers suggest that a racial war will erupt in the near future.

The government officials are bracing themselves against any attempts to overthrow the government and are preparing to take merciless and relentless action. The chief of the South African Defense Force (SADF) went on record as saying that even the present level of violence is a low-intensity undeclared war.

Other pronouncements of South African government leaders suggest that South Africa is also preparing to take action against any neighboring country that allows its territory to be used for attacks into South Africa. Anti-guerrilla task forces have been formed, and stricter security measures have been adopted at borders, airports, and other strategic locations.

There is a Soviet-backed African National Congress, a communist exile organization committed to the violent overthrow of white rule in South Africa. All this only firms the South African government's stance to prepare for a showdown by expanding the SADF forces that are officially over 65,000 in strength and can draw on 280,000 active reservists who are almost all white. Although South Africans of all races believe that the struggle ahead will be 80 percent political and only 20 percent military, the preoccupation with internal security and external threats make it difficult for South Africa to pursue the federation polices or implement any supercartel concepts except within its own territory.

Nevertheless should South Africa develop nuclear weapons it could by a combination of military and economic measures occupy or extend its control over most High Africa conutries in question. Because it has a surplus agriculture and an increasing industrial base such an entity could survive even under extreme sanctions for a very long time. Because Western capitalist countries would be the most damaged by such action the Soviet Union may encourage and even tolerate such an event. The rationale would be that such a supercartel would greatly weaken NATO and if controlled by white South Africans would be eventually doomed to failure perhaps even at a time when the West would no longer be in a position to react effectively.

WHAT THE WEST MUST DO TO PROTECT ITS INTERESTS

The prevailing popular opinions in the West call for increased political and economic pressures to demand faster reform and transition toward majority rule in South Africa. This objective is often seen as the panacea that will solve most problems in the region and remove all threats with one stroke. There seems to be a naive consensus that any black-majority government would be particularly well disposed to those who supported its coming to power and would assure stable supplies of strategic materials to such countries and end-users.

Reliance on the goodwill of revolutionary forces is irresponsible at best. Even advance agreements with revolutionary leadership that later may come to power cannot eliminate supply disruptions as a result of civil or racial wars and cannot guarantee access to supplies if "dirty" nuclear devices are used to destroy major mining and processing areas. Nor are those regimes particularly stable when they do come to power, and this policy is at best a stop-gap solution.

Because High Africa reserves are so vital to the West and present such an opportunity to the Soviet Union no matter what partial solutions are introduced the threat of a total takeover will continue until it is accomplished because the stakes are so incredibly high.

This is why the solution of Zimbabwe is unstable and may lead to further wars and revolutions in the region. A much more definitive long-range program is needed to assure unimpeded Western access not to one or two countries' resources but to all the reserves of High Africa for some time to come if the industrial democracies of the West are to survive in their present form.

If the West intends to confront and compete with the Soviet bloc with some measure of credibility in the future it must not only solve its energy dependence problems but also secure the reserves of High Africa for its exclusive use. This need not be forever but probably for at least 20 years through the year 2000 to provide sufficient lead time to determine whether alternative sources will be available in more secure parts of the world. In doing so the West must be prepared to forego its democratic and human rights policies in those areas and openly use its military power as the Soviets have been doing for years. The extension of NATO or a new security alliance such as the Trioceanic Alliance that would include High Africa as well as Japan, Australia, and perhaps Brazil would be one of the necessary steps to expand Western commitments. This type of approach is rapidly becoming a matter of survival of the Western democracies and may even prevent a nuclear war at a later date when the West may find itself reduced to the use of nuclear weapons or submission to a new world economic order under Soviet auspices.

During the next 20 years intensive exploration, mining, and conservation programs should be developed within at least NATO countries on a planned basis to eliminate unnecessary competition and duplication. Governments should face the problem by the introduction of special tax incentives to promote capital investment in these industries and to develop environmental provisions to bypass any restrictions that could hinder priority minerals development programs.

The basic objectives of these programs must be to ascertain that the West can survive in a confrontation with the Soviet Union even without the strategic materials resources of High Africa and despite the threat of a potential materials overhang contained within a Soviet-controlled strategic materials supercartel.

During those 20 years, however, the West must secure High Africa resources by supporting South Africa to prevent it from slipping into the Soviet orbit. This may mean investment, technology, and trade to make sure South Africa can maintain its hegemony over the subcontinent and perhaps even implement its federation concepts without fear of external aggression. The economic development of the area resulting from appropriate policies even if introduced by white-minority government could lead to a betterment of the living standards in High Africa and less desire to move into the Marxist camp by individual states. At the same time extensive Western and perhaps Japanese support would provide a means of exerting additional pressure on South Africa to introduce reforms leading to a more equitable society in that country.

REFERENCES

Fine, Daniel I., "The Soviets' New Foothold in Central Africa," *Business Week*, 10 March 1980, p. 59.

"Peace in Rhodesia—Or More of the Same?," *U.S. News & World Report*, 3 March 1980, p. 63.

"Rumblings of Race War in South Africa," *U.S. News & World Report*, 17 March 1980, p. 43.

Szuprowicz, Bohdan O., "The Danger of a Supercartel in Strategic Materials: It Could Make OPEC Seem Tame," *Canadian Business*, November 1979.

Szuprowicz, Bohdan O., "Fear Soviet Supercartel for Critical Minerals," *Purchasing*, 8 November 1978.

Szuprowicz, Bohdan O., "Soviet Squeeze on Strategic Materials," *Datamation*, October 1979.

Szuprowicz, Bohdan O., "Menace sur les Minerais Strategiques?," *Usine Nouvelle*, No. 38, 20 September 1979.

Szuprowicz, Bohdan O., "Russian Drive to Control Africa's Strategic Minerals," *Bulletin*, 15 May 1979.

Szuprowicz, Bohdan O., "Soviet Squeeze on Strategic Materials," *Datamation*, October 1978.

Szuprowicz, Bohdan O., "Strategic Materials Supercartel," *International Essays for Business Decision Makers*, Vol. 4, p. 176, Center for International Business, Dallas, Texas, 1979.

"We're Not Running Out—Just Short," *Purchasing*, 10 April 1980.

Western Massachusetts Association of Concerned African Scholars, *U.S. Military Involvement in Southern Africa*, South End Press, Boston, 1978.

CHAPTER
EIGHT

Pacific Basin Resources Geopolitics

The Pacific Basin in general and East Asia in particular is now expected to be the world's most dynamic region of growth during the 1980s. At the same time the region has undergone startling political changes during the 1970s, while the attention of the West was diverted by the instability in the Middle East, modernization of NATO, and U.S.–Soviet strategic relationships in other parts of the world.

Industrialization of the Pacific Basin will augment the demand for strategic materials in the future and increase the competition for available resources in Third World countries because the area is far from self-sufficient, in energy or raw materials. Until the 1970s the main economic development axis of the Pacific Basin existed between Australia and Japan. Those two countries developed a unique and little-realized dependence on each other, but in the partnership Australia is by far the more vulnerable. In any case the partnership is far from perfect because both countries continue to be dependent on energy supplies from the Middle East and many other strategic minerals from the Third World. However, now that Western competition for strategic materials is increasing Australia is clearly in a position to strengthen its stance vis-à-vis Japan as well as other free world capitalist countries that may increasingly look to Australia as a source of strategic minerals and an opportunity for investment.

During the 1980s increasing industrialization of North and South Korea, Taiwan, the Philippines, Hong Kong, Singapore, Malaysia, Indonesia, and Vietnam are bound to exert additional pressures on the demand for sources required for economic development of those countries. Another factor is the continued development of China, which presents only a potential source of strategic minerals in the future because it is more likely to need the supplies for its own requirements first before it will make them available for export.

Although the countries of the Pacific Basin produce at least 30 different minerals in significant quantities their cumulative shares of global production in most cases is relatively small. The Pacific Basin has a commanding supply position only in asbestos, bauxite, graphite, natural rubber, nickel, tin, and titanium ores. However, if Canada is excluded from consideration as a Pacific Basin country, the overwhelming supply position of the region is basically reduced only to tin, natural rubber, and graphite (see Table 8.1).

The Pacific Basin, outside China, is significantly short of oil, although its overall energy supply position is somewhat better because it produces almost 30 percent of the world's coal supply mostly in North and South Korea. Australia and Canada, however, are clearly the two most important contributors to the Pacific Basin minerals supply position, but even those two resource-rich countries cannot supply all the strategic minerals required by modern economies in the variety available from the High Africa countries or the Soviet Union.

The national interests of individual Pacific Basin countries have now replaced ideology as a major aligning force in international politics. The conflicts in the region are dominated by the Sino-Soviet confrontations, making them more East-East rather than East-West in character as China and the Soviet Union struggle to expand their influence in the Pacific Basin with an occasional threat or even the use of force. The major question is whether nationalist forces in the region will contribute to economic development or will increase tensions, resource rivalry, and arms and nuclear proliferation and eventually lead to destabilization of the area and a major Asian war.

INDUSTRIALIZATION OF THE PACIFIC BASIN

The industrialization of the Pacific Basin is accelerating as part of a growing interaction between the superpowers of the region, namely, Japan, China, the Soviet Union, and the United States and the remaining countries. An increasing role is already being played in the process by the newly industrializing countries of the region such as North and South Korea, Taiwan, Hong Kong, and Singapore and to a somewhat lesser degree by Malaysia, the Philippines, and Indonesia.

During the 1960s and 1970s several of those Pacific Basin countries have approached the "take-off" stage of economic development previously demonstrated by Japan. South Korea in particular has shown remarkable annual growth rates in excess of 10 percent, even as the rest of the world began slowing down as a result of inflation, recession, and continuing uncertainty about future energy and strategic materials supplies.

Some futurists believe that many of the so-called Neo-Confucian cultures representative of Pacfic Basin countries are better suited to rapid economic growth than Western cultures have ever been. These Neo-Confucian cultures are derivative of the Chinese culture and through overseas Chinese communities numbering about 20 million exert a strong influence in various states of the region. As a result the Confucian ethic is believed to be now at work playing a role in the modernization of the Pacific Basin not unlike that performed by the Protestant ethic in Europe and North America during the last century. It is also believed that this Confucian ethic will create much more spectacular effects in the Pacific Basin of the future.

Modern shipping, telecommunications, information systems, supersonic transport, and other international services are reducing the vast Pacific Ocean to the role of a common lake of the region, contributing more to the linking of various Pacific Basin interests at the same time that such modern services are separating different cultures, religions, races, and ethnic groupings. This function is not unlike that performed in the development of Western culture, trade, and technology by the Mediterranean Sea throughout the history of Europe and more recently by the North Atlantic in the development of the NATO community.

But the most important factor in the development of the Pacific Basin during the remaining decades of this century is the continuing economic growth, outstripping that of western Europe, the Soviet bloc, or most of the Third World countries.

If the associated rising expectations of the newly awakened Asian masses lead to demands for an increase in living standards comparable to those of the industrialized world the requirements of the Pacific Basin countries for energy and raw materials will be enormous. This is bound to create intensified competition for existing resources in the region that already are clearly inadequate. It will also create pressures on the market economies in the form of highly competitive manufactured goods produced by Pacific Basin countries that will have to be exported in even greater quantities to earn foreign exchange to pay for vital imports of energy and strategic materials not available within the region.

THE JAPANESE DILEMMA

The dominating economy of the Pacific Basin is Japan, but although Japan may even be considered as a regional superpower its lack of energy and mineral resources makes it an economy that is highly vulnerable to any strategic materials supply disruptions (see Figure 8.1). By comparison with Japan China's future superpower potential is considerably better because of its significant domestic minerals resources (see Figure 3.1 and Table 3.2 in Chapter 3).

Japan now faces a dilemma that has been increasing further in 1980 as a result of being pressured by the United States to stop buying oil from Iran and deteriorating U.S.–Soviet relations in the aftermath of the Soviet invasion of Afghanistan. At the same time rising protectionism in western Eu-

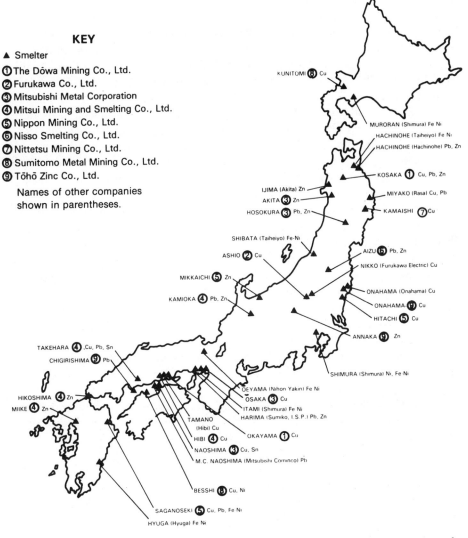

KEY

▲ Smelter

① The Dōwa Mining Co., Ltd.
② Furukawa Co., Ltd.
③ Mitsubishi Metal Corporation
④ Mitsui Mining and Smelting Co., Ltd.
⑤ Nippon Mining Co., Ltd.
⑥ Nisso Smelting Co., Ltd.
⑦ Nittetsu Mining Co., Ltd.
⑧ Sumitomo Metal Mining Co., Ltd.
⑨ Tōhō Zinc Co., Ltd.

Names of other companies
shown in parentheses.

KUNITOMI ⑧ Cu

MURORAN (Shimura) Fe Ni
HACHINOHE (Taiheiyo) Fe Ni
HACHINOHE (Hachinohe) Pb, Zn

KOSAKA ① Cu, Pb, Zn

IJIMA (Akita) Zn
AKITA ③ Zn
HOSOKURA ③ Pb, Zn

MIYAKO (Rasa) Cu, Pb

KAMAISHI ⑦ Cu

SHIBATA (Taiheiyo) Fe-Ni

ASHIO ② Cu

AIZU ⑥ Pb, Zn

NIKKO (Furukawa Electric) Cu

MIKKAICHI ⑤ Zn

ONAHAMA (Onahama) Cu
ONAHAMA ⑨ Cu
HITACHI ⑤ Cu

KAMIOKA ④ Pb, Zn

ANNAKA ⑨ Zn

TAKEHARA ④ ,Cu, Pb, Sn
CHIGIRISHIMA ⑨ Pb

SHIMURA (Shimura) Ni, Fe-Ni

HIKOSHIMA ④ Zn
MIIKE ④ Zn

OEYAMA (Nihon Yakin) Fe Ni
ŌSAKA ③ Cu
ITAMI (Shimura) Fe Ni
HARIMA (Sumiko, I.S.P.) Pb, Zn

TAMANO
(Hibi) Cu
HIBI ④ Cu
NAOSHIMA ④ Cu, Sn
M.C. NAOSHIMA (Mitsubishi Cominco) Pb

OKAYAMA ① Cu

BESSHI ⑧ Cu, Ni

SAGANOSEKI ⑤ Cu, Pb, Fe Ni
HYUGA (Hyuga) Fe Ni

Figure 8.1 Major Japanese nonferrous smelters and ferronickel plants that process mostly imported ores and minerals. Map shows locations, major metals processed, and principal operating companies. Source. **U.S. Bureau of Mines and Japan Mining Industry Association data, 1977.**

153

rope and the United States against a flood of Japanese imports is limiting export markets for Japanese goods that are the mainstay of its economy.

Recent political shifts in the Pacific Basin also pose several questions pertaining to Japan's security. So far the country has relied on the military umbrella of the United States, but it now appears almost certain that Japan will increasingly have to provide for its own defense. A military-industrial buildup in Japan will require additional secure sources of energy and strategic materials and may even cause Japan to move in the direction of becoming a nuclear military power. It is generally agreed that Japan has the technology to develop rapidly its own nuclear weapons and delivery systems and its decision not to do so has been purely political. Japan may quickly reverse its position, particularly as South Korea and Taiwan become nuclear powers and if the NATO-Soviet relationship further deteriorates.

Since the Pacific Basin is short of energy in general and oil in particular to sustain more rapid economic development of the region it seems very likely that Japan will continue on its course of nuclear power development. Japan is already the second largest nuclear power producing country after the United States and despite political and environmental opposition it seems certain that Japan will expand its nuclear power generating capacity. It may also transfer some of this technology to China and other Pacific Basin countries in return for access to resources, trade, and investment opportunities. Such a course of action, however, would nevertheless require increased imports of uranium, probably from Australia, Canada, and Brazil as well as acceleration of the development of nuclear fuel processing capacity and breeder reactor programs.

Given these developing conditions and uncertainties it is believed that Japan may move closer to China and the Third World countries during the 1980s. On the other hand Japan will probably want to continue relatively good relations with the Soviet Union because of its proximity, vast potential markets, and natural resources of Siberia that could be as readily available to Japan as those of China if it pursues an evenhanded policy toward both Asian superpowers. A realignment of Japanese policies and national priorities within the Pacific Basin will have a profound effect on the future of this region before the end of this century.

AUSTRALIA'S MINERAL RESOURCES

The Australian continent is sometimes called the "lucky country" because of its relatively abundant mineral resources, as well as political and economic stability that is conducive to the attraction of domestic and foreign investments. Among the Pacific Basin countries it is second only to Canada in the variety and abundance of minerals and is destined to play an increasingly important role in the region as competition for Australian resources intensifies (see Table 8.1).

Australia is now becoming aware of its growing importance as a major supplier of minerals to Japan, other Pacific Basin countries, and the industrialized West. It is also developing domestic policies to play an increasing role as a processor of minerals and metals by expanding local industries that will create additional investment and employment opportunities and enhance the value of its minerals and metals exports in the international markets.

Economic growth of the Pacific Basin has long-range implications for Australian infrastructure, transport systems, port development, shipping, mining equipment industry, and foreign trade. The development of Australia's mining industry is expected to play a crucial role in its future economic growth. Its strong agricultural base and long-standing position as a food exporter further enhances its chances of becoming a powerful economy in the future. Its relatively homogeneous and almost entirely white population assures the country relative internal stability, free from racial and ethnic·tensions that threaten South Africa or even the United States. Trade unions and labor problems are the greatest threat to disruptions of supplies from Australia, but under emergency conditions those could be handled in a special manner.

Australian national objectives are to increase minerals processing domestically and demand better access to the end-user markets in industrialized countries for upgraded minerals and metals products. This will threaten the minerals-processing industries of the industrialized countries, such as Japan, western Europe, and the United States, but the growing importance of Australia as a stable supplier of many minerals to the free market economies and the Pacific Basin countries gives it an advantage in future trade and investment negotiations.

Another objective of Australia in the future is to take advantage of its mining and minerals-processing technologies and become an exporter of its know-how, particularly to the Association of Southeast Asian Nations (ASEAN) group of countries in the Pacific Basin. Australians envisage opportunities for investment by Australian firms in joint ventures in foreign countries of the region whose resources may still be relatively unexplored and underdeveloped. As such Australia will present another factor in the Third World, competing directly with Japanese, American, European, and Soviet bloc interests. Nevertheless because of its relatively favorable domestic minerals resources Australia is well placed to take advantage of such long-term opportunities in strategic minerals exploration, extraction, processing, and trade.

Australia produces more than 70 different minerals and metals, and although it lacks deposits of some of the most critical metals such as chromium and platinum and has a relatively modest production of many other minerals, its resources go a long way to give Australia a good measure of

Table 8.1 Major Pacific Basin Minerals-Producing Countries and Their Share of Global Production

	Australia	Canada	Indonesia	North Korea	South Korea	Malaysia	New Caledonia	New Guinea	Philippines	Thailand	Pacific Basin Total (percent)
Aluminum	2	7	—	—	—	—	—	—	—	—	9.0
Antimony	—	—	—	—	—	—	—	—	—	6	6.0
Asbestos	—	29	—	—	—	—	—	—	—	—	29.0
Barite	—	—	—	3	—	—	—	—	—	5.5	8.5
Bauxite	35	—	1.4	—	—	1	—	—	—	—	37.4
Cadmium	—	7	—	—	—	—	—	—	—	—	7.0
Coal	3	1	—	17	8.5	—	—	—	—	—	29.5
Cobalt	—	5	—	—	—	—	14	—	—	—	19.0
Copper	3	10	0.8	—	0.2	—	—	2	3	—	19.0
Chromium	—	—	—	—	—	—	—	—	5	—	5.0
Fluorspar	—	—	—	—	—	—	—	—	—	3.5	3.5
Gold	1	4	—	—	—	—	—	2	1.3	—	8.3
Graphite	—	—	—	20	12	—	—	—	—	—	32.0
Iron ore	11	7	—	1	0.1	—	—	—	0.2	—	19.3
Lead	2	8	—	3	—	—	—	—	0.1	—	13.1
Magnesite	—	—	—	20	—	—	—	—	—	—	20.0
Manganese	6	—	—	—	—	—	—	—	—	—	6.0
Molybdenum	—	18	—	—	—	—	—	—	—	—	18.0
Nickel	11	30	2	—	—	—	14	—	1.2	—	58.2
Natural gas	1	7	—	—	—	—	—	—	—	—	8.0
Oil	—	2	2.4	—	—	—	—	—	—	—	4.4
Platinum	—	7	—	—	—	—	—	—	—	—	7.0
Silver	8	14	—	—	—	—	—	0.5	0.5	—	23.0
Sulfur	—	14	—	—	—	—	—	—	—	—	14.0
Talc	—	—	—	—	10	—	—	—	—	—	10.0
Tin	4	—	8	—	—	37	—	—	—	8	57.0
Titanium	26	22	—	—	—	—	—	—	—	—	48.0
Tungsten	—	4	—	6	8	—	—	—	—	5	23.0
Uranium	9	21	—	—	—	—	—	—	—	—	30.0
Zinc	8	14	—	3	0.8	—	—	—	0.2	—	26.0

Source. Compiled by 21st Century Research, based on data developed by the U.S. Bureau of Mines, 1980.

self-sufficiency. The country's surplus agriculture is also important in this regard and its most critical deficiencies are probably oil, water, and people (see Figure 8.2).

Although Australia imports about 70 percent of its oil requirements it is actually a surplus energy-producing country in the form of coal, uranium, and natural gas. Shale oil resources in Queensland are also believed to be so huge that they could last 12,000 years, and Exxon and other companies are planning to invest $7 to $13 billion in what is expected to become the biggest-ever mining project in Australia and is planned to produce 200,000 barrels of shale oil a day at full capacity.

Australia also possesses about 20 percent of the world's uranium reserves, although its current production represents a much smaller share of the global uranium output. Much of Australian uranium production is committed for export to Japan, West Germany, and the United States, and trade in uranium is strictly controlled by the Australian Uranium Export Office. Uranium-mining projects require a minimum 75 percent Australian equity and wholly Australian control.

Some Australian industry observers believe that the Soviet Union, which is well aware of Australia's minerals potential, intends to continue its efforts to reduce or prevent exports of uranium from Australia. Most Soviet influence in Australia is felt through communist-controlled trade unions and otherwise well-intentioned environmental and antinuclear movements. The growing Soviet naval power in the Pacific and Indian oceans is also of particular concern to Australia. This is so because Australia is wholly dependent on secure sea lanes to be able to export its minerals to the industrialized markets of Japan, North America, and Europe.

Australia is the leading producer of bauxite in the world, which gives it a commanding position in the aluminum industry. Australia produces 35 percent of the world's bauxite, and its known reserves represent 32 percent of the world's total. This means that no aluminum cartel can come into being without Australia's participation. Because aluminum is such an important basic metal on which modern industries and defense establishments depend Australia will most likely exploit its dominating position as a bauxite supplier to further develop its domestic aluminum industry.

This is probable because abundant energy resources exist in the country and such a development will allow Australia to sell aluminum products at higher prices than bauxite ores. Again such policies constitute a threat to aluminum industries in end-user countries, but foreign aluminum companies such as ALCOA, ALCAN, Reynolds Aluminum, Kaiser Aluminum, and Japanese companies are major investors in the expansion of Australia's aluminum industry.

Australia also produces 11 percent of the world's iron ore, making it one of the top suppliers in the world and certainly the largest exporter. Any cartel

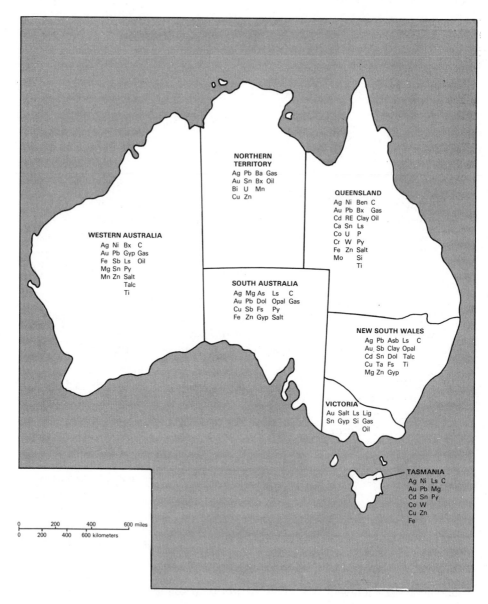

NORTHERN TERRITORY
Ag Pb Ba Gas
Au Sn Bx Oil
Bi U Mn
Cu Zn

QUEENSLAND
Ag Ni Ben C
Au Pb Bx Gas
Cd RE Clay Oil
Ca Sn Ls
Co U P
Cr W Py
Fe Zn Salt
Mo Si
Ti

WESTERN AUSTRALIA
Ag Ni Bx C
Au Pb Gyp Gas
Fe Sb Ls Oil
Mg Sn Py
Mn Zn Salt
Talc
Ti

SOUTH AUSTRALIA
Ag Mg As Ls C
Au Pb Dol Opal Gas
Cu Sb Fs Py
Fe Zn Gyp Salt

NEW SOUTH WALES
Ag Pb Asb Ls C
Au Sb Clay Opal
Cd Sn Dol Talc
Cu Ta Fs Ti
Mg Zn Gyp

VICTORIA
Au Salt Ls Lig
Sn Gyp Si Gas
Oil

TASMANIA
Ag Ni Ls C
Au Pb Mg
Cd Sn Py
Co W
Cu Zn
Fe

0   200   400   600 miles
0   200   400   600 kilometers

Figure 8.2 Distribution of major minerals-mining sources among Australian states. Source. **U.S. Bureau of Mines, 1979.**

158

Table 8.2   Major Minerals in which Australia
Had a Significant Share of the Total World's
Reserves during the Late 1970s

Mineral	Percentage of World Production	Percentage of World Reserves
Bauxite	35	32
Coal	3	17
Copper	3	2
Gold	1	1
Iron ore	11	7
Lead	2	13
Manganese	6	5
Nickel	11	3
Titanium	26	12[a]
Silver	8	15
Tin	4	3
Uranium	9	20
Zinc	8	13

Source.   U.S. Bureau of Mines.
[a] Combined rutile and ilmenite ores.

in iron ore would have to include Australia and Brazil to have any effect (see Table 8.2).

Another metal in which Australia appears to have a similar share of the world's production and in which it is the second largest exporter in the world is nickel, although Australia's share of the world's reserves of that metal is only 3 percent.

Australia is also a leading producer of titanium ores and accounts for 26 percent of the world's ilmenite production and additional output of rutile ores, the other major titanium material. Actually Australia is estimated to possess 6 percent of the world's reserves of ilmenite and rutile ores. As a result it is an important source of titanium ores, but titanium sponge, the primary metal, is produced mainly in Japan, the United States, and the Soviet Union. Because enormous amounts of energy are required for the production of titanium Australia may find it also profitable in the future to produce and export titanium metal rather than ores. This could create additional strategic problems for the United States and other NATO countries that depend on Australian titanium sources for their defense industries.

The Australian government already maintains export controls on bauxite, alumina, coal, iron ore, titanium ores, tin, uranium, petroleum products, and all raw and semiprocessed minerals. Decontrol of a wide variety is under consideration, which is likely to attract further foreign investment. This activity is also under the scrutiny of the Foreign Investment Review Board and Foreign Takeovers Act. In general at least 50 percent Australian equity is required, together with a minimum 50 percent of the voting strength of the board, except in the case of uranium projects where higher Australian participation and total control are mandatory.

By the end of the 1970s foreign subsidiaries in Australia controlled about 80 percent of the mining, smelting, and refining operations and most of the petroleum and natural gas projects. The dilemma of Australia during the 1980s may well turn out to be how to attract the necessary foreign capital for development and simultaneously try to retain or increase Australian ownership and control.

Japan is the major market for most Australian minerals, and in 1977 about 48 percent of Australia's minerals exports, representing over 50 percent of its export earnings, went to Japan. As a result the Australian minerals industry is greatly affected by Japanese economic growth, and it is commonly said in Australia that "when Japan sneezes, Australia catches pneumonia." The policy of the Australian governments is therefore to become less dependent on Japan by capturing more diversified foreign end-user markets for refined metal products rather than ores. Because domestic capital formation capabilities to finance the necessary investments for this purpose are limited by relatively a small population and economy, Australia must also depend on foreign capital for future expansion of its minerals industry and trade.

Although the existence of large reserves and future potential are attractive to foreign investors Australia's isolation as an island continent in the Pacific Ocean and its powerful and communist-controlled labor unions pose a certain political risk.

Supplies from Australia can be easily disrupted even in times of peace by well-organized, prolonged longshoremen strikes and other transportation workers' disputes, for without these workers Australian minerals cannot be moved to ports and shipped to foreign end-users. If the Soviet Union moves to exploit the unique correlation of forces in High Africa Australia would become a major alternative source for some minerals and as such a target for disruptive action.

Any disruptive Soviet policy in southern Africa, therefore, would be much more effective if strikes and labor disputes simultaneously could cripple Australia's ability to become an alternative source. Any such transportation and shipping problems in Australia would also automatically create additional disruptions, shortages, and price escalations in the aluminum industry throughout the world, because Australia has such a commanding position in bauxite mining and exports.

Although Australia is a viable alternative source for some minerals during potential future resource wars its isolation and labor union problems could present a danger to end-users overreliant on Australia as a dependable source of supply. It may well be appropriate for NATO to expand its responsibility along the Trioceanic Alliance concepts that would include Australia and Japan, as well as South Africa and Brazil, in a more comprehensive security arrangement of all crucial free market economy powers and resource supplier countries.

PACIFIC ROLE OF ALASKA AND CANADA

Alaska and Canada play a relatively minor role as minerals suppliers to the Pacific Basin countries, but their geographic location makes them part of the region. In this sense the United States, Mexico, Peru, and Chile are also Pacific Basin countries, and as the region develops all will play an increasing role in its economy.

Alaska is best known for its huge Prudhoe Bay oil and gas reservoir that is believed to be twice as large as any other oil field in North America. Significant in the Pacific Basin's geopolitics is the fact that Alaskan oil and gas are not available to foreign end-users but are parts of domestic American resources. Although the oil was found in 1968 it took almost 10 years and $7.7 billion before the Trans-Alaska pipeline was completed and Alaskan oil became available to the end-users. However, Alaskan oil could not be shipped to Pacific Basin countries such as Japan unless the U.S. Congress changes the laws governing the disposition of Alaskan oil supplies.

The Alaskan natural gas pipeline that would bring gas through western Canada to the northern United States is another controversial issue. Otherwise Alaska is a minor producer of non-oil minerals because of the proximity of Canadian and mainland United States deposits to the North American end-users. Nevertheless Alaska is believed to possess a large minerals potential, but environmental questions are keeping more intense exploration and production in check. It is inevitable, however, that with the worsening of the global minerals' supply situation Alaska will become a major area of future exploration.

Canadian Resources

Close to 70 percent of Canadian minerals exports are destined for the United States, whereas the United Kingdom and the rest of the European Community account for another 13 percent. Japan, the major Pacific Basin importer of Canadian minerals, obtains only 9 percent of all Canadian exports in this category. Thus Canada is not a major supplier of minerals to the Pacific Basin countries, but it may develop larger markets there as the economies of the region continue to grow.

The United States now obtains more than 90 percent of its asbestos and potash imports from Canada; 50 to 90 percent of its gypsum, iron ore, nickel, silver, sulfur, and zinc; and 30 to 40 percent of its copper and lead imports. In annual value Canada ranks third after the United States and the Soviet

Union, producing over 60 minerals and exporting about 60 percent of the industry's output to more than 100 countries.

Clearly when the resources of Canada are added to those of the United States and considered jointly as North American resources, the continent presents a somewhat more favorable import dependence position than the United States alone. Nevertheless Canada has serious deficiencies in bauxite, chromium, diamonds, manganese, mercury, phosphate, tin, tungsten, and vanadium. These deficiencies are similar to those of the United States; therefore the North American continent is vulnerable to supply disruptions of those minerals and metals. Canada also imports iron ore, iron and steel, coal, petroleum and natural gas, even though it has sufficient reserves of those minerals. This is done primarily for reasons of economics and geographic distribution of resources in the vastness of Canada (see Figure 8.3).

Canada is also energy self-sufficient, although some imports continue in the East for economic reasons. Otherwise it has adequate sources of petroleum and natural gas, coal, uranium, and hydroelectric power. Canadian oil

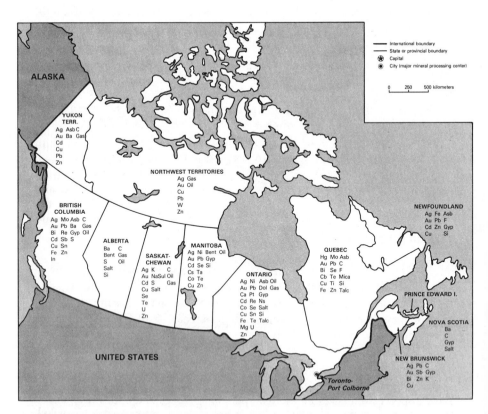

Figure 8.3 Distribution of major minerals-mining sources among Canadian provinces. Source. **U.S. Bureau of Mines, 1979.**

production peaked in 1973, and exports to the United States have been steadily reduced in recent years. The Canadian National Energy Board plans to phase out oil exports in the future to conserve oil reserves for domestic needs. The development of huge tar sands and shale deposits in western Canada are not yet economic, but should oil prices continue to escalate Canada is well endowed in such resources and could become again a major oil producer and exporter.

In non-oil minerals Canada has a truly commanding position in asbestos, nickel, potash, titanium ilmenite ores, and uranium. It also has significant reserves of cadmium, gypsum, iron ore, lead, silver, sulfur, tungsten, and zinc. Although cobalt, gold, and platinum metals are produced in Canada the country's share of the world's production of those strategic metals is relatively small, and its share of the world's reserves is even smaller (see Table 8.3).

The British North America Act put ownership of national resources under provincial jurisdiction in Canada, whereas the Yukon and the Northwest

Table 8.3 Major Minerals in Which Canada had a Significant Share of the Total World's Reserves during the Late 1970s

Mineral	Percentage of World Production	Percentage of World Reserves
Asbestos	29	43
Cadmium	7	21
Cobalt	5	2
Copper	10	6
Gold	4	4
Gypsum	11	21
Iron ore	7	13
Lead	8	10
Molybdenum	18	6
Nickel	30	14
Natural gas	7	3
Oil	2	9
Platinum metals	7	1
Potash	24	76
Silver	14	12
Sulfur	14	13
Titanium	22	27
Tungsten	4	11
Uranium	21	9
Zinc	14	19

Source. U.S. Bureau of Mines, 1979.

Territories, minerals trade and transportation, and some offshore exploration are administered by the federal government. Canadian objectives are to secure an adequate minerals supply for domestic use in the future, promote self-sufficiency by further exploration and diversification, introduce more domestic processing to allow the export of more advanced minerals and metal products, and maximize Canadian ownership and control of the industry.

In recent years federal and provincial corporations have been proliferating in Canadian minerals industry. Foreign companies nevertheless control about 50 percent of mining, smelting, and refining and 75 percent of the oil and gas industry in Canada. The United States and French companies are leading among foreign investors in the Canadian minerals industry.

Canada is regarded as a relatively stable supplier of minerals in the immediate future. Potential problems do exist if, for example, the province of Quebec were to secede from the federation and establish a socialist or even Marxist government. Quebec minerals resources would be an issue in this type of movement, and foreign ownership could be expropriated. On the other hand Quebec on its own produces exclusively only asbestos, mica, and titanium ores, whereas most other minerals are also available in other provinces of Canada.

STRATEGIC MATERIALS POTENTIAL OF INDOCHINA

Cambodia, Laos, and Vietnam are the three countries of Indochina under communist control that are also the most active Asian theater of Sino-Soviet confrontation. In contrast to the situation in southern Africa, however, strategic minerals play a negligible role, because the countries of Indochina produce very few minerals and their share of output is of no consequence to the world's minerals markets. In the future some significance may develop from offshore oil potential, but at present these projects are at best in the exploration stages.

Vietnam Resources Potential

Vietnam is the largest economy in Indochina, and since 1975 the country concentrated its efforts on the reconstruction of its war-ravaged infrastructure and the establishment of basic industries. These efforts have clearly been affected by the Vietnamese invasion of Cambodia and China's punitive military action against Vietnam in early 1979.

Major minerals produced in Vietnam are apatite, hard coal, chromite, salt, and zinc. However, the output of each of the minerals is relatively small and accounts in all cases for no more than 1 percent of the total world's output of those minerals. Vietnam exports anthracite coal to Japan, and most of its chromite output, but these are relatively small quantities in international trade. Nevertheless in 1976 a long-range geological plan was formulated to explore and develop Vietnam's natural resources. Japan, the Soviet Union, East Germany, Hungary, China, and France are major foreign countries involved in exploration and mine development.

Although Vietnam produces coal it must import most of its oil requirements to complement its energy needs and keep its relatively large armed forces operational. In 1974 oil was found in offshore regions of South Vietnam, whereas more recently Soviet exploration teams are believed to have found oil onshore as well. Some electric power is also available from hydroelectric power plants. Shortages of oil, fertilizers, food grains, capital goods, and machinery persist, and Vietnam relies on foreign aid to meet trade deficits, resulting from the imports of those products.

Most of the foreign economic and military aid comes from the Soviet Union and eastern Europe, but some also comes from other countries and international institutions. Vietnamese economy is predominantly based on tropical agriculture, and there is always a huge unsaturated market in Soviet bloc countries for tropical crops and fruits such as rice, bananas, vegetables, and other products. Among strategic materials Vietnam produces natural rubber, which the Soviet Union and other COMECON countries must import from rubber-producing countries such as Malaysia that require hard currency payment for their products.

Vietnam has already been made a member of the COMECON organization and can enter into barter trade agreements with other Soviet bloc countries. Given the natural rubber import dependence of the Soviet bloc it now seems logical to expect that the development of Vietnam as a larger natural rubber producing country may take place to provide COMECON markets with this product and save significant amounts of hard currencies. If that happens countries like Malaysia, Indonesia, Sri Lanka, and Thailand that are the major natural rubber producers in the world may find themselves facing declining rubber prices and diminishing markets.

The Soviet bloc will then find itself in a position to take advantage of low-priced natural rubber in world markets by buying in large quantities or on a long-term basis and at the same time controlling Vietnamese production. Such manipulation of the world's natural rubber trade could lead to civil unrest and even revolution in areas of Asia where economic conditions are heavily dependent on natural rubber production and export.

Cambodian Resources

Cambodia never produced any minerals for world markets except small amounts of gem stones. There are however commercial deposits of phosphates, iron ore, bauxite, manganese, silica, and gold. Copper deposits and coking coals also exist, but mining is a relatively minor industry, whereas agriculture plays the dominant role in the economy.

The energy resources of Cambodia have not been adequately surveyed, and the development of many mineral deposits must await the expansion of the country's infrastructure. Some oil wells have been drilled offshore by Elf-ERAP of France before the Khmer Republic fell to the present regime.

The future minerals industry of Cambodia depends on political stability and the reconstruction of an appropriate infrastructure. China extended a $1-billion loan over a period of five to six years, and the Cambodian government indicated an interest in receiving foreign aid from industrialized countries. Even so basic industries and agriculture are most likely to receive development priority in this war-devastated country when political and economic stability return to this region.

It is unlikely that Cambodia will become a significant producer of any minerals in the foreseeable future, although in the case of strategic materials it also possesses the potential to become a larger natural rubber producing country. At present, however, the development of agriculture to provide basic foods for the starving population is a much greater priority.

Resources of Laos

Agriculture is the mainstay of the Laotian economy. The country has no railroad and a very limited network of roads, making access to potential minerals-bearing regions extremely difficult and uneconomic. The country is landlocked with an uncertain political future that makes it unattractive to foreign investors.

Laos produces some tin for export that is smelted in Malaysia, but its share of the world's output is less than half a percent, and its reserves are small. In addition there are also deposits of lead, zinc, coal, iron ore, and potash; and some alluvial gold was found in previous years.

Because the country is undeveloped Laos' energy requirements are also relatively low. Coal and hydroelectric power present some future development possibilities, but the expansion of the sector depends on the availability of foreign aid and management assistance. Vietnam and Cambodia are more likely to receive development assistance before Laos because geopolitically those countries present more immediate opportunities, whereas the relatively small economy of Laos can easily be sustained with foreign aid from the Soviet bloc alone if necessary. As a base for possible future operation against Thailand, Laos nevertheless presents an excellent opportunity.

THE TWO KOREAS

Recent moves to resume the dialogue between North and South Korea may signal a new era of political and economic developments in the Korean peninsula. The two countries have been locked in an economic race since the partition of the region in 1945, and rapid economic development in both makes them an important growth area in the Pacific Basin. Nevertheless the possibility of a conflict between those two countries in the future with important consequences to the neighboring Asian countries of China, the Soviet Union, and Japan continues to exist.

Of the two Koreas the North is more powerful militarily, with per capita defense expenditures second only to Israel. Considerable resources have also gone into expensive underground construction programs that are being developed to protect vital industrial and military installations. South Korea by comparison relies on security guarantees of the United States and heavy imports of sophisticated military equipment that it can afford as a result of its export-oriented economy, modeled after that of Japan.

During the mid-1970s North Korea's minerals industry output was estimated at $1.1 billion in value, accounting for about 11 percent of its GNP. The most important minerals produced are anthracite and bituminous coal, barite, graphite, lead, zinc, magnesite, and tungsten. More than half of this output is exported, and although North Korea must import oil, aluminum, manganese, and other strategic materials to support its expanding economy and large military-industrial complex, it nevertheless had a positive trade balance in the minerals sector.

North Korea is the fourth largest steel producer in the Orient after Japan, China, and India and leads the world in magnesite output. It is the second largest producer in the world of anthracite coal and graphite and overall produces over 17 percent of the global coal supply. Although it is not a member of the COMECON organization of the Soviet bloc like Vietnam or Mongolia, North Korea apparently conducts some trade on a barter basis with those countries. Specifically it supplies barite to the Soviet Union under a long-term agreement. Domestic coal and hydroelectric power provide much of the energy required by the North Korean economy, and the country's oil requirements are met by imports from China via a special oil pipeline from the Daqing oil fields in Manchuria. The 1971–1976 five-year plan called for achieving "two-thirds" self-sufficiency in materials needed by North Korean industries. Whether this objective can be improved or even maintained in the face of attempts to double the output of steel, nonferrous metals, coal, and fertilizers is questionable, and chances are that North Korea will have to import increasing amounts of strategic materials from the Soviet bloc and China in the future.

South Korea's minerals industry is only half the size of that of North Korea, although its population is twice as large and its GNP almost four times that of North Korea. As a result of oil, steel, and other minerals imports South Korea has a negative trade balance in this sector. At present tungsten, bismuth, graphite, fluorspar, talc, and pyrophyllite are exported, but as the economy continues to develop rapidly more of South Korea's minerals production will be consumed domestically and minerals imports will escalate.

In the future South Korea's basic industries are expected to expand along the patterns established by Japan. This means that minerals processing, smelting, and fabricating plants will be built on the coast to process increasing amounts of imported materials for domestic consumption and re-export to end-users in more industrialized countries of the West. Again this is a threat to established minerals-processing industries in Europe and the United States, where labor costs are higher and restrictions more numerous.

The Koreas will remain the flash point of Asia for the conceivable future, particularly if the United States withdraws its security guarantees and its forces from the region. South Korea is already committed to nuclear power to assure itself the necessary energy to continue economic expansion in the future. This program is well along the way, with a nuclear scientific establishment in place, and there are many strategists who believe that South Korea will soon be in a position to develop its own nuclear weapons. Such a course of action is credible, particularly in the face of superior North Korean military and defense establishment possibly backed by China in case of another confrontation.

THE ASEAN TREATY COUNTRIES

The member states of the ASEAN organization include Indonesia, Malaysia, the Philippines, Singapore, and Thailand. These countries signed the Bangkok Declaration in 1967 that was designed to accelerate economic growth and promote regional security and mutual assistance in matters of common interest. The ASEAN countries promote a "zone of peace" in the region, relying on economic and diplomatic means without attempting to form a military alliance. They also form joint industrial programs for the production of fertilizers, soda ash, and certain manufacturing industries that benefit the group as a whole. In 1977 ASEAN countries concluded the Basic Agreement on the Establishment of ASEAN Preferential Trade Agreements. Under the agreement's terms the five countries will give each other priority in buying and selling their products at preferential rates during gluts or shortages.

Although ASEAN countries have some apprehension about Indochinese countries and particularly communist Vietnam, which is militarily superior to their collective armed forces, the main concern is to achieve a high rate of economic growth and some redistribution of wealth throughout their population to stave off radical forces in those countries. The economic policies of ASEAN countries are designed to induce capital investment and maintain favorable terms of trade for the export of their primary products such as minerals.

Except for rubber, which is also exported to the Soviet Union and China, the ASEAN countries have little dependence on communist markets, and their economic well-being is primarily linked to the vagaries of the free market economies. As a result ASEAN members have adopted common proposals that they submitted to the United States, western European countries, and Japan, concerning commodity price stabilization systems, and they also maintain a common position in negotiations on trade matters.

Indonesian Resources

Almost 50 percent of Indonesia's GNP is represented by the production of its famous low-sulfur oil that makes Indonesia about the tenth largest oil-producing country in the world. Most of Indonesia's oil is exported—much of it to Japan, which is also the purchaser of other Indonesian minerals.

Besides oil, which accounts for about 2.5 percent of the world's output, Indonesia produces 8 percent of the global tin output, 2 percent of the world's nickel, and 1.4 percent of the world's bauxite. There is some production of coal, copper, and iron sands, but the output of these is insignificant on a global basis. However, reserves of bauxite, nickel, and oil are believed to be large, and prospects for the production of additional oil and gas are excellent.

In addition to minerals Indonesia is the world's second largest producer of natural rubber and also exports tropical agricultural products such as palm oil, coffee, tea, rice, and spices. Indonesia remains undeveloped, and its infrastructure is inadequate, given the huge archipelago of tropical islands that make up the country.

Because of its oil production and strategic location at the crossroads of the whole Pacific Basin, Indonesia is probably the most important country of the ASEAN group. Its relatively large population of almost 150 million gives it the potential of becoming another Japan, whereas the fragmentation of its geography creates an excellent region for defense and control of the Pacific Basin.

Malaysian Resources

Malaysia is the world's predominant producer and exporter of tin and natural rubber. Any cartels or commodity stabilization arrangements for those two commodities are unthinkable without the participation of Malaysia. This is so because Malaysia's share of the world's output of those products is so large. Malaysia also produces small amounts of bauxite, oil, iron ore, and copper.

About 37 percent of the world's tin is produced in Malaysian mines, but almost 50 percent of the world's production of tin metal is refined in the country, which acts as a processing center for other tin-mining states in the region. Malaysian tin is exported primarily to the Netherlands, the United States, Japan, and the Soviet Union. Malaysia is a key member of ITC, which also includes Bolivia, Burma, and Thailand. The objective of ITC is to "stabilize" tin prices on international markets by establishing floor prices and maintaining buffer stocks of tin.

About 50 percent of the world's natural rubber output comes from Malaysia, and exports of rubber actually contribute almost twice as much to the Malaysian economy as exports of tin. Because of such a commanding position in those strategic materials Malaysia is extremely vulnerable as a target for subversion and supply disruption in case of an East-West conflict in the Pacific Basin.

Resources of the Philippines

Among the ASEAN countries the Philippines probably has the largest mining industry, accounting for about 4 percent of its GNP. About 15 percent of the Philippines' exports are made up of minerals, including chromite, copper, gold, iron ore, lead, nickel, and zinc.

The Philippines is the world's foremost producer of refractory chromite, but it also produces 1.3 percent of the metallurgical chromite that is so important to modern steel and defense industries. The country is also a leading producer of copper, accounting for 3 percent of the world's total. Gold and nickel are the only other minerals in which the Philippines produce slightly more than 1 percent of the global output, but nickel reserves are estimated to be extensive. In general, however, minerals production in the Philippines does not occupy a significant position in global markets, even though much of the output is exported.

Most of the Philippines' minerals are exported to Japan, but as the economy expands increasing amounts of fuels and other metals will have to be imported. Oil, steel, aluminum, and even copper consumption is going up, and it is questionable whether the Philippines can continue to export most of its minerals in the future.

Although most mining is in private hands the government is becoming more involved in such arrangements as trading copper and chromite for oil from China on a barter basis. Although minerals production is expected to increase, relatively meager domestic energy resources and expanding industrial demand are expected to dominate the Philippines' minerals policies for the conceivable future.

The Role of Singapore

Singapore is a small independent city-state that ranks fourth among ports of the world and where Southeast Asia's oil exploration activities are headquartered. It is the third largest petroleum refining center in the world after

Rotterdam and Houston, and as such is an extremely strategic target in the whole Pacific Basin. Much oil is imported, refined, bunkered, or exported through Singapore, and the Strait of Malacca itself is a strategic choke point on the vital shipping route between the Middle East and Japan, Taiwan, and Korea.

About 10 percent of Singapore's GNP is attributable to value-added activities in connection with oil such as refining, shipping, marketing, construction of rigs and vessels, and oil exploration. Aside from the oil industry and some insignificant steel production there is practically no minerals industry in Singapore. There is also a significant rubber processing and rubber products industry in existence as a result of the proximity of Malaysia, the largest natural rubber–producing country. In addition Singapore has significant entrepot trade and is a major financial services center of the Pacific Basin.

Thailand Resources

Thailand is a fairly important producer of antimony, barite, tin, metallurgical fluorspar, and tungsten. Two-thirds of Thailand's mining output value comes from tin whose production accounts for 8 percent of the global output. After Malaysia and the Soviet Union Thailand is also the third largest tin-smelting country, and its production of primary tin is comparable to that of Indonesia. Columbite and tantalite are by-products from tin smelting in the country.

The mining of other minerals is not significant, although Thailand produces 6 percent of the world's antimony, 5.5 percent of barite, and 5 percent of tungsten. The total mining activity accounts for slightly more than 1 percent of the GNP. Although most minerals are shipped abroad, export earnings are overshadowed by imports of oil and other metals required to run the economy.

There is great concern about Thailand's security because of its common borders with the Indochinese communist states of Laos and Cambodia. Vietnam is probably regarded as an even greater threat, and as a result China is seen as a force that can keep Vietnam in check. Political uncertainties in this country affect investment and further development in Thailand, although the prospects for mining other than for tin are considered good.

OTHER PACIFIC BASIN RESOURCES

Some Pacific Basin countries that produce minerals and have mineral deposits were not mentioned previously. These include Brunei, Fiji, Nauru, New Caledonia, New Hebrides, New Zealand, Papua New Guinea, the Solomon Islands, and Taiwan. Except in the case of New Caledonia, the min-

Table 8.4   Other Pacific Basin Countries and Their Mineral Resources

Country	Minerals Mined or Deposits
Brunei	Oil and natural gas production
Fiji	Silver and gold, tellurium and selenium by-products, copper deposits identified
Hong Kong	Financial and trade center No minerals of significance
Nauru	Phosphate rock production
New Caledonia	Nickel, cobalt, chromite production
New Hebrides	Manganese production
New Zealand	Aluminum, coal, natural gas, oil produced but imports required
Papua New Guinea	Copper, gold, silver production
Solomon Islands	Gold and silver production Bauxite and chromite deposits
Taiwan	Aluminum refining, coal and marble production

Source.   Based on U.S. Bureau of Mines data 1977–1979.

erals production of these countries is of no significance to world supplies, although it may be the mainstay of some small Pacific island nations (see Table 8.4).

Significance of New Caledonia

New Caledonia produces 14 percent of the world's nickel supply, but its reserves are estimated to be as much as 25 percent of the world's known total. The country ranks third in nickel production after the Soviet Union and Canada and is the second largest nickel exporter. It supplies its ores mainly to Japan, also a large refiner of the metal. New Caledonia also produces ferronickel and nickel matte for export.

Since 1973 New Caledonia also became a cobalt producer and accounts for 14 percent of the world's cobalt ore production, making it the second largest cobalt supplier to the world after Zaire. It is also estimated to have about 19 percent of the world's cobalt reserves, and in view of instability in southern Africa this makes New Caledonia a very important alternative source of cobalt for the West.

New Caledonia is also a minor producer of chromite, but its output is insignificant and reserves unknown. The island's economy is almost exclusively dependent on nickel exports, and mining accounts for about 40 percent of its GNP.

New Caledonia is a potential trouble spot in the Pacific Basin. This is so because it is French Overseas Territory, whereas only 40 percent of its population is French and a slightly larger proportion Melanesian, with the remainder made up of Vietnamese, Indonesian, Chinese, and Polynesian groups. Because of its important position as a major nickel and cobalt supplier and still quasi-colonial status New Caledonia could be singled out in a future resource war as a country to be "liberated" from capitalist exploitation. New Caledonia is politically represented in the French Parliament, but it may be tempted to become independent. There is a leftist Union Caledonienne political movement on the island, and some active communists were deported during the 1950s. Among the minorities there are also politically active Vietnamese elements.

France, Japan, the United States, and Australia are major trade partners of New Caledonia and process much of the nickel and cobalt ores produced on the island. In view of the special importance of New Caledonia as an alternative source of these strategic metals it should certainly be considered as a constituent member of the proposed Trioceanic Alliance, either through its association with France or as an independent entity in the future.

New Hebrides

New Hebrides is an Anglo-French condominium located in the vicinity of New Caledonia, and the country produces manganese ore concentrate that is mostly exported to Japan. It also depends on imports of oil to run its mining industry, but its output is insignificant on world markets. The population of these islands is predominantly Melanesian, and the major political party boycotted elections to the Representative Assembly in 1977, suggesting a possible political upheaval in the future. New Hebrides could join with New Caledonia to demand independence for their combined Melanesian majority, and as such New Hebrides is another potential trouble spot in this region of the Pacific, threatening major nickel and cobalt sources indirectly. In July 1980 New Hebrides attained independence preceded by a brief rebellion on one of the islands that was quickly put down by decisive Anglo-French action. Nevertheless the threat of further unrest in the future continues.

Solomon Islands

The Solomon Islands have been independent since 1978, and so far the mineral industry is primarily a small production of alluvial gold and silver. The government is interested in promoting investment in large-scale mining development, and deposits of bauxite and chromite have been identified that might present commercial potential. Because the population of the Solomon Islands is also predominantly Melanesian there is the possibility that this country may support New Hebrides and New Caledonia in their future demands for independence. As such the Solomon Islands must also be looked on as another potential trouble spot that might develop into a real threat to the nickel and cobalt supplies of New Caledonia.

Brunei

The sultanate of Brunei, an enclave country surrounded by Malaysian Sarawak territory, is a small oil and natural gas producer, and as a result is one of the richest (per capita) countries in Asia. Brunei's oil resources are exploited by Shell Petroleum, with 25 percent participation by the Brunei government. Brunei is the first country in the region to export liquefied natural gas (LNG) to Japan under a 20-year contract.

Fiji

Fiji is a remote Pacific island with minor production of gold and silver, but the future of the minerals industry is uncertain and requires government support. Potential copper deposits have been discovered and may lead to production during the 1980s, but the island requires imports of oil to provide energy for the expansion of its economy.

Nauru

Nauru produces phosphate rock that is primarily exported to Australia and New Zealand. As a result of this trade Nauru has one of the highest per capita incomes in the world, but it also depends entirely on imports of oil and petroleum products to run its economy.

New Zealand

New Zealand is not an important producer or consumer of minerals, but it is self-sufficient in iron and steel, coal, and natural gas. Otherwise the country's industries depend on imports of alumina, nonferrous metals, phosphates, potash, sulfur, and oil. Future expansion of industry is expected in the production of coal, lignite, natural gas, oil, and hydroelectric power to reduce imports of oil. However, New Zealand, although remote, is a large landmass and on further exploration may become an alternative source for some minerals in the future.

Papua New Guinea

The minerals industry accounts for about 16 percent of the gross domestic product and includes the production of copper, gold, and silver. The economy of Papua New Guinea is strongly influenced by the world's copper demand, and the country is an associate member of the CIPEC copper quasi-cartel. Australia's and the World Bank's foreign aid are also important to this large undeveloped country, and foreign investment in the mining industry is actively sought. Besides copper, exploration for chromite, nickel, and oil is also underway.

Taiwan

Taiwan is greatly deficient in minerals and depends on imports of oil, metal ores, and metals to run its economy. Concern about energy led Taiwan to develop nuclear power, and there is also belief that the country is well advanced in the development of its own nuclear weapons. Confrontation with the People's Republic of China, which claims Taiwan as one of its provinces presents one of the most serious flash points in the Pacific Basin, although Taiwan has no significance in global strategic materials markets. A blockade denying Taiwan its vital strategic imports could bring this island nation to the point of surrender very quickly without assistance from Western allies or could cause Taiwan to use nuclear weapons as an act of desperation if it is completely abandoned in the face of a takeover from mainland China.

ANZUS TREATY AND PACIFIC SECURITY

The Pacific Basin, although the fastest-growing economic region of the world today, is also replete with potential points of conflict as a result of ill-defined international boundaries, differing ideologies, numerous ethnic and racial groupings, and enormous population-growth pressures in most countries of the region.

To coordinate defenses as the first step to insure Pacific Basin security Australia, New Zealand, and the United States signed the ANZUS Security Treaty in 1951 that was also the basis for SEATO, which was developed further in 1954 but virtually defunct in recent years. The ANZUS treaty itself is similar in purpose and nature to the NATO treaty.

The annual meetings of ANZUS members deal with the formulation of military programs and take place in secrecy. As a result Vietnam and China have suggested in recent years that plans are being made to develop a politicomilitary alliance between the ANZUS treaty members and the ASEAN countries of Southeast Asia.

There is concern among Asian strategists about ASEAN countries developing into a military alliance independently or with ANZUS, since it is believed that such a move would only provoke the well-armed Vietnam into a more agressive posture that could threaten the internal or external security of ASEAN countries. Nevertheless advocates of these views propose the creation of the joint ASEAN Sea Coast Guard force to secure mid-Pacific shipping routes that are particularly vital to Japan. They also propose that

Japan should finance such a security flotilla and that Vietnam should be invited to joint to minimize suspicions of the motives behind the creation of such a force.

Participation of Japan in such an international security force is regarded as crucial since Japan reaps the bulk of the benefits from continued stability in the area. Together with Australia it constitutes the two most important countries for growth of the Pacific Basin. Indonesia, Malaysia, New Caledonia, and Singapore clearly play a role with regard to strategic materials and oil production and refining, but Australia and Japan are the prime movers in the economic equation of the region.

The ASEAN Sea Coast Guard force is a timely proposal because conflicts over exclusive control over continental shelf resources are already under way between Japan, South Korea, Taiwan, China, and Vietnam. Thailand, Cambodia, and the Soviet Union are also disputing coastal and island territories on the fringes of ASEAN area, and Indonesia and Papua New Guinea disputes could even involve Australia and the United States by triggering action under the ANZUS treaty.

These issues will remain the source of Pacific Basin tensions and insecurity, and intensified offshore exploration for oil in those disputed areas will only sharpen the differences in the future.

Because the Soviet Union is most likely to be the main beneficiary of any such conflicts and because its Pacific fleet and mobility is increasingly more significant, it is unlikely that token regional arrangements such as the ASEAN Sea Coast Guard are likely to remove the real threat from the region, particularly if the Sino-Soviet conflict were to escalate in the future.

What is more likely to stabilize Pacific Basin security is the extension of a NATO-like military alliance to include Australia, Japan, Indonesia, Malaysia, Singapore, and New Caledonia at the very least. The proposed Trioceanic Alliance that would extend NATO or even replace it with another organization that would include strategic countries such as Brazil, South Africa, as well as Australia, Japan, and other key Pacific Basin countries, is probably the only solution that is likely to provide the West with more secure sources of its strategic materials and shipping routes.

REFERENCES

"Australian Uranium: Symbolism and Reality," *Economist,* 16 June 1979, p. 93.

Barnett, Robert W., "ASEAN Unguarded Coasts," *Foreign Policy,* No. 38, Spring 1980.

"Black Gold and Greenies," *Economist,* 8 March 1980.

First National City Bank, *Asia-Pacific Overview,* New York, 1975.

Department of Trade and Resources, "Australian Trade and Related Policies," Unpublished Paper, Canberra, Australia, December 1978.

Garland, R. V., MP, "Overseas Trade and the Australian Mining Industry," Address given on the opening of Australia's First International Mining and Exploration Exhibition, 13 February 1979, Sydney.

Horsley, William, "Japan's Omnidirectional Diplomacy," *Listener*, 21 February 1980, p. 231.

King, Michael L., "Natural Rubber Price Rises Despite Boost in Output and Tire Industry Recession," *Wall Street Journal*, 13 February 1980, p. 38.

National Foreign Assessment Center, "Korea: The Economic Race between the North and the South," Research Paper ER 78–10008, Washington, D.C., January 1978.

Solomon, Richard H. (Ed.), *Asian Security in the 1980's: Problems and Policies for a Time of Transition*, Rand Corporation, R–2492–ISA, November 1979, Santa Monica.

U.S. Bureau of Mines, *Far East and South Asia*, MP-1 Mineral Perspectives, U.S. Department of the Interior, Washington, D.C., May 1977.

U.S. Bureau of Mines, *Mineral Industries of Canada, Australia, and Oceania*, MP Mineral Perspectives, U.S. Bureau of the Interior, Washington, D.C., July 1979.

U.S. Department of the Navy, *U.S. Life Lines*, Office of the Chief of Naval Operations, Washington, D.C., January 1978.

U.S. Department of the Navy, *Understanding Soviet Naval Developments*, Office of the Chief of Naval Operations, Washington, D.C., 1978.

CHAPTER
NINE

Latin American Minerals
Potential and Problems

Among over 25 countries of South America, Central America, and the Caribbean only a handful are presently significant in the world's minerals production and trade. These include Bolivia, Brazil, Chile, Peru, Mexico, and Venezuela. Guyana, Jamaica, and Surinam play an important role as major bauxite producers. Cuba as an outpost of the Soviet bloc's COMECON in the western hemisphere is also important as a nickel and cobalt producer, but its output does not normally reach Western markets. Argentina is regarded as one of the richest unexplored mineral potential areas left in the world, but its present contribution to the world's production is insignificant.

The main problem in the development of Latin America in all its aspects is the relative scarcity of energy resources despite the latest oil finds in Mexico, indicating huge reserves. In addition the region has the highest population growth in the world and intense migration of rural populations into the relatively few major cities. This trend creates extreme pressure on urban administrations for public services and maintains very high unemployment rates and at the same time depletes rural areas of agricultural labor.

Some political and social critics believe that Latin American countries are inherently unstable and that future solutions may lie in the introduction of China's Maoist development model in the area, forcing large segments of the populations to remain in agriculture, whereas industrial activity is centrally planned to develop according to political objectives and the availability of resources.

Attempts to change present Latin American regimes along such lines will probably continue with resulting unrest and changes in laws pertaining to minerals ownership, production, processing, and trade. As the rise and fall of the Marxist Allende regime in Chile has shown these changes in Latin America can occur in both directions, and it is not unlikely that communist Cuba may yet become a military dictatorship, whereas some of the more democratic countries could turn to Marxism or communism in the future along the lines of Nicaragua in 1979.

It is worth noting, however, that because Latin America does not have an overwhelming share in the production of any particular mineral, unrest and disruptions in that region do not have very much effect on minerals supplies on a global basis except in the case of processors or end-users that rely exclusively on particular sources that may be affected. All minerals produced in Latin America are always available in greater quantities from many other sources, and some of the most strategic minerals such as chromium, cobalt, platinum metals, or gold are only produced in very insignificant quantities if at all.

STRATEGIC MINERALS RESOURCES OF LATIN AMERICA

In comparison with southern Africa and the Pacific Basin, including Canada, Latin America is relatively poor in mineral resources, although as a region it produces about 20 percent or more of the global output of antimony, bauxite, beryllium, bismuth, copper, silver, and tin. In addition it produces between 10 to 20 percent of the world's output of molybdenum, nickel, and tungsten. In general Latin America as a whole commands much smaller shares of the world's production of much fewer minerals than southern Africa or the Pacific Basin. Only Brazil and Mexico produce a larger variety of minerals in significant quantities, but even their shares of the global output in specific minerals are in most cases relatively small (see Table 9.1).

Like the other regions of the Third World, Latin America is deficient in energy, although its total oil production accounts for about 8 percent of the global output, which is twice as much as the Pacific Basin's share of the world's oil production when China is excluded. However, whereas the Pacific Basin has large deposits and output of coal the comparable share of Latin America is not even 1 percent. In natural gas Latin America is also far behind, with only about 3 percent of the world's total output, although there are indications, notably in Argentina, that this situation will improve in the future.

This energy deficiency is compensated somewhat by extensive exploitation of hydroelectric power whose total potential is far from having been realized. There are also developments of nuclear power, particularly in Brazil and Argentina. Mexico, although together with Venezuela it is a major regional oil and gas producer, is also considering nuclear power in the future.

Bolivia, Brazil, Chile, Jamaica, Mexico, and Peru are the six most important non-oil minerals-producing countries, but each has a significant share of only one or a few of the minerals. As a result no single country enjoys a commanding position in more than one or two important minerals.

There is a certain similarity between Latin American countries and those of southern Africa because of their colonial heritage and ethnic composi-

Table 9.1 Major Latin American Minerals Producing Countries and Their Respective Positions in Percentage of World Production toward the End of the 1970s[a]

	Argen-tina	Bolivia	Brazil	Chile	Colom-bia	Cuba	Domin-ican Republic	Ecua-dor	Guyana	Jamaica	Mexico	Peru	Surinam	Vene-zuela	Latin American Total (percentage)
Antimony	—	21	—	—	—	—	—	—	—	—	3	(−1)	—	—	25
Barite	—	—	1	—	—	—	—	—	—	—	5	5	—	—	5
Bauxite	—	—	—	—	—	—	—	—	4	13	—	—	6	—	25
Beryllium	—	—	18	—	—	—	—	—	—	—	—	—	—	—	18
Bismuth	—	—	16	—	—	—	—	—	—	—	15	14	—	—	45
Cadmium	—	—	—	—	—	—	—	—	—	—	5	1	—	—	6
Chromium	—	—	2	—	—	(−1)	—	—	—	—	—	—	—	—	2
Coal	(−1)	—	(−1)	(−1)	(−1)	—	—	—	—	—	(−1)	—	—	—	(−1)
Cobalt	—	—	—	—	(−1)	7	—	—	—	—	—	—	—	—	7
Copper	—	—	—	13	—	—	—	—	—	—	1	4	—	—	18
Fluorspar	—	—	—	—	—	—	—	—	—	—	(−1)	—	—	—	(−1)
Gold	—	—	(−1)	—	(−1)	—	—	—	—	—	(−1)	(−1)	—	—	1
Iron ore	(−1)	—	10	1	—	—	—	—	—	—	(−1)	(−1)	—	2	14
Lead	(−1)	—	1	—	—	—	—	—	—	—	4	2	—	—	7
Manganese	—	—	4	(−1)	—	—	—	—	—	—	2	—	—	—	6
Mercury	—	—	—	—	—	—	—	—	—	—	6	1	—	—	7
Molybdenum	—	—	—	12	—	—	—	—	—	—	(−1)	(−1)	—	—	12
Nickel	—	—	1	—	—	7	3	—	—	—	—	—	—	—	11
Natural gas	(−1)	—	—	—	(−1)	—	—	—	—	—	1	—	—	1	3
Oil	(−1)	—	—	—	(−1)	—	—	(−1)	—	—	3	(−1)	—	4	8
Silver	(−1)	2	—	2	—	—	—	—	—	—	14	9	—	—	29
Titanium	—	—	(−1)	—	—	—	—	—	—	—	—	—	—	—	(−1)
Tin	(−1)	14	3	—	—	—	—	—	—	—	—	—	—	—	17
Tungsten	(−1)	6	1	—	—	—	—	—	—	—	1	1	—	—	10
Zinc	(−1)	—	1	—	—	—	—	—	—	—	3	1	—	—	5

Source. Compiled by 21st Century Research from data developed by the U.S. Bureau of Mines and American Metals Market, *Metals Statistics,* 1979. a (−1): means production is less than 1 percent of the world's output.

tions. Except in Argentina, Chile, and Brazil white populations are in the minority in Latin American countries. However, in most the remainder of the population consists of varying percentages of Indian, mestizo, mulatto, creole, African, and other minorities. These ethnic groupings differ in size, literacy, and political activity, but their existence guarantees the continuance of social unrest and instability throughout the continent for a very long time to come.

Legal and illegal communist parties that are pro-Soviet or pro-China are active in most Latin American countries. Cuba, as a communist state with party membership estimated at 200,000, is the focal point of the Soviet bloc's activity in the area. It must be remembered also that at the peak of the Allende regime in Chile that country's Communist party membership reached almost 250,000, which demonstrates the following that political forces demanding change can muster when they come to power. Perhaps Chile was the target of a Marxist takeover because it has such a commanding position in the world's copper trade. Similarly Peru, Jamaica, and Bolivia are equally vulnerable. On the other hand because those countries do not have a truly overwhelming position on world markets even in strategic materials on which their own economies depend, Western countries tend to belittle any threat to the supplies of strategic materials from Latin America.

If there exists any long-term strategy designed to subvert Latin America it probably follows the concepts of "liberating" small and relatively less important countries such as Jamaica or Granada before creating more significant upheavals in other countries that would require strong reaction from the United States or the West as was indirectly the case with Chile.

Actually Marxist control of small Central American and Caribbean countries such as Cuba, Jamaica, Nicaragua, Honduras, El Salvador, or Panama is not going to disrupt mineral supplies to anyone, but it could lead to a particularly annoying threat to the Panama Canal and the north-south shipping lines that are of strategic importance to the Western world. The most recent political developments in Central American and the Caribbean and new initiatives undertaken by Cuba since the Soviet invasion of Afghanistan suggest that such a policy may be implemented if there is continued uncertain and weak reaction on the part of the United States, the only dominant power in the area that could take any effective action.

THE GROWING POWER OF BRAZIL

Because of its size, population, and natural resources, Brazil is seen as the future regional superpower in Latin America. However, although it is relatively well endowed with several important minerals the major problem of Brazil is the lack of sufficient energy resources to continue its development programs at an increasing rate.

The Brazilian minerals industry represents only a very small part of the economy that is dominated by agriculture and manufacturing. On the other hand Brazil's ambitious industrialization programs already require the imports of some strategic and basic materials to keep up the development momentum. Besides oil, aluminum, copper, and wheat are major imports required to keep the economy operating.

Iron ore, manganese, and tin are the most important non-oil strategic minerals produced in Brazil, and their surplus contributes to the country's exports, but government policy appears to have been centered on development projects primarily designed to reduce Brazil's increasing imports of oil. As a result incentives and priorities are introduced to attract investment into the production of coal, nuclear fuels, and hydroelectric power. There is also an effort under way to produce gasohol by using sugarcane and manioc as raw materials for the production of alcohol. This program is designed to further reduce the consumption of petroleum products.

Although Brazil's production of some minerals is not very large by world standards, it is nevertheless possible that in this vast country that is still underexplored a much greater minerals potential exists, and in time such may come to bear on the economies of Brazil or even other Latin American states.

Of particular interest to the United States at present is Brazil's production and exports of such strategic minerals as quartz, lithium, columbium, beryllium, and manganese. Brazil ranks as the largest supplier of many of those minerals to the United States. It is also the second largest supplier of mica and third largest supplier of iron ore. Traditionally Brazil is also an important supplier of agricultural products such as coffee, cotton, sugar, soybeans, and cocoa. As such it is involved with the proposals to introduce various international commodity agreements to "stabilize" prices and developments in agricultural commodities and also direct attention to similar action in the mineral industry.

In basic metals, except tin, Brazil is not self-sufficient and is developing a larger production of aluminum, copper, lead, nickel, and zinc from domestic and imported ores. CONSIDER is a state organization that is planning and approving investments in nonferrous projects designed to increase Brazilian self-sufficiency in strategic metals. Japanese, West German, British, and American mining and engineering firms are particularly active in assisting in the development of Brazilian mineral resources.

Brazil's ambition to become a regional economic superpower depends on the availability of energy, and because the domestic production of oil, gas, and coal is insufficient Brazil emphasizes the development of hydroelectric and nuclear power. About 70,000 megawatts of nuclear electricity are expected to be required by the year 2000, which justifies Brazil's long-range nuclear development programs that includes the design and construction of a domestic nuclear fuels production and reprocessing industry.

There are uranium resources in Brazil that make the nuclear programs possible and attractive to the government which already strictly controls uranium mining in the country. Government controls also extend to the production and exports of such strategic materials as thorium, beryllium, lithium, and zirconium, all of which are of special significance in nuclear reactor manufacture and operation. Prospecting for uranium in Brazil is controlled by Empresas Nucleares Brasileiras S.A. (NUCLEBRAS), a government monopoly, that nevertheless can set up partnerships with private enterprises but always retains at least 51 percent of control.

Brazil's nuclear programs created international controversy when West Germany signed an agreement in 1975 to provide nuclear technology that would eventually allow Brazil to develop an autonomous nuclear industry. Because Brazil is not signatory to the international nonproliferation treaty there was immediate concern about the possibility that Brazil may become a nuclear weapons producer and supplier. The Soviet bloc countries also expressed their suspicion that the agreement between Brazil and West Germany was a cover to provide nuclear weapons capability to Germany in the future and thus create a new threat to the security of Europe.

More recently Brazil and Argentina, both of which have not signed the nonproliferation treaty, began discussions about cooperation between their respective nuclear industries. Whatever the present nuclear programs of those countries may be, there is little doubt that if unrest and revolutions in Latin America escalate and threaten the security of Brazil or Argentina, those countries could produce and deploy nuclear weapons without much difficulty.

POTENTIAL OF ARGENTINA

As a remote and large country in the southern hemisphere Argentina presents one of the world's largest untapped minerals potentials. Because it is one of the five richest agricultural areas of the world Argentina also has a sound base to develop into an economic power in the future. It is believed to be potentially richer than Australia or Canada, although it does not yet approach those countries in terms of economic development.

It is believed that only half of Argentina's potential mineral terrain has been explored so far. The lack of capital is one good reason, and new mining laws that are being proposed may create a climate more conducive to foreign investments. Much of the initial investment is also required to develop energy supplies, water, railways, communications, and other infrastructure projects. Argentina's minerals are considered to be a "new frontier" for the country that despite large potential is still importing almost $1-billion worth of minerals to keep its economy running.

Copper is Argentina's largest mineral potential at present. Molybdenum, iron ore, lead, zinc, and silver are other minerals mined, but their production is not yet significant on a global basis. In 1979 Argentina also began exporting small quantities of gold.

Besides surplus agriculture Argentina appears to have adequate energy resources in the form of oil, some natural gas, coal, uranium, and hydroelectric power. Domestic oil production supplies 93 percent of Argentina's requirements, and by 1985 it is expected that the country will be completely self-sufficient.

Natural gas production is expected to increase to a point where by the late 1990s Argentina hopes to operate liquefaction facilities for exports of its surplus natural gas.

Since 1974 Argentina has been operating the Atucha nuclear power station, and another plant is in the planning stages. There are uranium reserves estimated at 11,000 tons in 1979, and foreign investors are bidding to exploit the largest uranium deposits at Sierra Pintado at an estimated cost of $500 million over the next 15 years. Some observers believe that Argentina is among the nations that may develop their own nuclear weapons in the near future. In the case of Argentina there is some concern about this possibility because of the nuclear power fuels enrichment technology taking place in neighboring Brazil, the potential superpower of the area.

The new law for the promotion of mining that defines more precisely foreign participation in Argentina mining projects may prove helpful in attracting overseas investment if political stability in the country is assured and inflation is kept under control. Proposals to sell government-owned mines and deposits to private interests and tax incentives suggest that Argentina may become an attractive minerals supplier in the future for some minerals, but it is unlikely to play a major role in the world's minerals markets before the end of the twentieth century.

SIGNIFICANCE OF MEXICO

Mexico is one of the more important countries in Latin America, primarily because of its significant oil and gas resources located within easy reach of the huge U.S. markets. Besides oil, however, Mexico produces a variety of other minerals but only in silver does it have a significant share of the world's output of any one mineral.

Since the late 1960s Mexico implemented its policy of "Mexicanization" of mining industries that required a minimum of 51 percent Mexican ownership. If companies are interested in bidding for state-owned concessions the Mexican ownership requirement is increased to a 66 percent minimum. This policy was put into effect gradually, but by 1974 about 98 percent of Mexico's mineral output was controlled or owned by Mexicans.

Mexico produces about 14 percent of the world's silver and 15 percent of the global bismuth output, but in other minerals it does not have a very significant share of the total output. Nevertheless it is a source of antimony, cadmium, copper, lead, manganese, and zinc. Mexico is also one of the world's leading mercury producers, accounting for 6 percent of the global output. Mexican mercury producers did make an attempt at one time to join an international grouping trying to set a floor price for mercury, and other Mexican minerals producers have shown interest in joining other Latin American countries in setting up a more general producers cartel for various commodities.

Optimistic estimates of Mexico's current oil boom suggest that it may rival even Saudi Arabia's oil reserves, but the income from this oil bonanza has hardly been felt by the Mexican population that is growing rapidly and is expected to reach about 100 million by the end of this century. Social unrest is already a very serious problem because 4 of every 10 Mexicans are either without a job or underemployed. The massive illegal migration of Mexicans across the U.S. border is but a symptom of this problem.

As a result the Mexican government is appeasing active leftists in the country and introduced political reforms to even have communist representation in the Mexican Chamber of Deputies. This situation also prompted the Mexican government to disavow the Anastazio Somoza dictatorship in Nicaragua before it was firmly overthrown by the Sandinista rebels striving for socialist reforms, and now similar demands are being made for supporting Marxist rebels in El Salvador.

The main concern of potential end-users of Mexican energy and minerals is the fact that growing unrest in Central America and the Caribbean could spread north into Mexico and create another revolutionary change in that country, leading toward a Marxist centrally planned economy in Mexico itself. Political critics in many quarters feel that for many years the United States took Mexico for granted without too much concern about its potential or its problems. It is now clear that a much more creative U.S.–Mexican policy is needed that would benefit in the long run the economic development of both countries.

THE ROLE OF CHILE

Under the government of General Augusto Pinochet, which took power following the overthrow of the Marxist regime of Allende in 1973, Chile is following a policy of economic reconstruction toward a "social market economy." This concept provides for government subsidies to industries but is supposed to avoid price distortions that would interfere with the efficient allocation of resources.

Copper is the main export of Chile, accounting for 43 percent of the total $3.7 billion in exports during 1979. It remains the key industrial sector of

the country, although there are attempts to expand other industries to reduce the dependence of the economy on what amounts to be the vagaries of
the world's copper prices.

At present Chile is the second largest copper producer after the United
States and accounts for over 10 percent of the world's primary copper output. But because most of its copper is exported abroad Chile actually controls 30 percent of the international copper trade. It also possesses a very
significant position in copper reserves, estimated at 20 percent of the known
world total.

Major copper mines in Chile are administered by the state-owned National
Copper Corporation of Chile (CODELCO) that is investing heavily to expand production and reprocessing facilities of lower-grade materials previously discarded as waste. The major problem that can slow down this expansion is the rising cost of energy whose imports contribute to an adverse
trade balance. The existing oil production in Chile has been declining, but
Empresa Nacional del Petroleo is planning to increase the domestic output
to about 40 percent of requirements with new production from offshore oil
wells in the Strait of Magellan.

Overseas interests are again playing a growing part in major mining investments in Chile after years of disillusionment that followed the expropriation of the big copper mines from their previous American owners.
Afterward a period of violent political and economic instability kept foreign
investors away from the country, but now so-called small and medium mines
rely heavily on foreign participation for expansion.

Anaconda Aluminum and St. Joe Minerals are two American companies
already involved. Exxon Minerals, Falconbridge, Superior Oil, Noranda
Mines, and other North American companies are engaged in joint ventures
and exploration. In oil drilling and prospecting ARCO, Amerada Hess, and
Phillips Petroleum are involved on the Pacific continental shelf.

BOLIVIA'S TIN ECONOMY

The Bolivian government is very sensitive to the world's tin market fluctuations because tin production and exports are the mainstay of the Bolivian
economy. As a result rapidly changing regimes of the country usually take
up tin issues as soon as they come to power. In late 1979, for example, Bolivia's latest government immediately expressed great concern about U.S.
proposals to dispose of large amounts of tin from its strategic stockpile. Despite assurances that stockpile sales would be orderly Bolivia estimated that
it would suffer losses of up to $79 million and accused the United States of
"economic aggression," which was regarded as incompatible with the "human rights" issues promoted by the United States. At the same time Bolivia's
military regime pointed out that such behavior on the part of the United

States only delays Bolivia's return to a more democratic civilian administration as favored by the United States.

If this is tantamount to political blackmail it is also typical of how politics and the foreign policy of a small country dependent on a limited minerals industry are intertwined with that country's economy. The government in the case of such a country is more comparable to the management of a corporation that is checking out all the possible angles in trying to get the best prices for its products.

Bolivia's tin industry is dominated by the state-run Corporacion Minera de Bolivia (COMIBOL) mining corporation that controls almost 70 percent of the country's tin production. COMIBOL is also responsible for 65 percent of Bolivia's copper, 70 percent of lead, 86 percent of silver, most of the bismuth, 78 percent of cadmium, and 42 percent of tungsten ores. However, aside from tin and antimony most of the other metals produced in Bolivia do not represent a significant share of the world's output.

Although Bolivia accounts for 14 percent of the world's tin output and is active in ITC its tin industry is experiencing financial problems because of very high production costs. Bolivia's mining industry problems are expected to escalate even further as a result of failure to meet previously optimistic estimates for domestic oil production and the need to import energy at increasingly higher prices.

IMPORTANCE OF PERU

Peru is one of the few Latin American countries self-sufficient in energy as a result of domestic oil production in the jungle regions as well as offshore. This is an important factor in Peru's economy that centers around the mining of copper, lead, zinc, silver, and iron ore. About 50 percent of all the exports of Peru are accounted for by minerals, with copper being the largest revenue producer.

Peru also produces small amounts of tungsten, bismuth, molybdenum, antimony, cadmium, mercury, tin, manganese, and gold. Some diamonds and large coal deposits combine to make the country's significant minerals potential. Peru is probably the most promising region as an alternative supplier of some of those minerals, but additional investment would be clearly required to make Peru a significant producer of those other minerals with a larger impact on world production.

Perhaps because of its unique mineral potential Peru attracted the attention of the Soviet Union and China some time ago, and both countries have extended foreign aid to Peru in recent years. To China, Peru has been a supplier of lead and copper that China must import to supplement its inadequate production at home. For the Soviet Union, Peru has become an important market for military equipment in recent years; in large measure this is so because the United States and Western countries balked at supplying Peru with advanced supersonic fighter aircraft and other weapons that it requested.

JAMAICAN BAUXITE POSITION

After Australia Jamaica is the second largest bauxite producer in the world, accounting for about 13 percent of the global output. It is also an important member of the IBA that is sometimes regarded as the precursor of a bauxite cartel in the world's aluminum markets. The Jamaican government holds majority control of the country's bauxite industry, and it was instrumental in introducing the first export tax on bauxite in 1974.

Major aluminum producers such as ALCAN, ALCOA, Reynolds Metals, Anaconda Aluminum, and Kaiser Aluminum are also stockholders in Jamaican bauxite operations. Following the imposition of the bauxite export tax these companies have pointed out that such resulted in making Jamaican bauxite uncompetitive in world markets. This situation has worsened since recent oil price increases because Jamaica depends on imports of 95 percent of its energy that is manadatory for mining and bauxite processing.

As a result Jamaican operations have been losing money, and this in turn has seriously affected that country's economy. Such trends can be corrected by the reduction or elimination of export taxes, but any attempts to take such steps may not be popular among the political opposition to the Jamaican government. As a possible other solution of its problems Jamaica is known to have made overtures to the Soviet bloc's COMECON organization to become an associate member and develop barter trade. This is an interesting possibility because the Soviet bloc is a partial importer of aluminum and could offer equipment and machinery in return.

CARIBBEAN RESOURCES AND PROBLEMS

The mineral resources of the Caribbean countries are primarily the bauxite reserves of Jamaica, the Dominican Republic, Guyana, Surinam, and Haiti that jointly represent about 25 percent of the world's bauxite production. In addition Cuba is a nickel and cobalt producer, accounting for about 7 percent of the global production of each metal (see Table 9.1).

As far as nickel is concerned Cuba's share of the world's reserves is believed to be higher than its current production, and there is a significant production expansion program under way designed to increase the country's output by 1985. As a result Cuba could become a more important factor in the world's nickel trade in the future, particularly because the Soviet Union is already a leading nickel producer, accounting for 19 percent of the global output. As for its cobalt Cuba probably has a ready market within COME-CON. This is likely because the Soviet bloc has become an increasingly important importer of that metal in recent years.

Aside from this relatively limited minerals potential of the Caribbean the area is nevertheless an important producer and exporter of tropical agricultural commodities such as bananas, coffee, cocoa, sugar, and tobacco. Many of the countries in the area are truly "banana republics," dependent on their survival on but a few agricultural products and volatile foreign markets. As such they are extremely vulnerable to political opposition and proposals for change. Because most of these economies are very small they are also easily influenced by foreign interests.

There are in fact about 30 different political entities scattered around the Caribbean between Mexico and Brazil. These include fully blown republics; independent Commonwealth countries that recognize Queen Elizabeth II as chief of state; communist countries like Cuba; Marxist-leaning countries like Jamaica, Guyana, Granada, and Nicaragua; and territories in quasi-colonial status still dependent on the United Kingdom, France, and the Netherlands. The latter include Belize that remains a British colony; Guadeloupe, Martinique, and French Guyana that achieved the status of French departments; and the Netherland Antilles that remain self-governing Dutch territories. This political potpourri creates an explosive situation in view of the spread of nationalism and "liberation" movements throughout the Third World.

Some of the Caribbean countries made an attempt to diversify their economies, primarily by allowing foreign investment in mining and raw materials processing. Haiti, Jamaica, Guyana, and Surinam have bauxite mining and alumina production facilities. Antigua, the Bahamas, Curacao, Martinique, as well as Trinidad and Tobago, also operate oil refineries; and there is a French space center in French Guyana. All, however, must depend on imports of energy to keep such industries going.

The political fragmentation, economic uncertainty, rising expectations, and the influence of Cuba combine to make the Caribbean a volatile region with trends to develop more left-of-center and procommunist regimes in the region. Those political, social, and economic changes are supported by other Latin American countries and the Third World in general, and opposition to such changes is viewed as backing dictatorial regimes that conspire with capitalist interests to exploit whatever resources may exist in those countries.

SOVIET BLOC INTERESTS IN LATIN AMERICA

The major and most obvious interest of the Soviet bloc in Latin America is Cuba and its continued existence as a communist military and political power at the doorstep of the United States. The Soviet Union and Cuba both profit from their partnership. Cuba provides military bases close to

North America, armed forces for joint operations in Africa, and a superb jumping-off area for any activity throughout Latin America. Although the Soviet Union subsidizes Cuba to the tune of $3 billion per year it probably feels it is getting a much better deal than the United States gets from a similar level of assistance that it provides to Israel.

Since the late 1960s COMECON has advocated the development of long-term trade agreements with Third World producers and cooperation in establishing mining and processing facilities. Recent COMECON studies project future deficiencies of oil, iron ore, natural gas, nonferrous metals, minerals, and tropical foods in Soviet bloc countries. During the 1970s the Soviet Union particularly intensified its drive to develop new sources of bauxite and alumina for the growing COMECON industries. This policy is evident in Soviet initiatives in the bauxite and alumina industries domestically, in foreign trade, and countries like Guyana as well as other Third World countries. In general such Soviet initiatives provide investment and technology for costly infrastructure projects in return for long-term commitments for shipments of minerals to the Soviet Union or other COMECON countries.

Some insights into the objectives and policies that the Soviets are pursuing in Latin America can be gained from an analysis of the various economic and military assistance programs that Soviet bloc countries have offered to Latin American countries during the last 25 years. Of a total of about $26 billion in credits and grants to the Third World countries by the Soviet bloc, Latin America received a little over 10 percent. A relatively smaller proportion of Soviet arms went to Latin America, valued at about $650 million during that same period, but there was a marked escalation in both activities during the late 1970s. Soviet foreign aid programs include the sales of arms, the provision of military and economic technicians, credits for purchases of plants and equipment, and the training of Latin American students in Soviet bloc countries (see Table 9.2).

Communist countries' imports of Latin American minerals and agricultural products created a long-standing deficit exceeding $1 billion annually after 1973. As a result intensive campaigns have been undertaken by Soviet bloc countries to sell machinery and equipment under export credits granted to various Latin American countries, although most of those usually prefer to purchase Western equipment. This situation may change from country to country, however—particularly if energy costs continue to escalate and hard currency trade deficits become unbearable. Soviet bloc credits and equipment may look much more attractive in the future if economic conditions and inflation in the West continue to worsen. Political decisions about the sales of military equipment also affect these proposals.

The largest COMECON export-financing offer was made by East Germany to Brazil in 1978. The Soviet Union also negotiated contracts valued at several billion dollars' worth of electric power projects with Brazil and

Table 9.2 Soviet Bloc Activities in Latin American Countries

Country	Soviet Bloc Military Technicians in 1978	Economic Credits and Grants 1954–1978 (millions of dollars)	Soviet Bloc Technicians in Latin America	Latin American Students in Soviet Bloc Countries
Argentina		514		
Bolivia		121	125	170
Brazil		709		70
Chile		383		
Colombia		292		1020
Costa Rica		27		550
Ecuador				825
El Salvador				135
Guatemala				25
Guyana	10	30		80
Jamaica		66	15	
Mexico		35		
Nicaragua				125
Peru	150	241	185	595
Uruguay		83		
Venezuela		10		105
Total	160	2511	325	3700

Source. National Foreign Assessment Center, *Communist Aid Activities in Non-Communist Less Developed Countries 1978*, September 1979.

Argentina. Through another special arrangement the Soviets supplied oil to Venezuelan customers in western Europe in return for Venezuelan crude for Cuba and also diverted Soviet oil to Brazil.

Hungary offered to cooperate in building an alumina plant in Brazil and signed a $300-million three-year trade agreement to import Brazilian raw materials and products in return for Hungarian equipment. Poland also signed a three-year agreement, valued at $500 million that includes bartering coal for iron ore.

Peru has become a market for Soviet military equipment and assistance during the mid-1970s, and communist countries bought about 15 percent of Peru's exports in 1978. By 1977 Peru received 36 Soviet Sukhoi SU-22 supersonic fighter/bombers believed to be the most advanced aircraft delivered to a Latin American country. Soviet helicopters, transports, and tanks were also made available, helping Peru to attain its ambition to become a military power on the Pacific coast of South America. In addition the Soviet Union, Czechoslovakia, Hungary, and Romania are involved in proposals for developing hydroelectric power plants, chemical factories, and copper mining projects in Peru. Soviet military and technical personnel are estimated to number over 300, and almost 600 Peruvian students are studying in Soviet bloc countries.

In Bolivia the Soviets are completing the largest tin volatization plant in the world at Potosi, and a second Soviet tin-processing plant will be built at Marchamarca. The Soviets are expected to increase tin purchases from Bolivia, making them the third largest tin customer of that country after the United States and the United Kingdom. A Soviet–West German venture is also planning to build a $150-million lead and silver smelter, based on Soviet technology.

COMECON countries made some interesting inroads into the bauxite-producing countries of the Caribbean that may reflect Soviet policy to develop new long-term sources of aluminum. In Guyana a political shift toward the communist world is evident, and in 1977 the Soviet Union signed a 10-year protocol, providing credits for purchases of machinery and equipment. At the same time a Soviet team began studies of a 600,000-ton alumina plant and an associated power plant to be built in Guyana, much of whose output would go to the Soviet Union under a long-term supply agreement. Hungary, East Germany, Cuba, and North Korea are also involved in technical assistance and economic aid to Guyana's industries and agriculture with projects whose output could be bartered for COMECON equipment and machinery. In fact Guyana applied for association with the COMECON organization in 1977, following Jamaica and Colombia that also indicated interest in joining the Soviet bloc's group of which Cuba has already been a member for several years. The opportunity of signing long-term agreements for bartering commodities for machinery without the need for hard currencies is hard to resist for some of the poorer countries in Latin America caught in trade deficits and credit squeezes.

During the heyday of the Marxist regime in Chile under Allende that country was well on its way to develop close ties with all the COMECON countries and was granted several hundred millions of dollars' worth of foreign aid. Since the ouster of Allende trade with COMECON came to a halt, but Chile has renegotiated various COMECON debts and agreed on repayment terms in recent years.

Elsewhere in Latin America the Soviet Union is proposing assistance in developing power resources in Panama, Colombia, Guyana, Costa Rica, Uruguay, and Argentina. This particular field looks promising to the Soviet Union for several reasons. First, the Soviets have considerable experience in developing huge hydroelectric power projects, having done so in the Soviet Union itself for several decades. Second, they have a large electric power equipment manufacturing industry that can readily support any projects they undertake with adequate equipment. Third, and perhaps most significant in the context of Third World countries, hydroelectric power projects provide non-oil alternatives for supplies of energy where such is badly needed for economic development.

Such infrastructure projects are also being built by Western countries, but in most cases government foreign aid must be made available before capitalist enterprises can negotiate to undertake the projects. Because of centralization and a willingness to negotiate barter deals simultaneously COMECON countries can be serious competitors in such instances where Third World governments experience serious credit and balance-of-payment difficulties.

REFERENCES

"Argentina's Mineral Potential," Mining Journal, Vol. 294, No. 7538, 8 February 1980.

Central Intelligence Agency, "The Cuban Economy, A Statistical Review 1968–76," Research Aid, ER 76–10708, December 1976.

"Chile on a Firm Footing," Mining Journal, Vol. 294, No. 7548, 18 April 1980.

Clinton, Richard Lee, "The Never-to-Be Developed Countries of Latin America," Bulletin of the Atomic Scientists, October 1977.

Congressional Research Service, Project Interdependence: U.S. and World Energy Outlook through 1990, U.S. Government Printing Office, Washington, D.C., November 1977.

Financial Times, Mining International Yearbook 1979, London.

Lowrance, William W., "Nuclear Futures for Sale: To Brazil from West Germany, 1975," International Security, Vol. 1, No. 2, Harvard University, Fall 1976.

National Foreign Assessment Center, "Communist Aid to Less Developed Countries of the Free World 1977," Research Paper, ER 78–10478U, Washington, D.C., November 1978.

National Foreign Assessment Center, "Communist Aid Activities in Non-Communist Less Developed Countries 1978," Research Paper, ER 79–10412U, Washington, D.C., September 1979.

National Foreign Assessment Center, International Energy Statistical Review, ER IESR 80–008, 23 April 1980.

Niekrasz, Lech, "Brazylia pod Bronia . . . Jadrowa!?," Zolnierz Polski, Warsaw, 1975.

Pearson, John, "Latin America Can Stand on Its Own," Business Week, 9 November 1974.

"Powder Keg at Our Doorstep," U.S. News & World Report, 19 May 1980.

"A Setback for Bolivia," Mining Journal, Vol. 293, No. 7525, 9 November 1979.

U.S. Department of Commerce, U.S. Commercial Relations with Cuba, Bureau of East-West Trade, GPO Stock No. 003–009–00210–9, Washington, D.C., August 1975.

CHAPTER
TEN

What Are the Alternative
Solutions to Shortages?

Whenever there is a threat or a shortage of critical materials the actual end-users automatically turn to alternative solutions to take care of their supply problems. In fact whether or not shortages occur many large corporations and independent research organizations are constantly searching for alternatives that would improve the profitability of their operations. Many of those alternatives involve the use of new materials that are cheaper, easier to work with, require less energy in fabrication, improve product performance, are less toxic to the environment, and are readily available in the quantities required at short notice.

The search for such new materials is part and parcel of the innovative process, and the motivation is primarily economic, although increasingly environmental considerations are being taken into account. Whether an alternative solution is adopted under such conditions is often resolved by competition in the marketplace. Thus whereas the alternative search process is constantly under way, it is taking place relatively slowly, with ample time allocated for trying different alternatives before one is finally chosen.

Economics are not the main motivating factor in the world of raw materials geopolitics although their effect must be taken into account. End-users may not be even aware that a supply disruption of one or more of their critical materials is in the making. As a result they may or may not be prepared with an alternative solution to a shortage when it occurs. No end-users or others can protect their supply positions 100 percent anyway unless they actually own the sources of the raw materials and cannot be denied access to them at any time.

Nevertheless many organizations can and some do investigate various alternatives in advance as part of a contingency planning program. Such programs are very valuable as long as they are based on worst-case scenarios that could conceivably affect the organization. However, this type of contingency planning often differs from the more optimistic planning approaches that corporate marketing departments are so fond of implementing. The result is usually crisis management that could be avoided.

In general available alternative solutions fall into three categories, namely, technical, economic, and political. In practice it is often hard to distinguish between types of alternatives, because each may contain elements of all those factors. The recycling of used materials, for example, always requires a technical solution, but it may become economical only as a result of tax incentives that in themselves are a political solution (see Table 10.1).

Because many shortages and supply disruptions originate as a result of political action it is also important to keep track of pertinent political developments domestically and internationally when considering alternative solu-

Table 10.1 Major Technical, Economic, and Political Alternatives Available to Reduce Materials Shortages and Supply Disruptions

Types of Alternatives	Various Elements of Available Alternatives
Technical	Substitution
	Recycling
	Product redesign
	Innovation
	Technology transfer
Economic	Lower-grade reserves
	Research and development
	Exploration
	Materials management
	Stockpiling
	Trade agreements
	Contract renegotiation
	Undersea resources
	Remote region resources
	Space resources
Political	Tax incentives
	Government subsidies
	Risk insurance
	Investment policies
	Conservation programs
	Environmental restrictions
	Foreign aid programs
	Common markets
	Import-Export guarantees
	Tariff reductions
	Security treaties
	Military action

tions within contingency planning programs. Reliance on supply-demand and market competition factors alone for predicting future availability is not sufficient.

MATERIALS SUBSTITUTION

Except in the case of manganese, silicon, radium, and thallium there is one or more substitute materials that can be used instead of most other metallic minerals. In the case of nonmetallic industrial materials such as asbestos, diamond, graphite, mica, sulfur, and most industrial gases there are also substitute materials with similar characteristics. Among gases only oxygen is irreplaceable by any other gas for practical purposes.

However, materials substitution is not a simple matter and in most cases can only be made at the price of losing some unique characteristics in particular applications where the material is used. In many critical end-uses, despite the fact that substitute materials with similar characteristics exist, replacement is not possible.

For example, in the case of chromium, other metals such as cobalt, manganese, molybdenum, nickel, tungsten, vanadium, aluminum, cadmium, magnesium, titanium, and even zinc are generally considered to be substitute materials. But when it comes to the use of chromium for the production of corrosion-resistant, oxidation-proof, or high-temperature stainless steels, there is no known substitute. It may be possible to use something else in place of stainless steel, but stainless steel cannot be made without chromium. In fact during World War II steels containing boron were used as a substitute for high-strength alloy chromium-nickel grades, but there were many failures as a result because the fatigue properties of such steels were considerably lower than those based on chromium as an alloy metal.

It is possible to construct a matrix showing general substitutes for ferrous and nonferrous materials, but such a matrix does not reflect the criticality of specific materials for particular end-uses. Nevertheless such a device is a useful tool and a good starting point in critical materials contingency planning programs. For individual enterprises such a matrix can be tailored to reflect the critical materials used in the production process, and available substitute materials can be readily identified. An example of such a substitution matrix for general metallic minerals is shown in Figure 10.1.

Care must be taken when using such a matrix to identify those substitute materials that are even more critical from the strategic point of view than the materials they could replace in case of a shortage. For example, during the cobalt shortages of 1978 and 1979 certain magnetic alloys that use cobalt have been replaced by other alloys that use less cobalt but require a larger proportion of chromium. Although the immediate objective to reduce the consumption of cobalt has been achieved it was only made possible through the use of chromium that itself rates as a much more critical strategic material. In the case of magnetic materials the rationale for the use of chromium was based on the fact that the nature of this application requires relatively small amounts of chromium which is imported in very large quantities, primarily for use in stainless steel production and as refractory material. Had there been a shortage of chromium simultaneously such a choice would not have been wise.

Some materials are more likely to substitute for others than to be substituted for. Steels of all types based on iron are a good case in point. Aluminum is replacing steel in many applications such as transportation vehicles, where potential savings in fuel costs are a strong incentive. But besides aluminum there are no adequate substitutes for iron and steel in its myriad of uses all over the world. On the other hand iron and steel can replace not only aluminum but also beryllium, copper, lead, magnesium, silver, titanium, and zinc. Nevertheless aluminum and copper are more likely to be used as substitutes than to be substituted for because of their relatively abundant occurrence, large production, and availability.

Manganese is a particularly critical strategic material. This is so because despite intensive research no adequate substitute has been found for its use in steelmaking. Since the Soviet Union and South Africa control between them about 83 percent of the world's high-grade manganese ore reserves this makes it particularly strategic, along with chromium, cobalt, platinum, and gold. In the mid-1980s free market economies are expected to require more manganese than present suppliers are able to provide. This situation is at the roots of the programs to exploit ocean manganese nodules as one alternative in case shortages develop and manganese prices rise steeply in the future. As can be seen from the substitution matrix manganese can substitute for many metals such as chromium, molybdenum, nickel, vanadium, aluminum, cadmium, and mercury. This is most unlikely to happen, however, because shortages of manganese are more probable than of the other metals.

The whole domain of materials substitution is a vast and extremely complex subject. Depending on the application in question it extends beyond the use of metals and nonmetallic elements to their alloys and compounds. It also involves the use of such materials as plastics, rubbers, ceramics, glasses, and even woods as well as binding materials to produce resistant structures from such materials. Availability, price, strategic considerations, and technology determine the development and use of such materials.

Glass fiber used in optics is a good example of such a new material that is being introduced in telecommunications where it replaces copper that, along with some other metals, is by far the most universal and the cheapest electronic signals transmission material. But copper cable and wire connections have the disadvantage of radiating electromagnetic signals, and this capability makes them vulnerable to electronic detection devices and similarly al-

Nonferrous Substitutes / Ferrous — substitution matrix

Substitute	Chromium	Cobalt	Columbium	Iron	Manganese	Molybdenum	Nickel	Rhenium	Silicon	Tantalum	Tungsten	Vanadium	Aluminum	Antimony	Arsenic	Beryllium
Nonferrous Substitutes																
Zirconium											×					
Zinc	×												×	×	×	
Yttrium																
Titanium	×					×					×		×	×		×
Tin													×	×		
Thallium																
Tellurium														×		
Silver																
Selenium															×	
Scandium																
Platinum								×		×		×				
Mercury														×		
Magnesium	×										×		×			
Lead											×		×			
Indium																
Hafnium								×								
Gold																
Germanium																
Gallium																
Copper													×			×
Cesium																
Cadmium	×												×			
Bismuth																
Beryllium													×			
Arsenic																
Antimony																
Aluminum	×			×		×			×			×				×
Ferrous																
Vanadium	×	×	×			×	×	×								
Tungsten	×	×				×		×				×				
Tantalum			×			×		×		×						
Silicon						×										
Rhenium											×					
Nickel	×	×				×							×			
Molybdenum	×	×					×	×			×	×				
Manganese	×					×	×					×	×	×		
Iron													×			×
Columbium											×	×				
Cobalt	×															
Chromium						×	×						×	×		

198

Bismuth
Cadmium
Cesium
Copper
Gallium
Germanium
Gold
Hafnium
Indium
Lead
Magnesium
Mercury
Platinum
Rubidium
Scandium
Selenium
Silver
Tellurium
Thallium
Tin
Titanium
Yttrium
Zinc
Zirconium

Figure 10.1 General metallic minerals substitution matrix. Source. **Based on data from the U.S. Bureau of Mines.**

lows interference with such transmission. This weakness of all electronic transmissions, whether by wire or radio, is the basis of electronic countermeasures and electronic counter-countermeasures developed as part of electronic warfare capabilities by leading military forces in the world.

Fiber optics offer an inducing alternative to copper or metal transmission systems used in military applications. The fibers are made from glass which in turn depends on silicon that is widely available in all parts of the world. This reduces the need for copper for many strategic applications, but precision manufacturing technology and various critical mineral impurities may be required for the development of laser or LED (light emitting diodes) signal emitters, fiber connectors, splices, and photodiodes required to use such systems.

Continuous optical fibers are now available of such purity that repeaters in an optical fiber transmission system could be placed further apart than in land cables. All such electronic transmitters, repeaters, and receivers can be protected underground from hostile electronic intelligence and interference, and optical fibers can link the various points without any danger of signal detection. Soviet and eastern European electronics industries are known to be making considerable effort to develop a complete self-contained optical fibers technology and manufacturing capabilities because of these strategic advantages.

These few examples only illustrate the range of considerations and possibilities involved in materials substitution. Without more specific definition of a particular product and its expected performance and life cycle it is impossible to engage in contingency materials substitution planning. Nevertheless an assessment of vulnerable products and various alternatives today may prove to be more than a good investment in the uncertain future.

ALTERNATIVE SOURCES OF SUPPLY

When shortages threaten end-users are also prone to think of alternative sources of supply as an immediate solution. This is an obvious and logical alternative and is probably as popular as the search for substitute materials. Alternative sources of supply may in fact offer immediate short-term solutions but in cases where international cartel action is involved such alternative sources may become rapidly depleted or be persuaded to join the cartel. In any case the end-user is unlikely to escape paying the cartel-established price. This is clearly demonstrated by oil prices charged by Mexico or Canada, neither of which is a member of the OPEC oil cartel.

The end-user is usually dealing with minerals processors and suppliers that in turn depend on various sources for their raw materials and ores. In some cases these raw materials come from domestic mines operated by the suppliers or their subsidiaries. In other instances and particularly in the case of strategic minerals such as chromite or cobalt, these materials come almost exclusively from foreign sources. Other alternative sources of minerals such as undersea resources; deposits identified in Antarctica, Greenland, and other remote and hostile regions of the world; and moon, orbital meteorites, and space resources all represent only future potential. It is unlikely that those areas will contribute significantly to the global materials demand until the twenty-first century.

DEVELOPMENT OF DOMESTIC RESOURCES

Generally the supply of mineral resources is considered to be continuous over a period of time and depends on the availability of technology and capital that must be allocated to finding new resources as well as substitute materials. However, for specific industries, critical minerals, producing regions, and known deposits, are finite and are depleted as time progresses.

Whether adequate domestic supplies can be developed requires classification of known deposits as *reserves*, which by definition must be economically exploitable at current prices and with available technology. Such reserves may fall into many categories such as proven, probable, possible— sometimes also referred to as measured, indicated, or inferred, respectively. These categories define the degree of measurement or uncertainty of the deposits.

On the other hand *resources* include not only reserves but also other deposits that are known but cannot be economically or technologically recovered or that are believed to exist but have not yet been discovered. Resources are also categorized as recoverable, paramarginal, submarginal, conditional, hypothetical, or speculative. These categories reflect the uncertainty of the existence or feasibility of the recovery of these resources.

Reserves, therefore, are developed from resources through the application of technology and capital in response to changes in price. Because most free market industrialized economies have first developed their most economic reserves they have later ventured to less developed countries to take advantage of similar economic reserves in those areas.

What this means is that the development of additional domestic reserves is possible when the prices of minerals from foreign countries rise to a level that will make it economic and technologically feasible to reclassify some known resources and reserves. Of course this is quite meaningless when the resources of a mineral are negligible or do not exist as is the case with chromium in North America.

End-users face several problems if they want to assess the future domestic availability of mineral and material reserves that may be vital to their industries or companies. Announced reserve levels are always in question because of the nature of the industry. Mining companies generally prove reserves only sufficient to maintain medium-term production and do not announce mineral discoveries as soon as these are made. In the case of strategic minerals some countries maintain outright secrecy and impose those conditions on mining organizations operating in their territories. As a result there is considerable doubt about published reserves data for many minerals, and resource estimates are often regarded as grossly imprecise.

What end-users can do, however, is to determine the existence of domestic resources and their ownership in order to assess whether they are extensive enough to present supply potentials in case foreign sources are eliminated for political or economic reasons. If the domestic resources of a particular mineral are inadequate to assure supplies for at least several years this is a good starting point to consider product redesign and reduction or elimination of the vulnerable materials from the product lines whenever possible.

NEW EXPLORATION PROGRAMS

New exploration programs are not an immediate solution to a sudden shortage but are necessary to assure long-term supplies. There is widespread belief in the mining industry that any increase in reserves is a function of the amount of exploration being conducted in an area.

Exploration as such can take up to 10 years, depending on whether mineral discovery is accidental or proceeds in a region with already identified and worked deposits. The time between the start of exploration and commercial production can be considerable, and it is seldom less than about five years.

Exploration and feasibility work account for 5 to 10 percent of a mining project's cost, but in more recent years this ratio has reached 30 to 40 percent in some mining projects. Even when the exploration cost remains relatively low this phase is the high-risk element of a mining project. Because of the uncertainty of exploration the total risk in mineral resource development is often much higher than in manufacturing industries, and as a result it is difficult to attract risk capital to such ventures unless the potential rewards are also relatively high. This creates a problem in many less developed countries that control exploration and mining rights in their territories but cannot generate sufficient capital to embark on intensive exploration. Politically these countries cannot offer excessive returns for foreign capital that in turn looks to more lucrative investment opportunities in other areas. As a result moves to nationalize the mining industries in Third World countries had the effect of shifting the exploration capital to the remote regions of the developed world.

The availability of risk capital is crucial in mineral exploration, and adverse political or economic conditions may reduce or wholly cut off such funds in a country; the effects of such underinvestment may not become apparent until many years later.

It is interesting to keep in mind that during the 1970s exploration activities were heavily concentrated in the developed countries such as Australia, Canada, South Africa, and the United States, where about 80 percent of exploration expenditure took place. This preference is attributable to the stable political and economic conditions in those countries as perceived by private investment circles. If investment funds were made available on strictly technical evaluations and geological advantage then countries such as Chile, Peru, Zambia, and Zaire should have received a much larger share of the exploration capital.

Since the easiest deposits of minerals have already been discovered and exploited, exploration is becoming more difficult and expensive. This is one reason why government involvement in the exploration process is likely to increase in the future. Only with government support will it be possible in most countries to locate the best mineralization areas by satellites, detect ore bodies at very great depths or under the oceans, and develop access to more remote regions that require extensive infrastructure before the exploitation of resources can take place.

ANTARCTIC AND POLAR RESOURCES

It is not really certain who owns the minerals and fish resources of Antarctica. This is so because the Antarctic Treaty of 1961 has set aside territorial claims of all countries that were previously active in exploring this continent. Some now believe that an armed conflict could erupt in Antarctica in the future, particularly if significant mineral resources are discovered. Nevertheless it will be years before the recovery of Antarctica resources will be sufficiently economical to present a viable alternative source of minerals to anyone.

Antarctica's 200,000 square miles account for one-tenth of all the land surface on earth, and only a small fraction of this area has been explored. Minerals so far identified include gold, iron, platinum, copper, nickel, cobalt, uranium, and large quantities of coal. Recoverable oil and gas reserves have been found in the Ross, Weddell, and Bellingshausen seas off the Antarctic coast.

Much speculation about Antarctica's mineral potential is based on the so-called Gondwanaland theory, according to which Antarctica was at sometime joined to parts of South Africa, India, Australia, and Latin America. The landmass and minerals in Antartica must also have undergone similar geological processes.

A special resource of Antarctica is its ice cap, believed to contain 70 percent of the world's store of fresh water. A French engineering group conducted special studies for Saudi Arabian interests that demonstrated the possibility of towing large icebergs as far as the Indian Ocean and the Red Sea as a cheap supply of water. The other resource of Antarctica already being harvested is the protein-rich, shrimplike krill that occurs in these waters in immense quantities. Estimates suggest that between 100 to 150 million tons could be harvested each year without disruption to Antarctica ecology. This amount is more than twice the total annual fishing catch of the entire world.

Thus there are specific incentives that could further escalate the interest and exploration of Antarctica in the future. Since 1959 Antarctica has been "administered" by a dozen countries, including Argentina, Australia, Belgium, Chile, France, Japan, New Zealand, Norway, South Africa, the United Kingdom, the United States, and the Soviet Union.

The Antarctic Treaty does not explain what happens to resources anywhere in the continent if a commercial firm or a government decides to exploit them. It establishes an environment for free and open scientific research, bans all military activity, nuclear explosions, and disposal of nuclear waste but allows the use of military personnel for scientific or peaceful purposes.

As such it is an ambiguous treaty and clearly contains the seeds of its violation in the future. Already some territorial claims overlap; Belgium, Japan, and South Africa do not recognize any claims, and the United States and the Soviet Union "reserved their rights" and maintain the two largest outposts on the continent. Poland, Czechoslovakia, Denmark, the Netherlands, Romania, East Germany, and Brazil also acceded to the treaty, whereas West Germany and Uruguay expressed interest in doing so.

Among other polar regions Greenland, administered by Denmark, is a large unexplored island and already produces lead and zinc ores. Alaska, the Northwest Territories, and Siberia are also large polar land masses being explored by the United States, Canada, and the Soviet Union, respectively. Although harsh climate makes exploration and mining expensive and hazardous this activity will no doubt intensify as more accessible sources of minerals are depleted and prices escalate.

OCEAN RESOURCES

The minerals that exist in the seas include iron ore, copper, lead, zinc, silver, gold, cobalt, nickel, diamonds, manganese, tin, phosphate, bauxite, salt, potash, platinum metals, fluorspar, magnesium, chromium, tungsten, mercury, columbium, tantalum, rutile, ilmenite, barite, bismuth, and zircon. Among the most plentiful salt, magnesium, bromine, and oil are now being recovered in large amounts. A major obstacle to large-scale exploitation of other minerals is the high cost of recovery relative to land-based resources and numerous legal and political questions pertaining to the ownership and recovery rights of undersea resources.

Ocean resources fall into three major categories. Some are dissolved in seawater, and their recovery depends on processing vast quantities of water. In view of escalating energy costs this may not be feasible unless minerals recovery is combined with the production of fresh water from seawater, leading to major reduction in costs. The second category of marine minerals consists of subsurface bedrock deposits. Offshore oil and gas are the best examples, and these today account for the bulk of commercial exploitation of undersea resources.

The third category is made up of sediments on the ocean floor and holds out the greatest promise from an economic point of view. These deposits occur in relatively shallow waters and can be in the form of metalliferrous muds or manganese nodules. The nodules, which also contain nickel, copper, and cobalt, have received considerable attention in the media, and at least 35 major organizations from the United States, Japan, and western Europe are actively engaged in exploration, development, and equipment manufacture (see Chapter 12 for more details).

ORBITAL AND SPACE RESOURCES

There has been endless speculation that the space race between the United States and the Soviet Union was a race to discover very rich deposits of minerals on the moon and other space bodies. There are also persistent rumors that American astronauts brought back evidence from the moon that extremely rich deposits of the most strategic minerals exist there but that for political and strategic reasons this information has been suppressed and classified.

Even if the moon was in fact full of rich deposits of the most valuable minerals the cost of reaching, mining, and recovering such minerals for use on the earth would be staggering. Furthermore it would first require vast investments in energy resources based on the moon to implement such a program. It is much cheaper and more convenient to develop ocean and polar resources than those of the moon or even new technologies to process vast quantities of seawater. All these concepts, however, depend on the availability of energy at a reasonable cost.

More promising are some proposals to develop solar electricity in orbit and then transfer it to earth by means of microwave systems. Although the technology for such projects appears to exist today such orbital power systems are extremely vulnerable to hostile satellite attacks and are unlikely to come into being because of their strategic vulnerability.

Meteorite mining is also regarded as a future source of minerals. These concepts envisage solar and nuclear energy being harnessed in space from meteorite resources, some of which are believed to contain uranium.

Meteorites would provide the raw minerals for orbital processing into materials suitable for space structures, but it is unlikely that such materials could be brought back to earth economically in large quantities.

Two space programs are likely to have a pronounced effect on the minerals industry, however. These are the LANDSAT satellite series and the space shuttle program conducted by the National Aeronautics and Space Administration (NASA).

The LANDSAT satellites conduct a variety of earth resources observations from space. These include mineralogy, geography, mapping, and land use. LANDSAT satellites scan a strip on earth 115 miles wide in four bands of the spectrum that reveals much about the distribution of natural resources. Already researchers in about 50 countries of the world use LANDSAT data.

NASA's space shuttle offers opportunities to conduct economically experiments in the almost perfect vacuum of space under conditions not obtainable on earth. It is believed that new valuable alloys of metals of extreme purity may be obtained under those conditions which will exhibit unusual characteristics.

RECYCLING AND WASTE RECOVERY

Recycling and the reuse of materials are increasingly gaining wide acceptance as the soaring energy prices and raw materials scarcities occur. Already among the basic metals copper, stainless steel, aluminum, and ordinary steel are produced in very significant quantities from recycled materials and scrap. In the future the recycling of many metals may provide an even larger percentage of production as governments introduce further incentives in the form of tax deductions and low-cost loans for recycling enterprises (see Table 10.2).

The use of recycled materials has been increasing in recent years not only as a result of escalating prices and shortages but also because of environmental concerns and energy costs. This is particularly dramatic in the case of aluminum because a product made from recycled aluminum requires only 4 percent of the energy that would be needed if original bauxite were used. Experts in the aluminum industry believe that the recycling of aluminum could double in but a few years in a country like the United States, thereby offsetting the need to import increasing amounts of bauxite or alumina as raw materials.

In the case of steel it takes two to three times the energy to manufacture a steel product from virgin ore than from recycled metal. This explains the already significant steel scrap industry that accounts for 22 percent of all the

**Table 10.2 Percentage of Output
from Major Recycled Materials**

Material	Percentage of Output
Copper	40
Stainless steel	30
Aluminum	25
Steel	22
Paper	20
Rubber	4

Source. National Association of Recycling Industries.

steel output in the United States. Energy savings are also responsible for the considerable amount of copper, magnesium, titanium, and other metals that are also being recycled.

However, recycling may take many forms, not all of which produce additional output of the material being recycled. In the case of tin recycled from a detinning plant the metal can be used again as tin. In the case of steel scrap it is used to produce a lesser quality material such as iron castings. Other recycled materials are consumed without providing additional output as in the case of paper that can be burned to generate heat.

The biggest problem in the field of materials recycling has to do with the separation of mixed wastes and scrap before processing can take place. Reuse of metal scrap in a metals processing plant is relatively simple. But recapturing values from mixtures of unsorted waste at the household level is another matter altogether. If household waste can be classified at the source, collection and recycling are feasible on a local basis. However, if technological sorting is required, as would be the case of extracting small quantities of precious metals from electronics scrap, transportation and capital equipment become a serious cost factor.

Nevertheless, materials are too valuable to be discarded in such vast quantities as today, and it is inevitable that all levels of government will facilitate recycling and waste recovery in the future. Urban areas where most waste and scrap are generated are also facing the problem of space, that is, where to keep disposing of their waste. It is the belief of many city planning bodies that a shift in priorities from disposal to resource recovery is under way and that by the year 2000 a country like the United States will have widely installed municipally administered resource recovery systems that will include the collection, processing, and marketing of recovered materials and energy.

STOCKPILING

One alternative adopted by some Western industrialized nations to assure uninterrupted supply of strategic materials during a disruption of foreign sources is the national stockpile. This concept originated in the postwar United States as a measure to reduce dangerous and costly dependence on imports of strategic materials during a national war-connected emergency. A more detailed discussion of stockpiling is made in Chapter 11.

Originally the nature of the dangerous dependence involved the possibility of political instability or invasion of supplier countries and the disruption of sea lanes by enemy action. The first stockpile in the United States was conceived to assure the supply of strategic materials for five years under those conditions but was reduced to three and later one year. In late 1976 it was increased to three years again. Although originally military requirements were paramount the latest stockpiling policy objectives are to provide also for the needs of the civilian economy after some reasonable allowance for "belt tightening." The goals of the stockpiling program are to be reviewed every four years in peacetime or sooner if required.

More recent proposals are concerned with the creation of a national economic stockpile and international buffer stocks as distinct from the strategic stockpile. Among Western nations France and West Germany have developed national stockpiles, and Spain, Sweden, and Italy are considering such programs. Japan has no strategic stockpile, but two stockpile associations have come into existence since 1976 and are subsidized by a government agency.

CONSERVATION PROGRAMS

There are several approaches to conservation, each of which can be implemented by a combination of some of the alternatives that are discussed in this chapter. The first approach is simply nonuse of a particular material; this in fact means total substitution in the case of an industrial product. Another approach is the concept of limited use and prudent utilization of a scarce material. A third approach is basically an attempt to achieve an indefinitely sustainable pattern of use, presumably through some form of rationing. A fourth concept calls for using only a definite ratio of useful materials within a specific period such as a generation. The fifth concept is the allocation of scarce materials among different users according to priorities either based on national security objectives or relative social values.

During World War II and the Korean War it was necessary to adopt specific programs of materials conservation, and that experience provides several conservation approaches that are worth keeping in mind. Most were designed to extend available supplies of critical materials, with *critical materials* being defined as those that are necessary for essential projects but insufficient in supply to meet all needs. The following approaches were found useful:

1   Substitution of more abundant for less abundant.
2   Substitution of renewable for exhaustible.
3   Elimination of consumptive uses of the scarcest materials.
4   Avoidance of unnecessary uses of materials by reducing the size of components where size is not critical.
5   Avoidance of unnecessary uses of materials by reducing the need for inventories of replacement parts with minor variation.
6   Avoidance of unnecessary uses of materials by reducing the need for inventories of warehouse stock of shapes with minor variation of alloy content.
7   Use of alloys with the least content of scarce alloying additives.
8   Design to minimize the corrosion or other deterioration of a structure as a result of environmental exposure.
9   Design to eliminate premature failure through wear, cracking, or deformation.
10 Recovery of useful values from smoke and fumes.
11 Recovery and reuse of components.
12 Recovery and reuse of materials from municipal solid wastes.
13 Industrial symbiosis.
14 Classification of wastes at source.
15 Plating to repair worn parts and bring the parts within proper tolerances.
16 Elimination of low-volume categories of parts, alloys, shapes, and other stock.
17 Design for recycling.
18 Design of waste streams to facilitate reuse.
19 Salvage of high-energy materials to conserve both material and energy.
20 Reduction in the weight of moving parts.
21 Research to improve the properties of the most abundantly occurring materials.
22 Elimination of unnecessary packaging.
23 Use of systems requiring the least resources to perform the desired function.
24 Functional substitution.

25   Research into the mechanics of materials failure.

26   Research into the mechanics of materials corrosion.

27   Design to tolerate more dimensional variation and thus reduce rejects.

28   Use of fabrication processes that generate the least scrap.

29   Modular coordination of design in building construction.

30   Redesign of products using significant percentages of very critical materials.

31   Elimination of unnecessary performance requirements.

32   Research in the processing or uses of large-volume wastes or unused materials.

33   Development and application of a substitution index (of relative scarcity or relative abundance) to assess which of several alternative alloys represents the best conservation practice.

34   Systematic reduction of total throughput in an industrial process or production system.

PRODUCT REDESIGN

The redesign of existing products and the introduction of new products to avoid using critical materials that are in short supply are realistic alternatives but are not immediate solutions. The long lead times involved in product design, manufacture, and testing exclude these alternatives from being overnight remedies in case of a supply disruption unless they have been part of corporate research and development programs and introduction of new products are imminent. More often than not this is not the case unless the management has been involved in contingency planning for some time and envisaged possible shortages of its critical materials well in advance.

Traditionally in a relatively self-sufficient economy like that of the United States engineers and designers who know little or nothing about the short- or long-term outlook for the supplies of the materials they plan to use have been specifying into their designs many potentially scarce, unavailable, or price volatile materials. As a result corporate buyers are often unable to obtain sufficient quantities of such materials in time to meet design and production requirements.

There is also the danger that when such scarce materials are obtained the end-user company may find itself dealing in materials that are produced in small volume and whose production may be unprofitable to the supplier. As a result if even a threat of raw material supply disruption develops the supplier may withdraw completely from the market, leaving the end-user stranded and unable to find alternative sources of supply.

In the increasingly supply-short environment it becomes clear that design and production departments cannot operate independently. What is necessary is early coordination with the purchasing managers to discover that all critical materials can be obtained in a relatively uninterrupted flow at acceptable prices for the next one to five years. Only materials that can pass this test will insure some immunity from future shortages, although in the case of major disasters or military conflicts even this will not suffice.

Because of this need to depart from some traditional divisions of corporate functions in product design this may cause management problems in some organizations that must be identified, explained, and corrected. It can no longer be assumed that without adequate planning at the product specification stage it will always be possible to obtain all kinds of materials or fuels in quantities required when they are needed. If product redesign or new product introduction is to be a viable alternative corporations must learn to project specific critical materials availability for the duration of the planned project life cycle to insure uninterrupted production schedules and profitability.

This can only be accomplished if purchasing management is involved in the product's decision-making process from the very beginning, during the design and engineering stages. It is no longer practical for engineers to design a product and request the purchase of the materials they want. Recent shortages have demonstrated clearly that buyers cannot buy what is not available.

CHANGE IN ENVIRONMENTAL RESTRICTIONS

Since about 1960 significant importance has been attached to environmental quality, leading to the restoration or preservation of the purity of water and air and the natural beauty of the land. But since the mid-1970s these programs have come increasingly into conflict with other vital national goals such as the assurance of energy and raw materials to sustain accustomed levels of affluence and standards of living.

All materials are toxic under some conditions, but most materials are also essential to life. All pollution is basically materials misplaced, mismanaged, or wasted and can become a hazard to the environment at all points in the materials cycle as in mining, refining of ores, processing of materials into products, and disposal of wastes by industry and consumers (see Table 10.3).

Numerous environmental restrictions have come into being or are proposed to limit or eliminate various materials from the environment. There is little question that the toxicity of some materials makes them a serious threat to human health. Metals like beryllium, cadmium, lead, mercury, and plutonium and many chemicals are particularly toxic. But excessive constraints on their production and use also create political and economic threats that must be kept in mind.

Table 10.3   Environmental Pollution Resulting from Mismanagement of Materials Production and Use

Materials Activity	Type of Pollution
Extraction	Strip mining
	Coal washing
	Mine dumps
	Tailings, gangue, sinter, slime
	Toxic fumes
Processing	Fly ash
	Miscellaneous toxic fumes
Fabricating	Combustion products
	Solid wastes
	Process liquids
Transport	Consumption of space
	Pipelines
	Tracks
	Transmission lines
Consumer use	Packaging wastes
	Hardware and system operation
	Pesticides, fertilizers
Disposal	Nuclear radioactive wastes
	Toxic products of combustion
	Landfills
	Fly ash and fumes

What is required are special policies to control these dangerous substances not blanket environmental restrictions without regard to the greater threat posed by potential supply disruptions from foreign sources. The conflict can be resolved by the education and vigorous application of appropriate policies for the materials industry.

MATERIALS MANAGEMENT POLICIES

Any end-user accustomed to operating in an environment that assumes materials availability at all times will find it profitable to develop specific materials management policies designed to react instantly to critical materials shortages or supply disruptions. Not only will such policies and their implementation provide a modicum of insurance against sudden shortages but also they may reveal new opportunities for tightening up design, production, purchasing, and inventory procedures and contribute to cutting costs and increasing profitability.

All industrial processes involve the shaping of materials with various alternatives resulting in different levels of waste and energy consumption. Since almost all processes were developed during a period when energy was cheap there are bound to be numerous opportunities in process management to improve materials consumption levels. Casting, powder metallurgy, die casting, stamping, and drawing are therefore likely to offer better profitability incentives than reliance on machining.

There is a growing reliance on Materials Requirement Planning (MRP) systems designed to coordinate purchasing with manufacturing. Some are sophisticated data processing systems based on on-line computers and terminals to provide instant information where it is needed. But such systems are as good as the data that they process. More often than not MRP and other materials management systems tend to generate orders for materials and components on the basis of sales forecasts without much allowance for economic factors, supply bottlenecks, or political risk. Considerable improvement should be possible in the materials management function if such factors are included in these systems.

INVESTMENT AND TAX INCENTIVES

In a country like the United States where no national materials policy exists, numerous interests promulgate laws and regulations that may create as side effects the suppression or even demise of various exploration, mining, smelting, or materials processing industries. Only in recent years have a small number of the members of the U.S. Congress begun to introduce legislative proposals designed to stimulate the domestic production of minerals and reduce dependence on foreign sources whenever possible. The international atmosphere following the formation of the OPEC cartel, Soviet-Cuban adventures in Africa, the Iran crisis, and the Soviet invasion of Afghanistan also demands that serious consideration be given to reforms of restrictive mining laws, which has long been sought by the mining interests.

Although spot shortages of such strategic materials as cobalt, titanium, and aluminum in recent years focused the attention of the industries involved and some legislators on the need for reforms, it is unlikely that these will be introduced very soon unless there is a drastic deterioration in the international situation. It is likely, however, that a series of new studies will be getting under way proposing solutions ranging from changes in antitrust laws and environmental regulations to the examination of appropriate tax codes all designed to stimulate domestic production of minerals. One likely area to get considerable attention will be an attempt to permit minerals exploration in federal lands.

As a result investment and tax incentives that may result from new legislation are not likely to present immediate alternatives to sudden shortages or supply disruptions. Rather these are long-term solutions that will eventually create a better investment climate in the industrialized countries, but the lead times involved in opening up new mines and minerals processing plants is normally counted in years and requires hundreds of millions of dollars of investment.

SPECIAL TRADE AGREEMENTS

Western Europe and Japan have always had to face the import dependence problem in raw materials. As a result their governments and industries have often collaborated or at least coordinated their efforts to assure a relatively stable supply of raw materials from Third World countries. This often calls for special foreign trade policies and agreements with some form of government support in case of losses resulting from political changes or other government policies that could affect prior trade agreements.

In the United States mineral mining and processing companies are the prime movers in minerals trade and in 1977 were responsible for imports of about $10-billion worth of metals, up by 30 percent from the previous year. Already the United States is a net importer of metals, and there are projections that by the year 2000 the country's minerals trade deficit will approach $100 billion annually.

However, the developments of the last decade throughout the Third World have significantly reduced the freedom of the international minerals markets as a result of nationalization, the OPEC cartel, and Marxist takeovers in several countries. Government-subsidized enterprises in foreign countries may continue to expand their production and export of metals at low prices without regard to world demand. Such action often results in the closing of mines and production facilities in free market economies such as that of the United States.

Other industrialized countries such as Japan have developed extensive minerals processing industries based on government-sponsored–long-range trade agreements with raw material supplier countries. Such Japanese metals producers are now also competing in the world markets and can undersell producers of these materials in the United States even when tariff barriers are taken into account. Steel and titanium are two recent examples in which Japanese producers have been very successful.

In the case of titanium the Japanese were competing in recent years with the Soviet state monopoly that was able to undersell even the Japanese in the world's titanium markets. However, in 1979 the Soviet Union abruptly withdrew from world markets as a supplier of titanium, reportedly because a new program of Soviet nuclear submarine construction requires diversion of most Soviet domestic titanium production for its use.

Prior to this development Japanese titanium producers were offering long-term contracts for the supply of titanium, but most United States end-users continued to purchase their titanium on the spot market, whereas Japanese producers shifted their attention to European markets. When Soviet titanium sales were stopped many titanium users in the aerospace industries were suddenly caught short.

Now there is apprehension about developing long-term agreements with titanium ore producers and setting up additional titanium-processing capacity in the United States because of the potential Soviet titanium overhang. There is always the threat that the Soviet Union can reenter the global titanium market as abruptly as it left and prices for the metal would plummet, causing severe losses to the domestic titanium importers and processors. As a result titanium is viewed as another strategic metal that may require guaranteed support prices if domestic expansion and long-range trade agreements with foreign raw materials suppliers are to become attractive and profitable to the metals industry.

FOREIGN AID PROGRAMS

Since the end of World War II the United States extended over $195 billion in foreign aid throughout the world. The Far East, the Middle East, and South Asia received almost $110 billion of this total, and Latin America, Africa, and the Oceania received only slightly over $23 billion during the same period of time. This is comparable to the total American military and economic aid given to Vietnam before 1975.

After the United States, the largest donors are France, West Germany, Japan, the United Kingdom, and other western European countries, and they account for over 90 percent of all foreign aid drawings in the world. The Soviet bloc has a steadily increasing foreign aid program that is often tied to the development of hydroelectric and mining projects in the Third World (see Table 10.4).

Proponents of foreign aid claim that the world faces a somber future unless wealthier nations increase their aid to developing countries by $50 to $60 billion per year by 1985 and accept drastic trade and aid reforms. What this may mean is often funding sales of military equipment to Third World countries that see military power as a status symbol and a requirement for survival in regional wars and other "liberation" struggles.

The extension of foreign aid on its own, however, is a poor guarantee that a particular country will remain politically stable as events in Vietnam, Iran, South Korea, Afghanistan, and Nicaragua have recently made clear. As a result it is unwise to assume that sources of critical minerals in foreign aid recipient countries are any more reliable. Foreign aid programs may assist

Table 10.4   Gross Official Bilateral Capital Flows to the Less Developed Countries during 1977

Foreign Aid Donor	Aid in 1977 (millions of U.S. dollars)
World total	16,541
United States	5,072
France	2,540
West Germany	1,733
Japan	1,457
United Kingdom	683
Other countries[a]	3,831
Soviet Union	540
Eastern Europe	460
China	225

Source.   National Foreign Assessment Center, *Handbook for Economic Statistics,* August 1979.
[a] Including   Australia,   Austria,   Belgium, Canada, Denmark, Finland, Italy, Norway, the Netherlands, Sweden, and Switzerland.

in implementing foreign policy, but the end-user of strategic minerals should not rely on the hope that such foreign policy will endure or that it will succeed in the first place.

TRIOCEANIC ALLIANCE CONCEPTS

Those who believe that a resources war is being perpetrated by the Soviet bloc are also concerned about the NATO alliance and its vulnerability to strategic materials supply disruptions. According to this view the Soviet doctrine states that the best way to destroy the capitalist world is by gaining control of the Third World resources on which the Western world is dependent. Once that supply is cut off and markets for Western goods are eliminated an economic calamity is expected to occur in the noncommunist industrialized world, creating conditions for worker's uprisings and the establishment of communist governments.

To counteract this threat, a chain of sea-linked, NATO-type alliances of all nations commonly endangered by Soviet military power, subversion, and "liberation" wars is being promoted. This Trioceanic Alliance would provide collective security for all countries involved through the interconnecting sea lanes of the Atlantic, Pacific, and Indian oceans. Close cooperation between the armed forces of those countries and the emergence of Japan as a new military power would be required to make this concept effective.

Such an alliance is clearly a very long-range alternative and will be very difficult to bring about. It envisages bringing NATO countries together with Japan, Brazil, Argentina, South Africa, Australia, Indonesia, and the Persian Gulf states into a chain of security treaties designed to collectively counteract the Soviet bloc's expansionism and subversion. Although not an immediate solution it may, once it comes into being, assure considerable stability in the noncommunist world for several decades.

MILITARY ACTION

Military action of and by itself can be effective in assuring the continuing supply of particular strategic minerals if taken promptly, but it is a drastic and dangerous measure always inviting retaliation. By contrast to political or diplomatic alternatives it seldom offers longer-term resolution of international conflicts.

Nevertheless swift and decisive military action can be effective in the short term to buy time and turn to other alternatives. Increasing international tensions suggest that in the foreseeable future military action of this type will probably continue to play an important role in various local or regional conventional conflicts. One of the best recent examples of military action used to protect Western sources of strategic minerals was the French initiative to send troops to secure the Kolwezi copper and cobalt-mining region after the Katangan rebels invaded this area of Zaire from their bases in Angola during 1978.

In the Middle East Israel's occupation of the Sinai peninsula gave that country a badly needed independent oil supply to cover some of its demand, although the region has now been returned to Egypt. Military action may yet take place to occupy and secure Iranian oil fields if political instability in Iran and the surrounding oil-producing states further threatens oil supplies to the West. In such a case, however, a combined NATO force would have to be used to counteract any possible Soviet move that would almost certainly take place if only a single power tried to occupy the Iranian oil fields. The Soviets have made this quite clear by their invasion of Afghanistan, and Soviets' capabilities and will to act swiftly and decisively should not remain in doubt.

The most effective military measure that noncommunist industrialized nations can take is to create a special international military task force designed explicitly to occupy, secure, and operate the most important sources of strategic minerals whether these are the oil fields of Saudi Arabia or the gold fields of South Africa.

All the strategic minerals that form the lifeblood of the free market economies have been identified, and their major sources are well known. The special international military task force could be financed by all those countries whose import dependence makes them vulnerable to disruption of their sources of supply. Individual contributions could be proportional to respective national strategic materials vulnerability indices computed on a common basis. The task force should include technicians and engineers familiar with mining and processing technologies of all the strategic materials in question. The task force's training, aside from military preparedness, should include extensive familiarization with major strategic minerals areas and even field maneuvers in those locations to leave no doubt about the purpose and capabilities of such a force.

The existence of such a force either within NATO or the proposed Trioceanic Alliance would have a strong deterrent effect against resource war strategies of the Soviet bloc. It could be further strengthened by providing an opportunity for China to participate in such a force. China's mineral resources, strategic materials deficiencies, and geographic location next to its Soviet adversary would add significantly to the deterrent credibility of any specialized military task force of that nature.

REFERENCES

Bosson, Rex, and Bension Varon, *The Mining Industry and the Developing Countries*, Oxford University Press, Washington, D.C., 1977.

Christol, Carl Q., "The Moon Treaty: Fact and Fiction," *New York Times Magazine*, New York, April 1980.

Donohue, James F., "Nobody Can Ignore Material Shortages," *Purchasing*, 24 April 1980, p. 27.

Dowst, Somersby, "Who Says You Can't Substitute?," *Purchasing*, 7 January 1980.

"Exit Throwaway Era, Enter Recycling," *U.S. News & World Report*, 19 March 1979, p. 60.

General Services Administration, *Strategic and Critical Materials: Descriptive Data*, Washington, D.C., December 1973.

Harr, Karl G., Jr., "Space Manufacturing: A New Challenge," *Aerospace*, Aerospace Industries Association of America, Spring 1980.

International Institute for Environment and Development, *The Struggle for Antarctica's Riches*, Earthscan, London, 1977.

Lellouche, Pierre, and Dominique Moisi, "French Policy in Africa: A Lonely Battle against Destablization," *International Security*, Vol. 3, No. 4, Harvard University, Spring 1979, p. 108.

Library of Congress, *Materials Policy Handbook*, Science and Policy Research Division, U.S. Government Printing Office, Washington, D.C., 1977.

McCaskill, Richard C., "Fiber Optics: The Connection of the Future," *Data Communications*, McGraw-Hill, New York, January 1979.

McWethy, Jack, "Heating Up: Global Race for Antarctica's Riches," *U.S. News & World Report,* 28 February 1977.

Marsh, Acton K., "Domestic Production Stimulant Sought," *Aviation Week,* p. 51, 5 May 1980.

"Metals Supply Crisis Is Coming on Fast," *Purchasing,* 5 December 1979, p. 21.

National Strategy Information Center, *"NATO and the Global Threat—What Must Be Done,"* Proceedings of a Multinational Conference, Brighton, England, June 1–4, 1978.

"New Storm Gathering Over U.S. Foreign Aid," *U.S. News & World Report,* 31 March 1980, p. 59.

"Now the Squeeze on Metals," *Business Week,* 2 July 1979, p. 46.

Saxton, William A., and Morris Edwards, "Rapid Developments Make Fibre Optics a Practical Medium," *Canadian Datasystems,* May 1980.

Silverstein, Susan, "Out of Service Means a 10% Loss," *Purchasing,* 7 August 1973.

"Stretching Materials to the Limit," *Economist,* 17 May 1980, p. 77.

U.S. Government Printing Office, *Technical Options for Conservation of Metals,* Stock No. 052–063–00705–3, Washington, D.C.

"Watch Out for MRP's Purchasing Booby Traps," *Purchasing,* 29 May 1980.

"We're Not Running Out—Just Short," *Purchasing,* 10 April 1980.

"What Management Says It Wants Most," *Purchasing,* 24 April 1980, p. 31.

CHAPTER
ELEVEN

Stockpiling Policies
and Economics

Although materials substitution and diversification of supplies are two of the most appealing alternatives in case of strategic materials supplies disruptions, governments and industries are increasingly looking toward stockpiling as another method not only to assure critical materials availability but also to provide a domestic deterrent against excessive price manipulation by foreign supplier countries.

There are advantages and disadvantages in establishing and maintaining stockpiles, but with the increasing global instability and threats of supply disruptions and price escalations like those of the OPEC countries governments are more inclined to accept the cost of a strategic materials stockpile as an insurance premium against the potentially much greater political cost of economic disruption, unemployment, and civil unrest that would result from a denial of critical materials to an industrial economy even for a few months.

Although the original concept of a strategic materials stockpile was designed to provide the necessary inputs to the military-industrial complex to give it the capability to conduct a prolonged conventional war, it is now being extended to the operation of international minerals markets through buffer stocks, commodity agreements, and trade controls.

FINANCIAL REQUIREMENTS

The major disadvantage of a materials stockpile is the cost of its establishment, maintenance, and related transportation requirements. *Stockpiles* are essentially investments that bear no interest, although the value of the materials may appreciate. Stockpiles also require a continuing expenditure to keep them in good order, ready for use at a moment's notice. Manufacturing inventories are a small-scale analogy of a materials stockpile in a corpora-

220

tion, and in the world of business the objective has always been to optimize inventories by minimizing the cost of supplies that would at the same time guarantee adequate production to meet the expected market demand.

There are some arguments for stockpiling critical and precious metals at the corporate level that are required in manufacture, particularly if the metals' prices tend to increase with time. However, some studies made by the electronics industry manufacturers that use gold extensively suggest that losses or gains turn out to be surprisingly small when end-users simply buy gold when needed, regardless of price fluctuations. What this means is that the loss of interest on capital tied up in advance purchases may turn out to be greater than the average increase in the price of materials being stockpiled in a fluctuating market. The cost of storage, maintenance, and transportation must also be added to obtain the total cost of developing such an inventory on a short-term basis. The risks of holding it for a longer term are considerably greater and so are the costs.

Although the national strategic materials stockpile represents in fact a type of insurance premium against shortages, its cost could be staggering and requires funding appropriations at the highest levels. On the other hand if materials shortages continue to increase and prices of stockpiled materials escalate, such a stockpile also increases in value. Mostly this is only a paper profit, because stockpile sales are usually restricted and even when realized in part would substantially depress the market for such commodities unless special care is taken to conduct it in a controlled and orderly fashion.

As an example the American strategic stockpile was valued at about $13.7 billion in 1980. It has been increasing in value substantially during the 1970s from $7.4 billion in 1976 and $9.5 billion in 1978. But most of the materials in that stockpile were acquired prior to 1959, and by 1960 the cumulative expenditures amounted to almost $6 billion. If this capital were simply invested at a mere 5 percent interest over the last 20 years it would have increased to some $16 billion or at least $2 billion more than the current value of the stockpile. In addition if the stockpile were to be brought up to its stated goals another $6 billion would have to be invested right away.

By comparison other national stockpiles are but a miniature of the vast American program. Since 1975 the French government allocated $300 million to build up two months' stocks of all imported materials. Germany is also increasing its strategic materials stocks in industry with government support of financing and interest charges.

In the United States stockpile maintenance costs, administrative costs, and other expenditures represented over 10 percent of the cumulative stockpile expenditures from its inception through September 1977, and the breakdown of the costs gives a good indication of the amounts and types of expenditures involved. The size and dispersal of the American stockpile makes it unique; nevertheless these figures provide some guidance to the required funding levels necessary to maintain a significant stockpiling program.

Table 11.1   Total Cost of the U.S. National Strategic Materials Stockpile Cumulative from 1948 through 30 September 1977

Type of Expenditure		Cumulative Amount (millions of U.S. dollars)	Percentage of Total
Net total expenditure		6,075.3	100.0
Materials acquisition		5,444.0	89.6
Stockpile maintenance		494.8	8.1
Facility construction	43.8		0.7
Storage and handling	348.2		5.7
Net rotation costs	102.8		1.7
Administrative costs		119.9	1.9
Operations, machining		16.6	0.3

Source.   Federal Preparedness Agency, *Stockpile Report to the Congress,* Washington, D.C., April 1978.

Materials acquisition cost is of course the largest single item, but stockpile maintenance costs are not insignificant and require public funding for the construction of facilities, rental of storage space and handling equipment, and net rotation costs from all the transactions made. Administrative costs and operations, including machine tool program costs, amount to about 2 percent of the total expenditures over the year (see Table 11.1).

Clearly such levels of expenditures are very high, even for rich industrialized countries of western Europe or Japan, and public funds for such stockpiles are very hard, if not impossible, to obtain except under emergency wartime conditions. For example, if Japan were to establish such a strategic stockpile proportional in size to its GNP it would still have to spend immediately $6 to $7 billion for acquisition of the materials alone. A comparable figure for West Germany would be $3 to $4 billion, and if all industrialized countries tried to do this simultaneously the resulting market disruptions and shortages would probably be worse than those the stockpiles are designed to prevent.

U.S. STRATEGIC STOCKPILE

The Strategic and Critical Materials Stockpile of the United States consists of 93 minerals, metals, and other industrial materials stored at 122 locations throughout the United States. The purpose of the national stockpile is stated in the policy statement of the Strategic and Critical Materials Stockpiling Act of 1946, which reads in part as follows:

> It is the policy of the Congress and the purpose and intent of this act
> to provide for acquisition and retention of stocks of . . . materials
> within the United States and thereby decrease and prevent wherever
> possible a dangerous and costly dependence of the United States
> upon foreign nations for supplies of . . . materials in times of na-
> tional emergency.

Actually strategic and critical materials have been accumulated under the
authority of several statutes and exist in several inventories, including the
National Stockpile, the Defense Production Act Inventory, the Supplemen-
tal Stockpile, and the Commodity Credit Corporation Inventory. The stockpile is administered by the Federal Preparedness Agency of the General
Services Administration, and the goals and procedures adopted are based on
guidance from the National Security Council and other executive agencies
competent in estimating requirements and supply of materials.

The stockpile objectives have been established after a study of the estimated availability of U.S. production and imports in comparison with the
requirements for materials in time of emergency for military, atomic energy,
and defense-supporting and essential civilian needs; and for essential exports to allies of those materials for which the United States is the principal
source of supply.

Every major material in the stockpile is analyzed on a continuing basis to
determine whether it should be designated strategic or critical. Materials
may be added to or deleted from the list as technological, economic, or political changes occur that affect the design levels and composition of the
stockpile. The amounts held in the stockpile are determined by estimating
the difference between the quantities needed in a major war and the quantities available. If the supply of a material appears to be inadequate the shortfall is the amount that should be in the stockpile.

As of 1979 only 40 percent of the materials contained in the national stockpile were meeting their stated goals. Another 10 percent of materials met
their goals only by credits from materials that are held in the stockpile in
other forms such as bauxite and aluminum. A total of 43 material categories
were below their stated goals, 13 of which were below the 20 percent stockpile requirement levels (see Table 11.2).

The discrepancies in goals and percentage fullfillment in the American
stockpile also reflect the fact that the goals have been shifting in time. From
original five-year conventional wartime requirements they were changed to
three and even one year and since 1976 have been back to the three-year
contingency period again. During the whole time certain sales and purchases
have been authorized, creating additional imbalances.

The stockpiling act provides authority to maintain and administer the inventories, but funding for new additions or authority to dispose of materials
no longer considered critical rests with the Congress. After many years of
relative inaction a total of $170 million has been appropriated in the fiscal

Table 11.2   Some Major Metallic Minerals and Metals
Contained in the U.S. National Strategic and Critical
Materials Stockpile

Commodity	Percentage of Goal September 1977
Alumina	56
Antimony	202
Bauxites	2,706
Beryllium metal	25
Bismuth	269
Cadmium	25
Chromite (metallurgical)	77
Chromium (ferro)	170
Chromium (metal)	37
Cobalt	48
Columbium concentrates	56
Copper	2
Lead	69
Manganese (chemical grade)	91
Manganese ore (metallurgical)	177
Manganese (ferro, high carbon)	136
Mercury	370
Nickel	0
Platinum group (indium)	17
Platinum group (palladium)	51
Platinum metal	34
Rutile	22
Tantalum metal	15
Tin	628
Titanium sponge	24
Tungsten ores, concentrates	1,176
Vanadium (ferro)	0
Zinc	28

Source.   Based on the General Services Administration's report
to the Congress, April 1978.

year 1981 for additions to the stockpile and significantly larger appropriations are expected in the future.

It is believed by some critics that such controls limit the usefulness of the stockpile as a tool to deal with strategic materials shortages that result from situations not declared as national emergencies. Other observers claim that the stockpile is already being used as a political football to further specific regional or mining interests and fear that relaxation of controls to make it more effective in the case of emergency will only invite abuse of the program during peacetime. There is also considerable criticism of the physical state of the inventories and the associated logistics.

PROSPECTS FOR U.S. ECONOMIC STOCKPILE

Since about 1976 the concepts of an economic stockpile for the United States have emerged in Washington and have been discussed by administration and industry executives. This concept proposes that the U.S. government should act like a specialist in the stock market in certain critical materials. It should be buying such materials when the market drops and selling them on rising demand. This activity would be outside the strategic materials stockpile and designed primarily to dampen the fluctuation in materials markets by providing a floor price in falling markets.

It is argued that if the economy booms, end-users would have ready supplies of needed materials, and inflation would be moderated. The economic stockpile would also provide some protection against disruptions of supplies of critical materials from foreign countries for the civilian sector of the economy that would benefit from the strategic materials stockpile.

Because the concepts of the economic stockpile presume government involvement in the markets of many powerful corporations there is great controversy about the potential benefits and drawbacks of such a stockpile. Some compromise proposals suggest an economic stockpile for only 15 to 20 of the most critical items that would be changing, depending on the political situation and availability. The purpose of such a limited stockpile would be strictly the use and release of critical materials during abrupt and unanticipated interruptions of supplies. Such stocks would not be available for export in order not to disrupt international markets, where producer countries singly or in groups are also considering stockpiles of their own to stabilize such markets.

PRODUCTION AND BUFFER STOCKS

Stockpiling at the corporate level may also occur as shortages spread and companies tend to double and treble their orders, trying to obtain the materials they need from all available sources. When a sudden shortage of material takes place such corporate stockpiling can tighten the market even further and escalate the prices. Many manufacturers are willing to pay the costs associated with stockpiling because they know that continued shortages will cause suppliers to impose price adders or surcharges to reflect the soaring prices which result from such shortages.

An innovative approach to corporate stockpiling has been introduced in Sweden, which also depends on imports of many strategic minerals. The

Swedish government provides tax incentives to industrial companies that develop and maintain large inventories of certain strategic materials. Some taxes are paid eventually but only when the stockpiled materials are sold or used in production. This approach appears to have some merit and might be more acceptable to many corporations concerned with supply disruptions than the economic stockpile to be operated by the government.

Buffer stocks are usually understood to be stockpiles of a particular mineral maintained by an international producers group such as ITC. The objective is similar to that of the economic stockpile, namely, to maintain a floor price for the commodity and stabilize international markets. Buffer stocks for many minerals are being considered by Third World countries in connection with the NIEO movement centered on the United Nations.

FRENCH STOCKPILING PROGRAMS

Besides the United States, France has the largest national stockpiling program in operation, although it is relatively small in comparison with the American strategic materials stockpile. France, as one of the world's leading economies with a rather independent political stance on the international scene, is understandably concerned about assuring itself the greatest possible degree of economic independence with regard to strategic materials.

The domestic production in France of ores and nonferrous metals supplies only 15 percent of requirements, although a hefty 30 percent is obtained from the recovery and recycling of used metals. This still leaves France with a need to import 55 percent of its requirements, and an official study indicated French vulnerability in supplies of 13 strategic metals, including copper, cobalt, tungsten, chromium, titanium, tin, lead, and zinc.

Since 1975 France has embarked on a program to develop a national stockpile of the most critical materials whose ultimate acquisition cost is reported to be set at about $700 million. This is only about 5 percent of the current estimated value of the American national strategic materials stockpile. However, the French stockpile is designed to provide emergency supplies of the most critical materials during disruptions lasting no more than two months. They are to supplement commercial inventories, presumably maintained by the French end-users, and it is not yet clear how much of this stockpiling program has been implemented. A central purchasing agency GIRM buys materials from commercial suppliers and is responsible for management of the inventories.

GERMAN STOCKPILING PROGRAMS

The West German government basically relies on industry to provide supplies of all raw materials, and there is no overall planning at the national level. However, the government provides a favorable climate for minerals industries in the form of guarantees, loans, and special tax rates. In 1979 a special study was completed identifying political risks associated with the most critical imported materials, and a ranking index was developed to provide an indication of the relative "risk factor" among these materials. The most critical 15 materials for Germany include chromium, manganese, asbestos, tungsten, cobalt, vanadium, titanium, platinum, aluminum, nickel, molybdenum, copper, tin, lead, and zinc (see Table 15.3 in Chapter 15).

At least five of the forementioned critical materials that West Germany imports, primarily from southern African countries, are being stockpiled. Theoretically West German stockpiles of those critical materials are to provide supplies for four months of operations, but there are indications that the stockpile may be increased to assure supplies for a whole year. This suggests that Germany is not optimistic about the future stability of its critical materials sources in southern Africa.

The federal government bears two-thirds of interest charges connected with stockpiling these materials, and the Bundesbank provides $335 million over 10 years to refinance an organization that will subsidize the financing of those stockpiles. Although German manufacturers have reservations about the need to increase stockpiles of strategic materials it appears most likely that the German programs will continue to expand.

JAPANESE STOCKPILING POLICIES

Although Japan's import dependence for critical materials is greater than that of any other industrialized free market economy the Japanese government does not maintain a strategic materials stockpile. Rather the Japanese policy so far has been to pursue extensive diversification of foreign sources of supply. Japanese mining firms often work together in developing new projects abroad to spread the risks and are very often involved with the government, which establishes policy guidelines, provides tax incentives, low-interest funds, assumes some exploration and development risks, loosely regulates production and trade, and suggests stockpiling objectives. Many of those programs are supported by the government-industry Mineral Resources Development Company, formed in 1974 for this purpose.

Nevertheless by 1976 two stockpiling associations were organized in Japan to stabilize the import of basic metal ores and concentrates. One group specializes in aluminum, and another deals with copper, lead, and zinc. A government-funded Metal Mining Agency of Japan provides subsidies for various projects concerning those metals, ranging from exploration to the use of end products.

So far these Japanese stockpiles have a temporary status and are designed to be used up completely by 1982. Chances are that this will not happen because the all-powerful Ministry of International Trade and Industry believes that permanent stockpiles may be of great value to Japan. In view of growing political instability in many of the Third World countries supplying critical materials to Japan it appears more likely that Japan, like major industrialized countries in western Europe, will develop its own permanent stockpile to cushion the effects of potential supply disruptions that could be extremely damaging to the Japanese economy.

BRITISH STOCKPILING POLICIES

The United Kingdom presents a unique situation because its declining manufacturing base is responsible for a relatively complacent attitude of the industry toward potential critical materials shortages. This attitude is strengthened by the fact that London is the center of the world's minerals activity. In this city are the headquarters of many large international corporations, the London Metals Exchange (regarded by many as the leading metals trading mart of the world), and numerous international producers associations.

These factors combine to create what has been called "the North Sea Oil Syndrome" in the United Kingdom, whereby many end-users assume that whatever the minerals supply problems of countries like France, Germany, or Japan may be, the United Kingdom is assured of supplies by virtue of being the seat of so many elements of control of global minerals industries and their associated financing and trading circles. Old Commonwealth links with Australia, Canada, and some African countries also play a role in formulating these attitudes.

Nevertheless with mounting apprehension about future threats to strategic minerals supplies among the United Kingdom's major trading countries the British government began a program to try to develop a strategy to secure long-term supplies of critical raw materials. The initial stages will consist of consultations with end-users, mining firms, and financial interests about the future availability of critical minerals from foreign sources. There are no known plans, however, to organize a national strategic materials stockpile at this stage.

OTHER STOCKPILING PROGRAMS

In other countries critical materials stockpiles are also under consideration but because the issue is strategically, politically, and financially sensitive there is relatively little information available about the subject. Most smaller industrialized countries are highly dependent on imports of many critical materials but in many cases these are imported through the multinational mining and trading organizations operating from large European countries like France, Germany, and the United Kingdom. Some may also be subsidiaries of American multinationals.

It would also appear that many of the smaller countries would prefer not to become involved in strategic or critical materials stockpiling for political and financial reasons. The large initial cost is a major factor, but political considerations may be even more important. It is quite possible that Third World countries at some future date may withhold critical materials supplies from large powers like the United States, which they know already has the largest stockpile in the world. At the same time Third World countries may be willing to continue supplying smaller "friendly" countries that did not resort to stockpiling previously.

Nevertheless Italy, Spain, and Sweden have been reported recently as toying with the idea of starting strategic materials stockpiles of their own. South Africa has been reported to have stockpiled at least three years' supplies of crude oil anticipating possible sanctions and trade restrictions. South Korea also is known to have a strategic materials stockpile.

STOCKPILING AS A TOOL OF RESOURCES WAR

The Third World countries regard the stockpiling of critical raw materials outside their control as a means of market manipulation and retaliation directed against their best interests. It may even be possible that some of those countries will pass export control laws prohibiting the sales of their minerals for the purpose of stockpiling by consumer nations.

Similarly the organization of producer alliances or cartels and programs of international commodity agreements cannot be effective without some form of stockpiling among the producing countries. Therefore whereas existing stockpiles in developed consuming countries are regarded with suspicion the concept of a network of buffer stocks under the control of minerals-producing countries is viewed as a solution and a means to balance the needs and interests of both sides. For this reason these agreements are to come into being between producers and consumers, but a common fund required to establish and maintain buffer stocks will have to be financed by the developed nations, whereas the stocks will be under the physical control of producing countries.

The integrated commodity program, first proposed at the UNCTAD forum of the United Nations, is an expression of these Third World policies and is being invoked in the name of ultimate income redistribution through a massive upward readjustment of price levels for critical commodities—all in keeping with the concepts of NIEO.

The integrated commodity program encompasses 21 commodities of which only 6 are minerals at this time. These six include copper, iron ore, tin, bauxite, zinc, and lead and are nevertheless six very basic minerals, accounting for a very large proportion of the total value of the non-oil minerals trade.

Actually only tin and copper have been singled out so far for the creation of buffer stocks. Tin has already been subject to stocking under the International Tin Agreement implemented by ITC. The history of tin markets over the years is perhaps a good indication of the types of successes and problems likely to develop when other minerals are also handled in this way.

Another element that may affect and influence the emergence of other cartels or alliances of producers is the possibility of linking the action of OPEC oil-producing countries with that of major non-oil mineral supplier countries. This could be a very powerful combination of forces, particularly because it could lead to the solution of financing and energy problems of many non-oil minerals-producing countries of the Third World.

There are therefore powerful incentives and means to engage in various forms of stockpiling among both producing and consuming nations. However, if these trends continue it is certain that the markets for many of the critical materials will tighten significantly, and continued and aggressive price increases will become inevitable.

REFERENCES

"Buyers Try to Beat Precious Metals Prices," *Purchasing*, 14 February 1980, p. 18B9.

Federal Preparedness Agency, *The Strategic and Critical Meterials Stockpile*, General Services Administration Fact Sheet, Washington, D.C., October 1976.

"France Plans Creation of a Raw Materials Fund," *Wall Street Journal*, 13 December 1979.

General Services Administration, *Stockpile Report to the Congress April 1977–September 1977*, Washington, D.C., April 1978.

Gottlieb, Daniel W., "Economic Stockpile to Get Serious Study," *Purchasing*, 21 December 1976, p. 26.

Gottlieb, Daniel W., "Stockpile Shenanigans May Be Continuing," *Purchasing*, 7 November 1979.

"Nobody Loves the Stockpile Bills," *Business Week*, 2 August 1978.

Schwartz, Lloyd, "U.S. Officials Support 3-Year Strategic Stockpile Plan," *Electronic News*, 27 November 1978.

"Stockpile Gives Buyers Too Much Confidence," *Purchasing*, 5 December 1979, p. 20A14.

"Strategic Stockpiles: Who's Hoarding What?," *Economist*, 24 May 1980.

Strauss, Simon D., "Those Shifting Stockpiles," *New York Times*, 6 February 1977.

"Stockpile of Minerals Short of Goals," *Aviation Week & Space Technology*, 5 May 1980.

Thomson, Terri, "Angry Buyers Protest Precious Metal Adders," *Purchasing*, 8 May 1980, p. 21.

CHAPTER
TWELVE

Politics of Undersea
Resources

Ocean mining has been promoted over the last 20 years as the obvious solution for the mining industries concerned about political problems in mineral-producing countries of the Third World, continuous depletion of land-based reserves, and declining ore grades of new deposits.

Offshore oil extraction, which so far constitutes the bulk of undersea mining anywhere in the world, created expectations and concerns among the nations with a shoreline and is in no small way responsible for the extension of the previously familiar 12-mile territorial waters' limit to as much as 200 miles. That just about covers most of the continental shelves where most of the offshore oil is believed to be located, but in constricted coastal regions such as the South China Sea, where the promise of offshore oil is very high, these new limits were responsible for the emergence of numerous territorial disputes between governments and international oil companies.

The United Nations Conference of the Law of the Sea (UNCLOS) after 12 years of arguments and counterarguments appears to be nearing an international agreement on the mining of the seabed. Although this may finally remove many of the legal snags to undersea prospecting and mining, the economics and technical risks associated with these ventures remain the major obstacles to further progress. At this stage the earliest commercial mining of the seabed for non-oil minerals is still not expected to begin until 1990 at the earliest.

THE LAW OF THE SEA

The United Nations Conference of the Law of the Sea, which was first held in 1958, formulated several conventions that are the basis for the current sea law in the areas of fishing, conservation, the territorial sea, the high seas, the continental shelf, and the compulsory settlement of disputes. The Seabed Committee, created by the conference, declared a moratorium on all seabed exploration and also declared the seabed beyond national jurisdiction the "common heritage of mankind."

A proposed international organization, the International Seabed Authority (ISA), was created in principle to exploit the seabed resources. It is unique because it is the only international organization to be engaged in the mining business. It is directed by the Enterprise, which consists of representatives of 150 widely differing countries that are participating in the Law of the Sea Conference and are members of ISA.

Over 115 countries represented in this conference are from the Third World, and a majority of them belong to the Group of 77 that subscribes to the economic principles embodied in NIEO calling for the transfer of technology, capital, and profits from the industrialized to the developing countries. Whereas the developed countries possess technological and financial resources to mine the seabed the developing countries are more interested in limitations on the production of seabed minerals by artificial means. The concern of the developing countries is to protect the economies of those countries among them that are highly dependent on domestic mining of these same minerals.

The Group of 77 believes that its member countries have been deprived of technology and its benefits because of their colonial past. As a result the member countries demand to receive deep ocean mining technology through the Enterprise in exchange for undisputed rights to mine the seabed beyond national jurisdictions by private mining companies. They feel that unless they can exert this collective pressure and obtain the technology they will be further condemned to continue in poverty which they often ascribe to the lack of access to technology. Basically this effort is designed to use the United Nations to develop a Third World capability to mine the seabed in the belief that this will put those countries in a position to undertake sustained economic development.

Business consortia currently involved in undersea exploration claim that these approaches to deep sea mining would make it unprofitable for commercial enterprises to engage in such activities. Particularly annoying to business ventures is the proposal that the U.N. Enterprise would have first choice in picking among undersea mining sites already explored by private interests with considerable capital investment in previous years. In addition the U.N. Enterprise proposes to obtain operating capital from loan guarantees and funding contributions made by those commercial enterprises to the United Nations. Business firms competing in the free market economies simply do not believe these are viable business approaches to seabed mining.

UNDERSEA MINING CONSORTIA

There are five international consortia exploring and test-mining certain manganese nodule-bearing seabed areas of the Pacific Ocean, approximately 1000 miles south-west of San Diego in California. These consortia are not entirely opposed to legislation controlling seabed resources, but they are proceeding in the face of the moratorium imposed on seabed mining by the Law of the Sea Conference of the United Nations.

The five consortia involve large international enterprises from seven industrialized countries, including Belgium, Canada, France, West Germany, the Netherlands, the United Kingdom, and the United States. There are 23 major organizations involved in these consortia, mostly representing mineral mining and oil interests. Lockheed Missiles and Space Corporation as a high-technology company and some French government research organizations are also participating in some of the consortia (see Table 12.1).

These ventures are proceeding on the assumption that the legalities of the international seabed will eventually be settled and that the U.S. Congress will pass a seabed resources bill to give American-based companies protection against deep-sea claims by other competitors. Although the American legislature would not provide protection against foreign claims it seems that agreements will emerge providing for reciprocal multilateral recognition of claims between the seven countries whose companies and resources are already involved in the consortia. These legislative arrangements are necessary for companies to proceed further in their seabed exploration and mining activity; otherwise it would be extremely difficult to convince banking interests to provide additional financing for most of those ventures.

Whereas the consortia are engaged in the exploration and mining of manganese nodules on the ocean floor most of their efforts are directed only toward recovering nickel, copper, and cobalt rather than manganese ore that constitutes an average 32 percent of the nodule material. Only one of the consortia, Ocean Mining Associates (OMA) has been planning the production of high-purity manganese at some future date to compete with some existing manganese products. The reason for this is because there is a relative abundance of manganese reserves in land-based sources, although the richest deposits are located mainly in the Soviet Union, South Africa, Brazil, and Gabon.

Manganese is the twelfth most abundant element in the earth's crust, and manganese ores are produced virtually all over the world. Known world resources of manganese ore have been judged adequate to maintain current production levels and to support anticipated increases in demand for decades if not centuries. What makes manganese a strategic and critical mineral is the fact that most industrialized nations of the West must import large quantities of manganese ores to maintain their steel production. De-

Table 12.1   Major Organizations and Countries Participating in the Seabed Mining Consortia

Consortium	Constituent Organizations	Country	First Mining
Afernod	Centre Nationale pour l'Exploita- tions des Oceans Commissariat a l'Energie Atomique Bureau des Recherches Geologiques et Minieres Le Nickel France-Dunkirk	France	Test plant
Kennecott Copper	British Petroleum Consolidated Gold Fields Mitsubishi Noranda Rio Tinto-Zinc	United Kingdom United Kingdom Japan Canada United Kingdom	Little activity
Ocean Management (OM)	DOMCO INCO Metallgesellschaft Preussag Salzgitter SEDCO	Japan Canada West Germany West Germany West Germany United States	1990 to 2000
Ocean Minerals	AMOCO Bos Kalis Westminster Lockheed Missiles and Space Corporation Shell	United States Netherlands United States United Kingdom/ Netherlands	1990
Ocean Mining Associates (OMA)	Sun Company Union Miniere U.S. Steel	United States Belgium United States	1989

Source.   Based on U.S. Department of the Interior data, 1980.

spite this import dependence, however, the manganese reserves overhang is so large that mining manganese nodules for their manganese content would create a glut of the metal on world markets and depress the price levels to a point where it became unprofitable to continue with seabed mining. This would also have a disastrous effect on land-based manganese producers in some of the Third World countries such as Gabon, Ghana, Zaire, and India.

The most active of the five seabed mining consortia is OMA that plans to start production in 1989, using a dredging and airlift system at a depth of three miles. The Ocean Management (OM) venture, which relies on another dredging and hydraulic airlift system developed in West Germany, is not expected to begin commercial mining until 1990. Ocean Minerals plans to use similar technology but is also not expected to start commercial operations before 1990. Eventually Ocean Minerals hopes to produce 2.75 million tons of manganese nodules per year that would contain the equivalent of over 10 percent of the free world's manganese consumption as well as 7 percent of the nickel and 18 percent of the cobalt. This could have a significant impact on the world's output of those metals; however, at present price levels even energy-intensive–land-based projects producing some of those metals provide better investment opportunities because of lower overall costs. Political instability, particularly in cobalt-producing areas, however, could change this situation. Therefore in a way the existence of those seabed-mining consortia acts as a political deterrent against excessive demands and price escalations on the part of producing countries of the Third World.

Of the remaining seabed-mining ventures Kennecott Copper has reduced its activities significantly, and there are some questions whether it will proceed with the project. The all-French Afernod makes no bones about the fact that ocean mining at present is not economic and does not have plans beyond conducting pilot plant tests using a continuous line bucket system developed in Japan for picking up manganese nodules from the ocean floor.

MANGANESE NODULE POTENTIAL

Billions of tons of manganese nodules are scattered over vast areas of ocean floor in the Atlantic, Pacific, and Indian oceans. These nodules are generally 1 to 10 centimeters in diameter, are very porous, and consist essentially of aggregates of colloidal particles of manganese and iron oxides and hydroxides and clays deposited in concentric onionlike layers around a central nucleus of volcanic debris or fish remains.

The nodules contain appreciable concentrations of nickel, copper, and cobalt, with the nickel and copper being associated with the manganese minerals and the cobalt being associated mostly with the iron minerals. The average metal content of those nodules varies, depending on their source, but the North Pacific region contains the most commercially valuable nodules because of their relatively high nickel and copper content (see Table 12.2).

Accumulations of nodules of up to 100 kilograms per square meter have been reported, but in areas most favorable for seabed mining concentrations range between 10 to 30 kilograms per square meter. The greatest concentrations, however, are in areas with the least detrital materials and tend to be far from land in the deeper parts of the oceans at depths of 13,000 to 20,000

Table 12.2   Average Metal Content of Seabed Manganese Nodules in Various Areas

Ocean Region	Area	Percentage of				
		Manganese	Iron	Nickel	Copper	Cobalt
North Atlantic	Blake Plateau	14.5	13.7	0.50	0.08	0.42
Ocean	Red Clay Region	13.9	—	0.36	0.24	0.35
	Seamount	13.5	—	0.39	0.14	0.36
South Atlantic Ocean		7.2	—	0.14	0.09	0.05
Indian Ocean		16.3	—	0.54	0.20	0.26
North Pacific	Red Clay Regions	18.2	11.5	0.76	0.49	0.25
Ocean	Siliceous Ooze	24.6	8.2	1.28	1.16	0.23
South Pacific Ocean	Deep Water Clay Region	15.1	—	0.51	.0.23	0.34
	Submarine Highs	14.6	—	0.41	0.13	0.78

Source.   National Materials Advisory Board, National Research Council.

feet. Some of those sea bottoms are very rugged and are not conducive to seabed mining.

The pacific nodules found in the North Pacific region are considered at present the best mining sites from the viewpoint of nodule abundance, metal content, favorable sea floor topography, and relative depth. This region lies about 600 miles southeast of Hawaii, with nodules at an average depth of 16,000 feet. The Pacific nodules are most likely going to be the first to be exploited commercially.

Other nodules of interest are located on the Blake Plateau only about 125 miles east of Georgia and Florida at an average depth of 2600 feet. Although more accessible these nodules are less desirable metallurgically than the Pacific nodules because they have a lower metal content and contain calcium carbonate, which is undesirable in hydrometallurgical extraction processes. However, these nodules have the strategic advantage of being accessible for domestic exploitation under the control of the United States in case of an emergency.

The Pacific nodules that lie in the high seas are not considered an American domestic deposit. They present a potential source of several critical metals that could discourage any cartel action against American end-users. Even if only nickel, copper, and cobalt are extracted commercially, the processing plant tailings if stocked would constitute a major potential source of manganese that could also act as a political deterrent. This is why the United Nations–sponsored proposals insist on the U.N. Enterprise having the first choice of seabed-mining sites. Only then could this deterrent be removed from the control of the Western industrialized countries.

THE GLOMAR EXPLORER STORY

Although seabed mining for manganese nodules is not yet commercially feasible the investments made by the ocean-mining consortia give some credibility to those programs as possible deterrents against cartel or other political action by some of the Third World producers of critical materials imported by the industrialized countries. By 1980 OMA, the most active of all undersea consortia, is believed to have invested $70 million on research and development of its seabed-mining system and another $100 million is to be spent to further develop the project that will ultimately cost about $1 billion. The total investment made by all the five consortia is believed to be over $150 million already. Several seabed-mining vessels have been built for these projects since 1970, including OMA's *Deepsea Miner* and *Deepsea Miner II* and OM's *Sedco 445*, a converted offshore drilling ship.

But by far the most sensational technological development in deep-sea exploration was the construction of the *Glomar Explorer* by Howard Hughes in 1973. This ship was built at a cost of $200 million, ostensibly for the purpose of mining manganese nodules, and no expense was spared to equip this vessel with the latest and most efficient technology. It included the most sophisticated pipe-handling equipment and an entire section amidships was superbly stabilized with the best available electronic and navigational equipment. Using a submersible barge and a giant claw assembly 60 meters long this ship could lower 4.5 kilometers of pipe section to pick up objects at the ocean's bottom with extreme stability and positional accuracy.

It was later revealed that the real purpose of the *Glomar Explorer* was to retrieve a sunken Soviet Golf-class submarine, at least part of which containing Soviet code books was retrieved from the ocean floor into the hull of the ship. The owners and operators of this exquisite technical equipment turned out to be the CIA. In 1978 it was announced that *Glomar Explorer* has been leased to Lockheed Missiles and Space Corporation, one of the leading partners of the Ocean Minerals consortium, and there is little doubt that it will be a superb tool for seabed-mining operations.

The existence of the *Glomar Explorer* and other ocean-mining ships as well as sophisticated computerized exploration systems and technical expertise give the consortia the required credibility vis-à-vis other attempts to form seabed-mining enterprises such as the proposals of the United Nations Law of the Sea Conference. The magnitude of investments required provide another measure of the challenges involved, and it is quite clear that only a few very rich countries could afford to become involved in deep-sea mining with any chance of success. Because of the magnitude of the investment and the uncertainty of the outcome these countries are naturally reluctant to share this expensive technology with other countries that cannot contribute to this effort but whose actions often provoked the search for alternative sources of critical materials.

It is obvious that the existence of this technology and expertise in the hands of the industrialized countries with high strategic materials import dependence is a clear warning to the Third World countries and particularly the Group of 77 members that there are limits beyond which developed countries will not be held hostage by unreasonable demands of their raw materials suppliers.

PROSPECTS FOR MINERALS FROM THE SEA

At least 30 important minerals exist in seawater, but only a few are at present extracted in any significant quantities. Salt, magnesium, and bromine are the three that are recovered in large amounts, but the oceans also contain enormous amounts of iron, copper, lead, zinc, silver, gold, cobalt, nickel, diamonds, manganese, tin, aluminum, platinum metals, chromium, tungsten, mercury, columbium, tantalum, rutile, ilmenite, bismuth, uranium, and zircon.

Various techniques for the extraction of these minerals from seawater exist, but in most cases the prohibitive factor is the enormous cost in energy required to process very large quantities of seawater. German and Japanese interests have already launched projects to obtain uranium from seawater since it offers some potential to produce more energy than required for its extraction, particularly when uranium is used in nuclear breeder reactors.

The prospects for recovering minerals directly from seawater are very slim as long as land-based reserves continue to require relatively less energy for extraction. This is so because ore deposits contain minerals in very much higher concentrations than those dissolved in seawater. However, there is some promise that minerals production from seawater may become economical in cases where it is combined with the processing of seawater for the production of fresh water. On the other hand such facilities are not likely to be widespread because underground water and natural sources, including rain, provide cheaper methods of obtaining fresh water. In most cases such systems would be limited to relatively sparsely populated regions of the Middle East or isolated islands, and the volumes of seawater processed may not be large enough to provide any economically significant output of minerals.

Besides the oil and gas exploited from offshore oil fields in many parts of the world and the potential of the manganese nodules the only other undersea deposits that show promise are the metalliferous muds. These belong to the superficial deposit category of relatively recent origins and are found in or near beaches and continental shelf regions, mainly in protected shallow waters and submerged extensions of streams flowing into the sea. Recently discovered muds associated with hot and saline brines of the Red Sea have been found to contain extraordinary concentrations of iron, zinc, copper, lead, silver, and gold.

The question is no more whether mineral markets will be affected by competition from such seaborne and undersea resources but how soon, to what extent, and by how much. It is being argued that even if these minerals were eventually available at lower prices from the oceans it is questionable that this would have any appreciable impact on the economic well-being of developed industrialized countries. Similarly if ocean mining succeeds to destroy land-based minerals industries in poor developing countries like Zaire or Zambia that heavily depend for their income on mining activities, then the ultimate cost of ocean mining may turn out to be inordinately high in terms of civil unrest, further political instability, and foreign aid requirements. On the other hand technological breakthroughs may find new uses for manganese and nickel that will result in the spectacular growth of both the land-based and ocean sources of such minerals.

REFERENCES

"Cashing in on the Ocean—The New Manganese Klondike," *Listener,* 7 September 1978.

Chemical Bank, "New UNCTAD Rules Will Regulate Investment in Developing Countries," *Report from Europe,* January 1980.

DeHuff, Gilbert L., *Manganese,* MCP Mineral Commodity Profile, U.S. Department of the Interior, Bureau of Mines, Washington, D.C., 1979.

Dykstra, Franz R., "Manganese—Its Strategic Implications," Statement before the Subcommittee on Energy Research and Development of the Senate Committee on Energy and Natural Resources, Washington, D.C., 29 March 1979.

Kahn, Herman, William Brown, and Leon Martel, *The Next 200 Years,* William Morrow & Company, New York, 1976.

National Materials Advisory Board, *"Manganese Recovery Technology,"* Publication NMAB–323, National Academy of Sciences, Washington, D.C., 1976.

"Ocean Mining—A Long Way Down," *Economist,* 31 May 1980, p. 86.

Richardson, Elliot L., "The Challenge of Managing the World's Deep Seabed Resources," *The International Essays for Business Decision Makers,* Vol. 3, Center for International Business, Dallas, 1978.

U.S. Department of State Library, *International Relations Dictionary,* Washington, D.C., 1978.

Foreign Policy Implications

The decade of the 1980s is emerging as a new era in international relations. The rules of the game are changing under pressure from new raw materials supplier nations that base their actions on nonbusiness considerations and are ready to threaten or withhold supplies of critical materials for purely political reasons. The OPEC cartel, oil from Iran, cobalt from Zaire, or coconut oil from the Philippines are but a few initial examples of the new international plays that are more likely than not going to multiply as the decade progresses.

The supplier countries are becoming more nationalistic, and the wave of the future is a variety of joint-venture projects between Third World governments, Western and Japanese businesses, or COMECON state monopolies as these governments become more active in their economies. As time goes on they are also bound to become more adept at playing off various potential partners and investors against each other without any concern for the traditional business ethics, particularly of the Anglo-Saxon variety.

Political risks associated with these developments may influence manufacturing firms from disinvesting or withdrawing from a country, but minerals mining, processing, and trading corporations do not have the luxury of walking away from the sources of their business. They must continue to operate under all conditions and can best conduct such business when supported by appropriate foreign policies and adequate investment incentives and risk protection programs of their own governments. Japan Incorporated, with its superb government-industry collaboration, provides the best example of how this is done.

CONFLUENCE OF POLITICAL AND ECONOMIC OBJECTIVES

The developing countries possessing mineral resources that are needed by industrialized countries of the West are under great pressure to exploit their positions and maximize their incomes to finance the general development of

240

their countries. The host governments are taking increasingly more agressive attitudes toward multinational corporations that are nevertheless a vital source of the capital and technology required to exploit mineral resources.

In previous years international mining companies negotiated and even made personal agreements with one or a few political leaders in power in a developing country. Under the new concepts and rules such arrangements are no longer safe or even advisable. The reasons for this are not hard to understand if one only analyzes the debacle of Iran. Whoever is in power today in a Third World country is not necessarily going to be in that position next year or even next month. One political risk research organization reported recently that one-third of all the governments in the world change every year and that more often than not such was not done as a result of predictable democratic processes.

To further complicate these conditions Soviet bloc political and commercial organizations are increasingly active in Third World countries. Acting in concert they can always sponsor a "liberation" movement to subvert whatever government is in power in any developing country in the name of returning the riches of the land to the people. Capitalist interests may also do that, of course, but representing private interests they lack the popular excuse and appeal.

Since the Soviet bloc countries do not yet rely on critical materials supplies from Third World countries to any significant degree they can afford to play the role of watchdogs influencing the developments without the necessity of becoming directly involved or taking any commercial risks.

Typically there are three major elements involved in various Third World development projects. These include the host country itself, technology and management suppliers, and financial resources. The interests of those three groups of players are not necessarily identical, although they overlap on several common issues central to each project. In all instances, however, it is a combination of political and economic interests, but whereas the political aspects of each project are becoming increasingly important, the political stability of most developing countries is always in question.

The host government of a country controls its natural resources and therefore possesses the strongest bargaining chip in any particular situation. Whether or not it is democratically elected the host government's main objective is to remain in power, and to do so this government will engage in all activities that will consolidate its power and provide the wherewithal to maintain it indefinitely. The natural resources of a country are in the host government's eyes a means to an end and so are the land and its people, armed forces, communications media, transportation network, and whatever industry there may exist.

To develop such natural resources massive amounts of capital, technology, management, mining skills, training, and maintenance are required from foreign sources. However, since the minerals are not for use in the countries of their origin there is considerable concern that no matter what price is paid for the resources it is not really adequate compensation for a depletion of what may turn out to be only a temporary treasure. It now occurs to the Third World countries that they would like to exchange some of their resources for technology and industrial plants that will raise the levels of their economies to those of the industrialized nations. They often ignore other vital factors such as the existence of markets and other necessary resources such as energy at reasonable cost.

Technology and management suppliers, on the other hand, are normally Western companies that often also provide a certain amount of their own risk capital to finance these projects. In most cases such sponsoring companies are interested in developing the mining projects and sometimes in processing the minerals into products that can be marketed to end-users in developed countries. In some instances these companies are also the final end-users of those minerals, but in all cases the companies' objectives are to seek returns on their investments for their shareholders.

Because the end-user market for minerals and end products is all important to the profitability of these projects the mining companies are also interested in identifying all potential customers and try to lock them in with long-range purchase contracts for their output. This provides an important measure of creditworthiness to the mining companies that are required to obtain appropriate financing from banks and other investment sources.

The financing of these projects also takes place from foreign sources. This is so because most developing countries are too poor to generate sufficient capital domestically. The exceptions are some of the rich oil-producing countries such as Saudi Arabia, Libya, or Kuwait, but others, like Mexico, Indonesia, or Nigeria, despite oil revenues in the billions of dollars each year, are also confronted with large and poor and rapidly growing populations.

Commercial and government banks provide short-term capital, and their objectives are to get repaid on time and earn their interest on loans advanced. Banks do not seek larger returns such as equity holders in the mining projects and certainly have no use for the output. Nevertheless the banks are interested in providing their capital to the least risky enterprises, and the commitments banks make are usually for no longer than 7 to 10 years and are widely diversified throughout the world.

RECOGNITION OF CRITICAL GEOPOLITICAL SITUATIONS

Whereas Japan, France, West Germany, and some other western European countries and their political leaders are well aware of threatening geopolitical patterns that are developing in the world, the Anglo-Saxon world in general and the United States in particular appear to show great complacency and often disbelief about the situation. Perhaps this is the legacy of the unique characteristics of the Anglo-Saxon heritage. These characteristics include the concepts of fair play, the Protestant work ethic, and trial by jury, all of which are neither practiced nor expected to develop in most other cultures.

The United States in particular is putting itself at a great disadvantage relative to the rest of the world. The U.S. government and business community in many cases continue to operate under the rules developed during a long period of self-sufficiency, although the economy is increasingly dependent on the whims of foreign politicians, suppliers, and manufacturers. In addition, the policies and objectives of business and government are not coordinated and often are unrelated to long-term national interests. What is more, business is increasingly suspicious of big government and its policies and would like to see less government interference and regulation.

All these factors combine to confuse and disorient public opinion and even some legislators. Needless to say the rest of the world, keenly competing for new markets, raw materials, and political influence, is quick to take advantage of these institutional weaknesses as it unbelievingly wonders at the naivete of much of the American political leadership.

Even within government itself departments and agencies may pursue policies affecting foreign supplies and markets that are at odds with each other. The classic example is the intense promotion of trade, joint ventures, and other exchanges with the Soviet bloc countries during the 1970s by the U.S. Department of State and some parts of the U.S. Department of Commerce. At the same time export controls administration of the same department, as well as the U.S. Department of Defense, and parts of the intelligence community voiced great reservations about such trade and demanded stricter export controls on transfers of valuable technology. The concepts of unilateral disarmament in the hopes of inducing the Soviets to do likewise was probably the acme of American naivete in the international geopolitics of that era.

Businesspeople who get caught in the middle of such debates are naturally frustrated, and since they are free agents in a democratic system, sooner or later they take matters into their own hands, perform their own research, and arrive at their own conclusions, primarily motivated by the profitability of their enterprises and the well-being of their stockholders. This is a natural and logical development within the current system that fails to provide clear-cut guidelines because the government does not speak or act with one voice.

This does not mean that dissension and argument do not abound within government agencies of other countries that are more sophisticated in dealing with geopolitical realities in the international arena. What is important to remember is the fact that once decisions are made a solid and common front is presented by all government agencies, businesses, and industries vis-à-vis a foreign entity.

The Japanese government-industry relationships are famous for this type of behavior, and it is little wonder that Japan, despite being one of the largest have-not nations in the world performs so admirably in the international markets. It is irrelevant that some of those arrangements are unacceptable to the United States because they would violate antitrust legislation. This only emphasizes that Japan assesses realistically its import dependence position and acts in its national interest. It is also futile to naively expect that negotiations for fair trade will succeed in the long run. Although the Japanese concede on some issues pertaining to individual products or quotas, they are also extremely busy inventing other combinations of factors that will more than compensate for lost advantages. Most important is the fact that throughout these proceedings the government and industry act in unison.

Another factor that often goes unrecognized is the relative mediocrity of American government officials, particularly those who have to deal with their foreign counterparts on a day-to-day basis. In many cases this criticism can be extended to corporate international management, particularly among companies with recent or relatively limited experience in foreign markets. It is often believed that a brief visit by a government or corporate executive to a foreign capital is sufficient to provide insights into the markets, politics, and economics of a foreign industry, and many business decisions have been made based on such subjective, incomplete, and often purposely provided erroneous information.

In contrast foreign service employees of foreign governments are usually very shrewd, well educated, and older men who grew up in countries that are constantly searching for means to maneuver toward a less-dependent status in the international arena. This is the dilemma of all industrialized countries that do not possess sufficient domestic raw materials or energy. This is the reason for import controls, tariffs, foreign exchange restrictions, and other regulations designed to minimize foreign dependence on other countries. Foreign diplomats, government officials, and businesspeople learn to operate in such environments from the very beginning, and they are aware that acting in concert representing their country in foreign arenas is a mandatory tactic for national survival.

Geopolitics is almost a dirty word in the United States because it implies self-interest, whereas a naive missionary fashion demands the furthering of human rights and democratic principles on much of a world that neither believes nor has any significant track record of such principles. However noble such policies may have been in the past, only a self-sufficient and unquestioned world power could afford the luxury of promoting them without risking national security. But those days are over, and reliance on multinational alliances will not substitute because those foreign partners are knowledgeable about the harsh realities and recognize the world like it is.

SETTING NATIONAL PRIORITIES IN FOREIGN POLICY

Clearly the 1980s is a time for the United States to define national priorities that must be pursued in its foreign policy that reflect its weakened position as a result of growing raw materials and energy import dependence on so many politically unstable Third World countries. These national priorities should address the inseparable issues of energy, strategic and critical materials, and national security. Closely associated is also the issue of foreign trade which is even more important to the United States now that it is no longer a self-sufficient superpower.

One of the simplest and most effective solutions to the problem is probably the creation of a new Department of Foreign Trade that would combine several pertinent government agencies now operating within the Department of Commerce, Department of the Interior, Department of Energy, Department of State, and other organizations. Such a department could provide the American businessperson operating in foreign countries much more specialized support in the form of up-to-date political and commercial intelligence and would be in a position to better confront foreign governments, most of which operate through highly specialized foreign trade ministries of their own. It should not simply promote foreign trade but also analyze potential and real threats to domestic industries as a result of the policies and actions of foreign governments.

The emphasis in such a department may well be placed initially on the most critical foreign trade sectors—such as energy and strategic materials. This will concentrate the department's resources on issues of significance to national security and at the same time minimize its interference in other trade sectors where ordinary international market forces do not threaten national security, domestic markets, or employment.

SECURITY OF SHIPPING ROUTES

The question of the security of vital shipping lanes has been often discussed in connection with political and military developments all over the world and most recently came once again to the attention of global strategists following the Soviet invasion of Afghanistan. The Soviet potential to expand their position in that area and eventually to dominate the Strait of Hormuz through which a large proportion of the world's oil must be shipped is of great concern to many countries dependent on those supplies.

There is little argument about the fact that certain strategic shipments such as oil present important targets to an enemy who might want to embargo supplies of such resources. But an embargo, if enforced, is generally regarded as an act of war. The question of making an embargo effective then becomes most important, and certain constricted passages in the generally traveled sea lanes provide unusual opportunities to control such shipments. However, most oil and raw materials are shipped from Third World countries and are destined for Western industrialized nations and Japan. Therefore the threat of an embargo can primarily come from the Soviet Union which is probably aware that such action would invite the retaliation of the West.

Although the Soviet Union is developing its navy and merchant marine to become the largest and most modern in the world it is doubtful that it would risk a global confrontation. Such action would most certainly unite all NATO countries into presenting a common front against the Soviet bloc. Rather it is much more in the Soviet bloc's interest to continue supporting local "liberation" movements or other political activity in strategic minerals-producing countries. Such actions are less provocative, easier to stage, and if successful obviate the need for embargoes of shipments that can be stopped at the source.

In a resources war those endangered shipping lanes are not as important as they would appear. The shipping lanes make a good argument for increasing the budgets of Western navies by those who are unaware of modern warfare. The possession of a powerful navy by NATO countries of itself is still not a guarantee of keeping the lanes open unless there is a will to enforce the threats to do so. Recent attempts by the United States to try and embargo trade with Iran jointly with NATO countries demonstrated the futility of such postures. No adequate answer has been given so far to the question of Soviet warships escorting ships of other countries to break such an embargo.

The concern about shipping lanes also becomes less revelant when the capabilities and ranges of modern armed forces are taken into account. Satellite intelligence systems, of which the Soviet Union has by far more than anyone in the world, can readily spot and monitor all shipping throughout the high seas. Intermediate or intercontinental missiles armed with quite conventional warheads and aided by satellite guidance systems can threaten, reach, damage, or destroy such shipping selectively or collectively according to political expediency, thus getting around any defenses designed to protect the vulnerable straits.

From this point of view the protection of vital shipping lanes is really nonexistent in the face of a determined enemy; however denying the control of critical materials-producing areas is possible. For this reason it is also necessary to maintain a powerful navy that is capable of easy access to Third World countries. There is also a case for Japan, whose global investments are expanding rapidly, to become a major contributor to security forces in the Third World and even deploy a navy to protect its own interests rather than rely on that of the United States.

POLITICAL RISK INSURANCE

Because of political instability in Third World countries private enterprises are facing political as well as commercial risks when they become involved in various mining or mineral-processing projects. As a result no single partner, whether the host government, mining company, or financial sponsors, is willing to accept all the risks. It might be pointed out here that COMECON enterprises, which are state monopolies, do not have this problem to the same degree, whereas many Japanese ventures are often sponsored and to a degree are guaranteed by their government. There are also many companies in western Europe that are owned by various governments or in which specific governments have a significant equity and control.

All such organizations enjoy an advantage over American multinationals in having their respective governments directly involved in overseas critical minerals ventures from the start. By virtue of such arrangements those companies possess a certain form of political risk insurance in the sense that they would not be involved in such ventures if their respective governments did not consider it vital to national interest and were prepared to accept their share of the risks.

This is important because political risks are associated with actions and interactions of governments. In politically unstable Third World countries the major political risk is that of a new government seizing power and renouncing the obligations of a previous government. Whatever the government in power, there is also the risk of expropriation or some equivalent actions such as legal harassment, discriminatory taxation, or even government-sponsored terrorism.

Political risks also include the possibility of a crisis in foreign exchange and the inability of central banking authorities to provide foreign currency to repatriate profits. This can occur regardless how sound and profitable a project may turn out to be and can be motivated purely by political decisions to acquire exchange for other purposes such as the purchase of weapons.

There are also several other events that could be classified as political or commercial risks, depending on the motivation. For example, strikes are commercial risks in developed countries, but they would very often be considered political events in most developing countries. Various forms of taxation or pressures to renegotiate existing contracts or arrangements as well as transportation slowdowns and port congestions may be politically motivated.

It could be argued that the existence of competing enterprises in a country like the United States provides in fact a means of spreading political risks and hedging bets by the opportunity to enter into various agreements with different political entities of a host country without an overt commitment of the U.S. government. This assumes that private corporations are in business to look after the national interests, which they are not. The apparent advantage exists only in theory not in fact because private corporations may readily withdraw from an overseas venture when the risks or even competition is excessive. For private industry to remain involved, as national security reasons may sometimes dictate, and despite political risks, the government must provide not only special profit incentives but also some form of political risk insurance.

The multinationals in the 1980s are therefore looking for better means to assess and control political risks associated with foreign ventures in developing countries in order to decide what form of political risk insurance is most appropriate. This activity requires anticipating trends and changes abroad to prepare the company to react timely and appropriately. Economic forecasting alone does not suffice because nationalism, religion, race, and personalities come into play and more often than not have a greater impact on a small developing economy than market forces alone.

Some multinationals, such as banks, already have some form of risk assessment organizations in operation, but the involvement of such organizations is not as great as that of an equity partner. These groups take the form of advisory councils and consist of prominent foreign experts, politicians, and government officials or risk committees evaluating foreign loans with in-house country specialists. Such councils perform the useful task of evaluating political risks before commitments are made, although they offer no protection once a decision is taken and conditions change at a later date. The effect is political risk insurance by virtue of noninvolvement in a venture if it is deemed too risky, but this approach does not offer a solution when an investment is necessary because of national interests.

Political risk insurance has been growing in popularity in recent years. The Overseas Private Investment Corporation is an agency of the U.S. government that insures investors in developing countries against war damage and foreign exchange problems. There are also a few private insurance corporations that provide political risk insurance on such foreign ventures, but premiums for such coverage in the most dangerous places may be expensive, running up to 6 percent or more.

No matter what risk insurance policies are written there are few if any that will cover all possible risks a company may be exposed to in a foreign country. One of the most effective ways, therefore, to avoid maximum risk is to operate private intelligence systems and political risk assessment task groups.

There is usually a great amount of information available about the political and economic developments in any country, practically on a daily basis particularly if radio and TV broadcasts and publications of the country are monitored intelligently and in a systematic way. The problem is to analyze the information and try to predict the impact of developments on a particular industry and corporations operating within that enviromnent.

Such intelligence activity within corporations is a form of political risk insurance also because it brings to the attention of corporate decision makers important facts that they should know about a country which are normally outside the scope of their activities. If such facts point to the possibility of a radical change in government or taxation then project evaluators should consider an additional return on investment as a hedge against uncertainties and analyze the project from that point of view.

Although political risk analysis within corporations seems to be a necessary tool for corporate managements of the 1980s it also poses problems and increases tensions internally. It is inherently a "negative" activity, and various executives who may have already developed some activities in foreign countries may be held responsible for previous uninformed decisions. This suggests that political risk and intelligence activities within a company should have the freedom of access to top management at all times to be effective with new and unsolicited assessments of developing situations that may impact the company's operations.

There is also a positive side to political risk assessment activities. The evaluation of individual countries and changes in their political and economic systems also uncovers opportunities that may develop in the future. Investment conditions may not be conducive to involvement at present, but trends may be identified that may suggest serious consideration of investment in the future. Early identification of such trends and conditions could give a company a significant advantage relative to its competition in a particular country or even a whole region of the world.

MEANINGFUL FOREIGN TRADE POLICIES

The United States lacks a coordinated nonfuel minerals policy that embraces the needs of national security, foreign policy, domestic mining policy, international trade, and foreign aid programs. Although a nonfuels minerals policy review was initiated by President Carter it has been severely criticized as an explanation of current government attitudes rather than a serious attempt to envisage a worst-case scenario and propose measures to create appropriate conditions for pertinent national contingency planning programs.

Other countries recognize the importance of strategic materials imports to their economies, and the governments of such countries assist their companies in negotiations and trade with Third World supplier countries. The United States expects to import half of its supplies of all raw materials by 1985, yet there are many uninformed people in the country who cling to the belief that the United States is largely self-sufficient as a nation. This is the legacy of previous eras during which the United States could have abandoned foreign trade completely without any appreciable impact on the lives of its population. Today this is impossible because of America's interdependence with other nations, and if serious attempts were made to abandon foreign trade in a new wave of isolationism the adjustments in the standard of living would be so great that civil unrest and major political changes would be inevitable. This is why the U.S. government must take the lead in formulating and implementing meaningful foreign trade policies that will create the best possible conditions for American companies to adjust to the growing interdependence of the American economy.

In the area of foreign trade policies with regard to strategic materials imports national security should be the paramount criterion until such time that the nation's vulnerability is significantly reduced. Reliance on the existence of the strategic stockpile should not be considered as adequate for long-range economic planning by American industries.

This consideration alone requires that several foreign trade policies be reexamined and streamlined to reflect the need to satisfy vital national interests, not chimerical objectives of the liberal establishment. Many foreign trade policies have been formulated in the past on the assumption that foreign countries in general and developing countries in particular cannot get along without imports of American equipment and technology. Nothing can be further from the truth. There is almost not a single exportable American product for which an equivalent or similar product is not available from Japan, western Europe or even COMECON countries. This competition will only get tougher in the future.

Besides competition American exporters and importers face several legislative and regulatory restrictions that hinder the expansion of foreign trade and give the advantage to foreign competitors. These include trade boycotts, heavy taxation of foreign-source income, promotion of human rights through trade policies, trade sanctions and embargoes, illegal payments legislation, and export controls. All these have laudable objectives in themselves, but the measures are not considered effective in the real world of international trade.

In addition to giving away international markets to foreign competitors these measures serve to assuage the guilt or temporary political objectives of special interest groups. Collectively the effect of such measures is damaging to foreign trade in general and to strategic foreign trade in particular.

These foreign trade restrictions exist at a time when foreign governments are also under intense pressures of protectionism. Foreign countries are constantly erecting new barriers to imports, and at the same time they embark on aggressive export drives not seen in international trade since the worldwide depression years of the 1930s. The overall effect is that while the rest of the world is developing various nontariff trade barriers and assisting its industries to expand exports the United States is moving in the opposite direction.

In a free market economy there are always great apprehensions about government intervention in foreign trade, particularly in activities where private market forces may allocate resources more effectively than government bureaucrats. Nevertheless the U.S. government's inaction should not give foreign industries and governments an advantage, particularly in trade sectors that are strategically important to the country as a whole. Unless more meaningful foreign trade policies are evolved that favor and support vital national interests of the United States, American industries will become even more vulnerable to foreign political forces and subject to price manipulation and political blackmail by unstable and unpredictable Third World countries.

REFERENCES

Beim, David O., "Risk-Sharing in International Minerals Projects," *International Essays for Business Decision Makers 1977*, Center for International Business, Dallas.

"Can World Head Off a Trade War?," *U.S. News & World Report*, 23 April 1979, p. 43.

Chemical Bank, "EC Proposes to Insure Companies against Risks Run in Third World Investments," *Report from Europe*, May 1978.

DeYoung, Henry G., "New Supplier Nations Will Behave Differently," *Purchasing*, 14 February 1980, p. 25.

Gottlieb, Daniel W., "Needed Badly: A National Policy on Metals," *Purchasing*, 14 February 1980, p. 33.

"Japanese Multinationals, Covering the World with Investment," *Business Week*, 16 June 1980, p. 92.

Kraar, Louis, "The Multinationals Get Smarter about Political Risks," *Fortune*, 24 March 1980, p. 86.

Morgan, James P., "Tactics in Times of Uncertainty," *Purchasing*, 28 February 1980, p. 29.

U.S. Department of the Interior, *Report on Issues Identified in the Nonfuel Minerals Policy Review*, Office of the Assistant Secretary, Energy and Minerals, Washington, D.C.

Vogl, Frank, "Protection against Political Upheaval," *New York Times*, 28 January 1979.

New Investment Opportunities

The threat of materials shortages in the future and associated price escalations present unprecedented challenges to corporate managers and investors alike. Management is eager to identify future problem areas and plan in advance to develop secure sources of supply or innovate with substitute materials and new product designs. Investors, looking for the greatest return on their capital, are facing a large number of opportunities, most of which are influenced by unpredictable political as well as economic forces (see Table 14.1).

These opportunities must be kept in proper perspective, depending on the impact of particular strategic minerals on the economy. Energy resources, exploration, production, and associated equipment manufacture are the most important from this point of view, because energy in the form of oil, gas, coal, and nuclear fuels accounts for over 70 percent of the total value of the world's minerals production.

Metallic minerals represent another 23 percent of that total, but the most important among them are copper, iron ore, gold, zinc, nickel, lead, tin, silver, platinum metals, bauxite, uranium, and manganese. Some other metallic minerals are very critical and include chromium, cobalt, tungsten, but the value of these metallic minerals relative to the other metals is somewhat smaller, usually less than 1 percent of the world's total output. Among nonmetallic minerals salt, potash, diamonds, phosphates, asbestos, and sulfur account for the bulk of the remaining 6 percent of the total value of the global minerals output.

Another investment approach might be based on predictions that metals are in danger of running out by the year 2000. Some industry observers believe that platinum, gold, zinc, and lead will not be available in sufficient quantities to meet the global demand by the end of the century. Silver, tin, and uranium are also expected to be in short supply by the year 2000. Such predictions lead into considerations of investment in gold in various forms, gold-mining stocks, precious metals, and potential substitutes.

More sophisticated investment policies might be based on analyses of industries and corporations with the least exposure to strategic and critical

Table 14.1   Major Categories of Investment Opportunities in Minerals and Associated Equipment Manufacturing and Service Industries

Major Category	Types of Enterprises in Category
Energy	Major oil companies Independent oil companies Drilling and service companies Oil exploration and production equipment Energy construction Uranium mining and nuclear fuels Coal mining and equipment Synthetic fuels
Basic metals	Copper mining and processing Aluminum production Other basic metals production Iron and steel
Precious metals	Gold bullion, coins, jewelry Gold-mining companies Silver mining and production Platinum metals Other precious metals production
Equipment	Mining machinery Transportation systems Marine systems and structures Seismic exploration systems
Technology	Materials substitution Recovery and recycling systems Satellite resource mapping systems Computerized logging systems
Electronics	Communications substitution systems Data communications Telecommunications
Defense	Aerospace companies Electronic warfare systems Shipbuilding Major weapons systems

materials import dependence. Similarly companies that control domestic assets, such as land that contains strategic materials deposits, are particularly attractive to investors because those assets will increase in value with the escalating prices of energy or particular minerals. Many small American independent oil and gas producers operating in the United States fall into this category.

There is also a whole range of investment opportunities based on the manufacture of substitute materials, more efficient exploration and production equipment, new transportation systems, and infrastructure development opportunities connected with the opening up of new mining and processing facilities in previously remote or uninhabited areas.

Electronics and telecommunications systems offer certain unique opportunities because they can provide more efficient minerals exploration systems and can also substitute for energy-intensive communications over long distances. The defense industry also offers unique opportunities because of national security priorities that must guarantee the availability of strategic materials to certain corporations engaged in the manufacture of crucial weapons systems.

CORPORATIONS WITH SMALL IMPORT DEPENDENCE

Among the end-users that are not directly associated with the minerals industry, the ones least vulnerable to strategic and critical materials shortages and supply disruptions are those which do not depend to any significant degree on inputs of materials or products containing strategic or critical minerals that must be imported from politically unstable foreign countries.

Strictly speaking there are no such end-users, since it could be argued that the economy as a whole is dependent on imports of about 50 percent of its oil demand from abroad. But even here some sections of the country use predominantly imported oil for transportation and electric power generation, whereas other regions may depend primarily on local supplies of oil, gas, or nuclear power. Industries based on such domestic energy supplies theoretically are somewhat safer from supply disruptions, but they will not escape energy cost escalations as the deregulation of oil and gas prices and further OPEC price increases impose higher costs on operations.

Aside from energy supplies different end-user companies experience varying degrees of import dependence on foreign non-oil minerals required for the production of their products, but in most cases they are not very much aware of the degree of their vulnerability. This is so because of minerals mining, processing, and trading corporations that form a buffer between the actual end-user and the sources of minerals. Roughly speaking there are three groups of end-user corporations that can be categorized according to their vulnerability to disruptions of foreign supplies.

Those end-users that depend on materials from suppliers whose sources are exclusively foreign are the most vulnerable, whereas those that get their supplies from domestic sources are much more secure. Most end-users are probably partly vulnerable because they depend on suppliers whose sources are both foreign and domestic. In those cases it becomes important to ascertain supplier import dependence for specific minerals (see Figure 14.1).

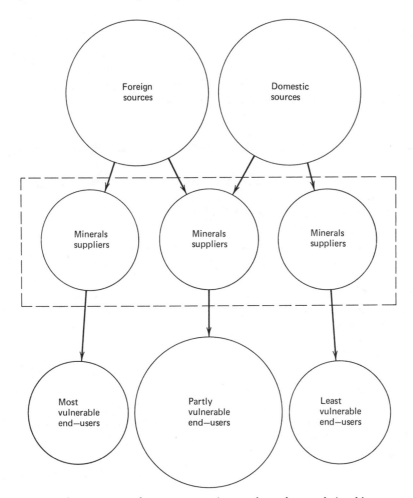

Figure 14.1   End-user company import dependence relationships.

To determine the degree of exposure of a particular end-user to unstable foreign supplies it is necessary to identify all that end-user's minerals and critical materials suppliers—most likely these are other domestic multinational corporations—and determine to what degree those suppliers depend on foreign sources and for what minerals. It is also important to determine what prospects, if any, the suppliers have of developing or increasing supplies from domestic sources in the future.

Investors can then rate end-user companies according to an import dependence vulnerability index to determine which group of companies is the least exposed to shortages or supply disruptions from foreign sources. This analysis is not easy to perform because end-users are free to change their suppliers, and minerals mining, processing, and trading companies are also diversified, having holdings and contractual arrangements with many sources in various countries. Nevertheless, end-users that rely on a single supplier that in turn depends on only one or a very few foreign sources must be regarded as risky investments until they diversify their supply sources and reduce their direct or indirect import dependence.

CORPORATIONS WITH DOMESTIC STRATEGIC MATERIALS ASSETS

This type of company is one of the most attractive investment vehicles, provided its natural resource assets are sufficiently diversified. Some oil- and basic metals-producing companies fall into this category. Other corporations such as iron and steel producers, pulp and timber companies, and railroads may also possess control over domestic resources by virtue of extensive land holdings in various areas of the country. However, environmental, taxation, or labor problems may make the exploitation of such assets unattractive, and these factors must be taken into account when evaluations are made.

Some basic minerals-producing companies have been diversifying with the objective of becoming all-around resource companies. Several American nonferrous metals producers fall into this category, but not all such diversified resource companies control the mining sources for all their products in the United States. About 10 nonferrous metals producers, however, do control significant domestic resources and mining operations primarily engaged in the production of copper, lead, molybdenum, silver, and zinc. Other important minerals such as gold, platinum, palladium, tungsten, and vanadium are also mined by those companies in the United States, but the output levels of those materials are not very significant relative to foreign production levels, and in many cases they are by-products of the production of large quantities of copper (see Table 14.2).

The existence of domestic sources of ores does not in itself mean that a company is not dependent on foreign sources for at least part of its ore supplies. In the final analysis it is necessary to determine what proportion of the total output is derived from domestic ores, and in this way it is possible to define the specific corporate import dependence on foreign sources. Two companies importing raw materials from abroad may not be equally vulnerable. This is so because when there are several sources of supply it matters which are involved in providing inputs to a particular company. Some are politically much more stable than others.

The Aluminum Industry

For example, there are several large aluminum-producing companies in the United States, and although ALCOA mines some bauxite domestically it is

Table 14.2   Major American Nonferrous Metal-Producing Companies with Some Mining Operations in the United States

Corporation	Metallic Ores Mined in the United States
ALCOA	Some bauxite, gallium
AMAX	Lead, molybdenum, tungsten, zinc
Anaconda	Copper, gold, silver, uranium
ASARCO	Copper, lead, molybdenum, silver, zinc
Atlas Corporation	Uranium
Cominco Ltd.	Lead, silver, zinc
Cyprus Mines Corporation	Copper, molybdenum, silver
Du Pont	Titanium ores, zircon
Gulf Mineral Resources	Uranium
Hanna Mining	Nickel
Hecla Mining	Lead, silver, zinc
Homestake Mining Co.	Lead, gold, silver, uranium
Kaiser Aluminum	Magnesium
Kennecott Copper	Cadmium, gold, lead, molybdenum, platinum, palladium, selenium, silver, zinc
Kerr-McGee	Molybdenum, uranium
Magma Copper	Copper
NL Industries	Barite, ilmenite
Phelps Dodge	Copper, gold, silver
Reserves Oil & Minerals	Uranium
Reynolds Metals	Some bauxite
St. Joe Minerals	Copper, lead, zinc
Sunshine Mining	Antimony, copper, lead, silver
Union Carbide	Copper, molybdenum, tungsten, uranium, vanadium
United Nuclear	Uranium
U.S. Antimony	Antimony
Western Nuclear	Uranium

Source.   Compiled by 21st Century Research from various sources, 1980.

negligible compared to the levels of imports from abroad. Since IBA is pushing toward a common pricing formula it would appear that all aluminum-producing companies in the United States and Europe are facing a similar bauxite supply and pricing situation. However, this is not necessarily so; companies whose major sources are in Australia are probably feeling more secure than those that rely on supplies primarily from Jamaica, Surinam, or Guyana.

In the case of aluminum, domestic producers are also developing new methods of extracting the metal from kaolinitic clays in case the overseas bauxite supplies are threatened by political or economic forces beyond their control. ALCOA also developed a new smelting process that uses almost 50 percent less electric power to produce the same amount of aluminum. The introduction of these new technologies in the future may make aluminum-producing companies in the United States much more attractive investment vehicles than they are at present.

Major Copper Developments

American copper-mining companies are probably among the better future investment values in the nonferrous metals industry. This is so because the United States is the largest copper producer in the world, and virtually all domestic copper mine output is from ores that are primarily mined for their copper content. However, copper ores also provide many by-products in fairly large quantities, some of which are valuable strategic metals. These include gold, silver, molybdenum, selenium, rhenium, and tellurium.

Nevertheless the recent problems experienced by the American copper industry result from increased foreign competition from Canada, Chile, Zambia, and Peru that are all expanding their copper-smelting and copper-refining capacity. This tends to keep copper prices low and in the face of rising operating costs makes marginal mines unprofitable, and producers are reluctant to invest in new copper-mining ventures until prices increase. A better investment climate is expected to develop in the copper industry later during the 1980s when the demand begins to outstrip supply once again. Kennecott Copper, Phelps Dodge, Cyprus Mines, and Newmont Mining are the leading American copper producers with domestic and foreign sources of ores.

Lead Producers

Companies involved primarily in lead production present an uncertain investment opportunity. On the one hand global shortages of lead are predicted before the end of this century, and at the same time environmental considerations reduce the use of lead as an additive in gasoline, and stricter pollution standards are being imposed. This, however, also brightens the prospects for larger-scale development of lead-acid–battery-powered electric vehicles that would significantly increase the demand for lead. Already storage batteries account for about 60 percent of the total lead consumption. Even so there are new developments in alternative power storage batteries, including fuel cells; nickel-iron and nickel-zinc batteries and zinc-air batteries—all of which may turn out to be cheaper and more efficient that may in turn inhibit the demand for lead in the long run.

Another important factor is lead scrap recovery; in the late 1970s this accounted for about 44 percent of the lead demand. St. Joe Minerals is the largest American lead producer, and a substantial portion of this company's output comes from domestic mines located in Missouri. AMAX, ASARCO, Cominco Ltd., Newmont Mining, and Gulf Resources and Chemical are the other major suppliers with important overseas interests.

Decline of Zinc Output in the United States

America's capacity for smelting zinc has decreased by half since 1968 because operators of smelters decided to shut down rather than incur the costs required to meet very stiff pollution standards. This resulted in the increased dependence of the United States on foreign zinc supplies, much of it from Canada, a major zinc-mining country. Cominco Ltd., Hudson Bay Mining and Smelting, and Texasgulf are the major zinc-mining firms in North America. Zinc slab from domestic and imported ores is also produced in the United States by AMAX, Gulf Resources and Chemical, New Jersey Zinc, St. Joe Minerals, and U.S. Steel.

The Ferroalloys Industry

Ferroalloys are used extensively in the steel industry to remove oxygen and sulfur and to provide special strength properties, corrosion resistance, and high-temperature resistance. The metals that provide this alloying function for improving steel properties are primarily nickel, chromium, and molybdenum. As a result the demand for those metals follows the demand for steel whose production consumes by far the largest amount of ferroalloys.

INCO Ltd. of Canada is the largest nickel producer in the world. Other major producers are Falconbridge Nickel Mines Ltd., also of Canada, and the only producer of nickel in the United States, the Hanna Mining Company. Since Canadian nickel production accounts for about 30 percent of the world's output it is unlikely that other nickel mines will be opened in North America unless the demand increases dramatically, possibly as a result of increasing steel-production capacity in Third World countries.

There is practically no chromium or manganese production in the United States because of a lack of economic deposits of those minerals. Chromite and increasingly ferrochrome are being imported from South Africa, Zimbabwe, Albania, Turkey, the Philippines, and even the Soviet Union. A once-thriving ferrochrome industry in the United States based on imported chromite has also been eliminated by competing output from ferrochrome-producing plants in foreign countries. Ferromanganese is produced also from imported ores by Ohio Ferro-Alloys, Union Carbide, Engelhard Minerals & Chemicals, Satra Corporation, Interlake, and Diamond Shamrock.

Molybdenum is abundant in the United States, which is also a major exporter of this metal. The major American producers of molybdenum are AMAX, Molycorp, Kennecott Copper, Duval, and Hudson Bay Mining and Smelting.

The Precious Metals

Gold production in North America accounts for less than 7 percent of the global output that is dominated by South Africa and the Soviet Union. In the United States, Anaconda, Homestake Mining, and Kennecott Copper produce gold that accounts for only a small part of the companies' precious metals output. Among Canadian gold producers the leading firms include Campbell Red Lakes, Dickenson Mines, Dome Mines, Kerr-Addison, Giant Yellowknife Mines, and Sigma Mines. There is also considerable interest in the West in investing directly in the South African gold-mining industry that is controlled by seven large mining enterprises. These include the Anglo-American Corporation, Anglo-Transvaal, Central Mining Finance Ltd., Consolidated Gold Fields, General Mines Finance, Johannesburg Consolidated Investment, and Union Corporation.

Silver is produced in the United States by Hecla Mining, Callahan Mining, Sunshine Mining, and Day Mines. Other silver-producing companies whose output also includes silver among other metals include ASARCO, Anaconda, and Homestake Mining. Some of those companies also have silver mining interests in Canada, Peru, Mexico, and Australia.

Platinum is not mined in the United States, but INCO Ltd. produces platinum as a by-product in Canada that accounts for 8 percent of the world's platinum output. However, the leading platinum producer in the world is Rustenberg Platinum Mines, followed by Impala Platinum, both in South Africa. Japanese industrial and jewelry demand is a very strong influence in the market because Japan accounts for up to 50 percent of the global platinum consumption.

In the United States platinum is used in catalytic converters to reduce pollution, and this market is dominated by Engelhard Minerals and Chemicals that imports platinum for this purpose. However, a new investment opportunity may develop in the near future as a result of increasing numbers of automobiles now being scrapped with catalytic converters that contain about 0.05 ounces each of mostly recoverable platinum and palladium. It is being estimated that nearly 200,000 ounces of platinum metals will be available from used converters by about 1985, and this amount will continue to increase with time. About 90 percent of converter platinum metals are recoverable, providing a new source of platinum in the future.

CORPORATIONS WITH DOMESTIC ENERGY RESOURCES

Because of the continuing price escalation of oil as a result of the OPEC cartel many major international and smaller independent companies that produce, refine, and market oil present unusual investment opportunities. This is particularly true of the lesser-known, so-called independent oil companies that depend on oil resources located in the United States and Canada. Many of those companies are also involved in the mining of other energy resources such as coal, uranium, tar sands, and oil shale that may significantly contribute to earnings and profitability in future years, particularly when rising prices will make synthetic fuels really economic. Some oil companies have also diversified into nonenergy minerals that may represent valuable assets, particularly if they include mineral deposits of some of the critical minerals located in North America.

There are basically two groups of oil companies of importance to investors, both of which appear to have excellent prospects for continuing growth in earnings. This is especially true of companies with resources located in the United States, the Alaskan North Slope, Canada, and the North Sea, since these areas are considered politically and economically much more stable than the Middle East and other Third World countries. Shell Oil—although 69 percent owned by Royal Dutch Petroleum, a British/Dutch combine—is a good example of such a company because its oil and gas reserves are large and strategically located in North America (see Table 14.3).

Nevertheless about 75 percent of all crude oil imports into the United States comes from Saudi Arabia, Nigeria, Libya, Algeria, Indonesia, Mexico, Venezuela, and the United Arab Emirates. All these are Third World countries whose future political stability is in question in varying degrees. As a result large oil companies that depend to a large extent on crude oil supplies from those countries are clearly more vulnerable than those that have only a fractional dependence on those sources for their crude supplies.

Most of the so-called large integrated oil companies control oil- and gas-producing properties in many parts of the world, including North America. It is possible to determine foreign crude dependence with a little research, although it is not a simple matter because most international oil companies market their products in many countries and some of their crude never reaches North America at all.

Companies with significant production from some domestic oil fields like those of the Alaskan North Slope and other newly discovered oil fields are also benefiting from price decontrols and are able to obtain world market prices for their oil. Such prices are in fact dictated by OPEC. Some production from marginal oil wells and tertiary oil-recovery projects are now also becoming profitable because oil from those areas can also be sold at world market prices. All this means that it is necessary to assess the major oil companies not only by their degree of dependence on politically unstable foreign sources of crude being marketed but also by the types of oil- and gas-producing properties controlled by them in North America.

Whereas the large oil companies are regarded as sound investment opportunities in general, many of the smaller independent firms offer unusual growth opportunities, although of a more speculative nature. In fact many

Table 14.3 Major Oil Companies Having Annual Sales over $1 Billion, with Their Oil and Gas Resources in North America

Corporation	Sources of Crude and Other Interests
Amerada Hess, New York, NY	California, Midwest, Canada
Ashland Oil, Ashland, KY	United States, Canada, North Sea—shale oil, coal
Atlantic Richfield, Los Angeles, CA	California, Alaska—copper
Cities Service, Tulsa, OK	Oklahoma, Texas, Midwest
Continental Oil, Houston, TX	Worldwide—coal, uranium, copper
Crown Central Petroleum, Baltimore, MD	Gulf of Mexico, Canada
Diamond Shamrock, Amarillo, TX	United States, Alaska, Canada
Exxon, New York, NY	United States, Alaska, North Sea, Venezuela, Mexico
Getty Oil, Los Angeles, CA	California, Alaska, Gulf of Mexico, North Sea, Canada
Gulf Oil, Pittsburgh, PA	Texas, Oklahoma, Canada—coal, uranium, tar sands
Kerr-McGee, Oklahoma City, OK	Gulf of Mexico, Canada, North Sea—coal, uranium
Marathon Oil, Findlay, OH	Midwest, North Sea
Mobil Corporation, New York, NY	Canada, Middle East
Murphy Oil, El Dorado, AK	Louisiana, Canada
Occidental Petroleum, Los Angeles, CA	California
Penzoil Company, Houston, TX	United States, Canada—copper, molybdenum, sulfur
Phillips Petroleum, Bartlesville, OK	United States, six foreign—coal, uranium, oil shale
Quaker State, Oil City, PA	United States
Reserve Oil & Gas, Denver, CO	United States, Canada
Shell Oil, Houston, TX	Large U.S. oil resources—coal, chemicals
Standard Oil (California), SF, CA	United States, Latin America
Standard Oil (Indiana), Chicago, IL	Midwest, California, Canada
Standard Oil (Ohio), Cleveland, OH	Midwest, Alaska—coal
Sun Company, Radnor, PA	United States, Canada, North Sea
Superior Oil, Houston, TX	United States, Canada—oil shale, coal, minerals
Tesoro Petroleum	Canada
Texaco, White Plains, NY	Texas, Oklahoma, Latin America
Union Oil, Los Angeles, CA	California, Midwest, Latin America, Australia

Source. Compiled by 21st Century Research from various trade directories and corporate annual reports, 1980.

of those smaller oil companies are merging with each other, and some are being acquired by the larger firms in programs to expand their production base in the United States and Canada (see Table 14.4).

Several of the independent domestic oil companies are already sizable operations with sales of several hundred million dollars annually. A few own their own marketing and distribution systems, selling their products on a regional basis, whereas others have a ready market for their crude oil and gas with the large integrated oil companies they supply. It is also possible that some companies may be keeping their assets "in the ground," waiting for oil prices to increase still further before expanding production. Several of those companies also diversified into the production of coal, uranium, sulfur, copper, silver, gold, and other minerals.

There are other companies still operating in different sectors of the economy that have acquired energy and mineral resources and are beginning to derive increasing earnings from such production. Some of the railroads such as Union Pacific or Burlington Northern fall into this category. Freeport Minerals, Reynolds Industries, Seagrams, and Santa Fe Industries all possess assets that include oil, gas, uranium, and other minerals. Some of those companies already derive a significant portion of their revenues from the sales of minerals, and the character of these companies' operations may change in the future, either through the acquisition or sale of their nonminerals-producing assets and operations.

Uranium-Mining Companies

Several companies operate uranium mines and ore-processing mills in the United States and Canada and may also present investment opportunities in the future as use of nuclear power continues to grow. Among the most important of those are Anaconda, the Atlas Corporation, the Exxon Corporation, Kerr-McGee, Homestake Mining, Gulf Mineral Resources, Reserve Oil and Minerals, United Nuclear, and Western Nuclear (see Table 14.2).

American uranium reserves are estimated to be in the order of 890,000 tons at a cost of $50 per pound or less, and it is estimated that it takes 6350 tons of uranium to fuel a nuclear reactor for 30 years. This suggests that up to 150 reactors could be operated on known American uranium reserves until the year 2000 at least if a high enough price could be obtained for the uranium ore.

Uranium resources could be greatly extended by the use of fast breeder reactors, but there is much opposition to this type of nuclear power plant because it produces and uses plutonium in the process that can be utilized for the construction of nuclear weapons. This is a ridiculous argument, particularly when applied to the American nuclear power program, since plutonium and nuclear weapons have been produced and existed in American strategic arsenals for years.

Table 14.4 Representative Independent Oil Companies with Annual Sales between $50 million and $1 billion Whose Resources Are Mostly Located in the United States and Canada

Corporation	1978 Revenues (millions of U.S. dollars)	Sources of Crude and Other Interests
Apache, Minneapolis, MN	96	Texas, Louisiana, North Dakota
Aquitaine Canada, Calgary, AL	150	Canada
Barber Oil, Carlsbad, NM	112	Texas, Louisiana, Florida—coal
Belco Petroleum, New York, NY	443	Midwest, Canada
Bow Valley Industries, Calgary, AL	233	Canada—coal, uranium
Canadian Superior, Calgary, AL	229	Canada—sulfur
Dome Petroleum, Calgary, AL	639	Canada, United States
Dorchester Gas, Dallas, TX	368	Canada—coal (United States)
Earth Resources, Dallas, TX	406	United States, Alaska—silver, gold
Energy Reserves Group, Wichita, KA	76	United States—coal, uranium
Forest Oil, Bradford, PA	61	United States, Canada
General American Oil, Dallas, TX	155	Texas, Louisiana, Gulf of Mexico, Canada
Hamilton Bros. Petroleum, Denver, CO	77	United States, Canada, North Sea
Helmerich & Payne, Tulsa, OK	126	Oklahoma, Texas
Home Oil, Calgary, AL	201	United States, Canada
Houston Oil & Minerals, Houston, TX	326	Texas, Louisiana, Atlantic Coast
Hudson Bay Oil & Gas, Calgary, AL	394	Canada (Conoco Subsidiary)—sulfur
Husky Oil, Calgary, AL	703	Canada, United States
Inexco Oil, Houston, TX	71	Louisiana, Texas
Louisiana Land & Exploration, New Orleans, LA	550	Gulf of Mexico—copper, coal
Mesa Petroleum, Amarillo, TX	167	Louisiana, Texas
Mitchell Energy & Development, Houston, TX	273	Texas, Ohio, Colorado
Pancanadian Petroleum, Calgary, AL	325	Canada—sulfur
Pogo Producing, Houston, TX	144	Louisiana, Texas, Oklahoma, Alaska
Sabine Corporation, Dallas, TX	56	United States, Canada—uranium, coal
Southland Royalty, Forth Worth, TX	184	Gulf of Mexico, Canada
Texas International, Oklahoma City, OK	143	United States, Canada—oil field equipment
Texas Oil & Gas, Dallas, TX	899	United States—gas transmission
Total Petroleum, Calgary, AL	570	United States, Canada—coal
Trans Ocean Oil, Houston, TX	50	United States (subsidiary ESMARK Corporation)

Source. *Standard & Poor's Stock Reports,* New York Stock Exchange, American Stock Exchange, Over-the-Counter, February–April 1980; and *International Petroleum Encyclopedia 1979,* Petroleum Publishing Company.

In 1977 three domestic firms and 10 foreign uranium producers were accused of fixing the world's uranium prices and allocating markets. So far it has not been proved that an international cartel of uranium producers exists, since there is a lack of cooperation from foreign governments on this matter. However, this emphasizes the highly political nature of the uranium industry.

MODERN EXPLORATION AND DRILLING TECHNOLOGY

The effects of the OPEC cartel and the decline of the oil output from Iran following the Islamic Revolution combined to keep crude oil prices high and finally prompted the government to institute phased price decontrol of U.S. oil and gas reserves. These events are responsible for increasing oil- and gas-drilling activity and resulted in greater demand for exploration and drilling technology products and services. Above-average profitability is expected as a result to continue in this industry until the 1990s.

Service companies that can offer the latest seismic exploration techniques are in great demand, but the oil and gas exploration activity consists of numerous companies serving the petroleum industry as a whole. Major products and services involved include drilling bits and tools, drilling muds and other well cementing and stimulating materials, well-logging services, offshore and onshore drilling contractors, and companies that provide engineering and construction services for building refineries, pipelines, and associated equipment. American companies that dominate this industry on a worldwide basis are performing the bulk of this work and are fairly immune from foreign competition because of their extensive experience and technological advantages (see Table 14.5).

Because most of the easy-to-find oil and gas have already been found the trend now has been to drill deeper wells and operate in harsher physical environments that call for the use of tungsten carbide drilling bits that last longer. Associated tools that include drill collars, drill pipes, tool joints, shock absorbers, reamers, stabilizers, and other components of the string of downhole tools must also be of better quality. Hughes Tool Company, Smith International, Dresser Industries, and Reed Tool (a subsidiary of Baker International) are the major companies involved in the manufacture of such equipment.

Drilling muds are used for the cooling and lubrication of rotating drills and must be pumped from the surface to the drilling bit. There is much use of barite in drilling muds, some of which are complex fluids, depending on the location. About 7 percent of the drilling costs is represented by these fluids. Cementing materials, acids, and other substances are also required in drilling.

Well-logging services assist in the measurement of the physical properties

Table 14.5   Major Corporations Engaged in Oil and Gas Exploration, Drilling, Construction, and Services

Activity	Corporation
Drilling bits and tools	Hughes Tools Company Smith International Dresser Industries Reed Tool (Baker International)
Drilling muds, cementing, and stimulating materials	Magcobar (Dresser Industries) Baroid (NL Industries) Milchem (Baker International) IMCO (Halliburton)
Well-logging services	Schlumberger Ltd. Gearhart-Owen Dresser Industries Halliburton NL Industries Teleco Oilfield Services
Offshore drilling	Global Marine, Ocean Drilling Kanab Services Reading and Bates Rowan Companies Santa Fe International SEDCO Inc. Western Company of North America Zapata Corporation
Onshore drilling	Helmerich and Payne Noble Affiliates Parker Drilling Rowan Companies Santa Fe International Schlumberger Ltd. SEDCO Inc. Tom Brown
Pipelines	Reading and Bates
Refinery and processing plant construction	Bechtel (private) Brown and Root C. F. Braun Dravo Corporation Fluor Corporation Foster Wheeler Company Kellogg (Pullman Company) Lummus (Combustion Engineering) McKee Corporation Parsons Corporation

of underground strata to predict where commercial quantities of oil and gas may be found. This activity involves the most advanced technology in this industry and is dominated by Schlumberger Ltd. throughout the world for onshore and offshore operations. Companies like Gearhart-Owen, Dresser Industries, Halliburton, NL Industries, and Teleco Oilfield Services share the remaining market. The conversion to computerized mobile well-logging systems and the development of measuring techniques simultaneously with drilling will give an advantage to companies that can provide services using these techniques.

Offshore drilling activity is increasing, creating new opportunities during the 1980s as a result of the growing demand for drilling rigs and platforms. Submersible drillings rigs used in depths of 10 to 70 feet are in great demand. Jack-up rigs used in depths of 20 to 300 feet are also fully used, while Mexican and Chinese offshore operations may create additional demand in the future. Platform rigs are more permanent structures, built to develop offshore oil fields. Semisubmersibles are the most sophisticated floating drilling rigs, generally operating in water depths up to 1000 feet.

Drillships are also mobile units and when equipped with "dynamic positioning" systems are able to drill at great depths. The demand for this type of unit is declining, but it is likely to be used in very deep waters, in remote parts of the world, in Arctic waters, and for ocean mining (see Chapter 12). Marathon Manufacturing is the largest builder of jack-up rigs. Other builders include Avondale Shipyards, Levington Shipbuilding, and Bethlehem Steel. Companies manufacturing motion compensation equipment, blowout preventers, and marine drilling assemblies are also going to benefit from the expansion of undersea drilling, because their products are expendable and must be replaced very four years or so.

In onshore drilling about 90 percent of the wells being drilled is in the United States and Canada, and this trend is expected to continue during the 1980s. As long as the OPEC cartel continues to increase prices and limit oil production, drilling activity will increase in North America, Mexico, and South America. Land drilling is performed on a contractural basis and is highly competitive. Drilling rates are much higher outside North America because of higher investment and political instability risks. National oil companies in foreign countries operate their own drilling subsidiaries, whereas private oil companies prefer to use drilling contractors. Major land rig manufacturers include National Supply, IDECO, Skytop/Brewster Rig Company, and Continental Emsco.

Production platforms, pipelines, oil refineries, and associated processing plants are designed and built by major engineering firms. However, those corporations are also engaged in the construction of petrochemical complexes, natural gas facilities, synthetic fuel conversion plants, deep-water ports, and LNG facilities. In recent years U.S. firms have been losing markets to competitors from South Korea, Japan, and West Germany. These countries' companies are in a better position to receive foreign contracts because the Foreign Corrupt Practices Act forbids American firms from paying foreign government officials for expediting contracts. Yet such practices are a normal way of doing business and in some countries even a tax deductible expenditure.

MATERIALS AND PRODUCTS SUBSTITUTION PROGRAMS

Investment opportunities connected with the development of substitute materials and new products are of a different nature than investments in stocks or equity of companies producing strategic minerals or specialized equipment for exploration and mining operations.

Research and development activity into materials and new products requires specialized technological skills as well as risk capital and is more likely to take place at research institutes, universities, and research and development departments of large corporations that are both suppliers and end-users of critical materials. Various government agencies in the United States and in foreign countries are also pursuing research of this type.

However, much of this research in recent years has been performed as part of the normal process of innovation, the objective of which is to find new products and materials that will cut the costs of production and contribute to the increased profitability of corporations. This process has been going on for many years in an environment of abundance and self-sufficiency of energy and raw materials without regard to the possibility of shortages or supply disruptions as a result of foreign political action.

Under the present circumstances, and in view of potential resources wars that might develop during the next decades, it may well turn out to be a very good investment for end-user corporations in particular to initiate materials and products substitution programs that take into account corporate vulnerability to strategic and critical materials shortages and supply disruptions as well as the potential cost reduction of the company's product line.

FINANCING NEW FACILITIES

The large size of mining and minerals-processing projects that normally range from $250 million to over $1 billion and commercial as well as political risks involved limit the financing of new facilities primarily to large mining enterprises, banks, and governments. More often than not such projects are joint ventures between mining corporations with the necessary technology, host governments that control access to the resources, and large multinational banks that provide syndicated loans often guaranteed by their own governments.

Because the easiest deposits of minerals have already been found and often depleted new discoveries and mining must increasingly take place in remote or hostile environments that require the development of a source of power or even a complete infrastructure, including roads, water supplies, and housing before exploitation can commence. These are immense projects that require very large amounts of capital, sometimes for several years, before minerals can be mined and revenues start coming in. For example, of $800 million invested in Western Australia during the 1960s on 11 mining projects over $500 million was spent on the development of the necessary infrastructure.

Exploration for minerals is most often financed from the cash flow of large mining companies, with some financing from institutional and private speculators. The role of governments in this activity, although widely publicized, is relatively small. The United Nations established an exploration fund to assist developing countries in systematic exploration for resources, but this financing is also relatively small compared with the other sources.

During the exploitation stages of a project the major sources of financing are the mining companies themselves, although quite often they spread their risks and minimize individual exposure by forming mining consortia. This procedure is widely practiced by the oil companies whose investment requirements in the search for new oil are very large.

In several Third World countries major multinational corporations have come into existence based on local oil or minerals production, and these are also engaging in projects outside their own countries, particularly in the Third and Fourth World, consisting of the poorest countries in the world, where local governments and investors are concerned about being accused of selling out to imperialism. Typical of those are the National Iranian Oil Company, Petroleos de Venezuela, Petrobras of Brazil, Pemex in Mexico, Indian Oil of India, Chinese Petroleum of Taiwan, Zambia Industrial and Mining Corporation, The Lucky Group and Korea Oil of South Korea, Steel Authority of India, Turkiye Petrolleri of Turkey, Kuwait National Petroleum, CODELCO in Chile, and Philippine National Oil. All these are already at least billion-dollar corporations, often being the largest enterprises in their respective countries.

Additional financing is also increasingly coming from end-user and trading companies that want to assure themselves of minerals supplies through long-term purchase agreements and financial institutions of developing countries such as the various Arab development funds that reinvest petrodollars in Third World projects. Suppliers credits are also a form of financing mainly extended to large mining enterprises and usually guaranteed by interested governments. Financing by speculators, local governments, and through foreign aid extensions provides a relatively small portion of the overall funding requirements.

TECHNOLOGY TRANSFER PROGRAMS

Most Third World countries believe that they are being oppressed and humiliated by their dependence on technology and know-how that basically come from but a few industrialized countries. This persistent attitude is based on the facts that only about 15 percent of the world's population in advanced countries controls 90 percent of the global manufacturing capacity, 85 percent of the world's patents and innovations, and nearly 80 percent of the global food production.

The non-oil-producing countries of the developing world experienced severe economic setbacks since the OPEC cartel began escalating the price of oil in 1973, and many are now heavily indebted to the Western banks, and their foreign trade deficits continue to increase. This, coupled with rising nationalism and worldwide inflationary pressures, is the motivating factor behind the moves to institute NIEO that calls, among other things, for transfers of technology and know-how to Third World countries.

These pressures are particularly strong whenever a developing country happens to be a major supplier of minerals to the industrialized world that is rich in technology and scientific resources. Nationalization of mining operations can be regarded as the first phase of a development program in such instances. Once this is accomplished further pressures usually build up demanding the establishment of minerals-processing plants that could utilize cheap local labor and realize higher export revenues that result from the value added to the raw materials.

Many of the joint-venture proposals from Third World countries are in fact attempts to blackmail industrialized countries into providing technology in return for temporary, unimpeded access to some minerals without any guarantees that such arrangements will last beyond the next coup d'etat.

Because of worsened economic conditions in the industrialized countries in recent years it is often feared that the transfer of the latest technology, whether in the minerals or other industries, will only mean a loss of employment opportunities and a further worsening of economic conditions in the West. As a result industrialized countries are more willing to transfer the so-called adapted technologies that are considered second best and outdated by the Third World. Otherwise, it is feared, the possibility of creating several "new Japans" in countries like Brazil or even India is inevitable. And this in turn will inundate the world with a surplus of manufactures that could not be consumed locally and will destroy many Western industries.

This continuing struggle is only likely to escalate in time as developing countries acquire more control of their resources and a scientific-technological base of their own. Soviet bloc countries that possess some technology probably comparable to the second-best technologies that Western multinationals are willing to transfer to the Third World are bound to continue to exploit this situation both politically and economically. Until these issues are resolved in such a manner that they satisfy the social, cultural, and development needs of the developing world, political instability and the threat of strategic materials shortages and supply disruptions will remain.

REFERENCES

Beim, David O., "Risk-sharing in International Minerals Projects," *International Essays for Business Decision Makers 1977*, Center for International Business, Dallas.

Bosson, Rex, and Bension Varon, *The Mining Industry in the Developing Countries*, World Bank, Washington, D.C., 1977.

Brown, Lester R., "The Limits to Growth of Third World Cities," *Futurist*, December 1976.

Bryant, William C., "A Rush to Buy Mining Shares," *U.S. News & World Report*, 15 October 1979, p. 118.

Central Intelligence Agency, *"Least Developed Countries: Economic Characteristics and Stake in North-South Issues,"* Research Paper, ER 78–10253, Washington, D.C., May 1978.

Chemical Bank, "EC Proposes to Insure Companies against Risks Run in Third World Investments," *Report from Europe*, New York, May 1978.

Chenery, Hollis B., "Restructuring the World Economy," *Foreign Affairs*, January 1975.

"Dealing with the Third World—Will the New U.S. Strategy Work?," *U.S. News & World Report*, 25 July 1977.

Farnsworth, Clyde H., "Third World Companies Achieving Global Reach," *New York Times International Economic Survey*, 3 February 1980, New York.

Friedman, Irving S., "International Lending to Developing Countries," *The International Essays for Business Decision Makers, 1978*, Vol. 3, Center for International Business, Dallas.

"Holes in the Ground," *Economist*, 4 August 1979, p. 74.

International Petroleum Encyclopedia 1979, Petroleum Publishing Company, Tulsa, Oklahoma, 1979.

"Investing for Tomorrow," *Economist*, 21 April 1979, p. 47.

Janssen, Richard F., "Political Forces Increasingly Influence Investment Decisions of James Sinclair," *Wall Street Journal*, 22 January 1980, p. 9.

Jones, C. N., "Formulating Plans for Joint Venture Companies in Saudi Arabia," *The International Essays for Business Decision Makers, 1979*, Vol. 4, Center for International Business, Dallas.

National Foreign Assessment Center, *Non-OPEC LDC Terms of Trade 1970–77*, ER 79–10145, Washington, D.C., March 1979.

"New Mine Analysis System to Be Launched by Eminent Economist," *Computerweek*, Johannesburg, 27 August 1979.

"Prospects for the Future of the Third World," *Partner*, AMK Berlin, October 1979.

Rowe Price New Era Fund Inc., Investment Prospectus, Baltimore, May 1979.

Rudnitsky, Howard, "How High Is High?," *Forbes,* 16 April 1979, p. 87.

Standard & Poor's, *Stock Reports,* American Stock Exchange, New York Stock Exchange, and Over the Counter series, February–April 1980, New York.

"Sunshine Mining Sets First Offer Backed by Precious Metals Since the Late 1800's," *Wall Street Journal,* 5 February 1980.

"Those Other Japans," *Economist,* 10 June 1978.

"Where Stock Market Goes from Here," *U.S. News & World Report,* 5 May 1980, p. 65.

How to Assess Your Vulnerability

Traditionally materials supply disruptions result from wars, labor disputes, civil unrest, and revolutions. End-users of raw materials operating in the free market economies during formal peacetime generally concentrate their attention on optimum inventory levels, timely deliveries, and cost of materials. Much less attention, if any, is given to the political risk factor, particularly if it results from developments in distant countries. The general belief is that all materials will always be available at some price that most end-users will be willing to pay.

Although this is basically true end-users who are unaware of political trends and have not bothered to engage in contingency planning may experience considerable losses as a result of short-term supply disruptions of critical materials that are directly or even indirectly required in the manufacture of their products or the delivery of their services.

It is relatively simple to minimize potential losses resulting from materials supply disruptions. What is required is a realistic assessment of the vulnerability of the organization to a worst-case scenario and preparation of contingency plans that could be put into effect well ahead of time as soon as threatening trends are detected. The basic data required for such an assessment are the identification of critical danger points inherent in the materials being used and of events and conditions that are conducive to a future crisis.

CRITICAL DANGER POINT INDICATIONS

Critical danger points are certain characteristics or statistics pertaining to a particular material and are inherent in its physical properties and natural distribution in the world. These danger points may change in time, primarily as a result of the development of new resources, new technology, or substitute materials. Critical danger point evaluation is useful in comparing alter-

Table 15.1   Critical Danger Point Indications

1. Lack of domestic reserves
2. Lack of known substitutes
3. Small number of primary producers
4. Single or sole supplier
5. Few foreign suppliers
6. Remote location of foreign sources
7. Hostile ideology of foreign suppliers
8. Low production levels
9. Small trade and sales volume
10. High energy requirements
11. Extended transportation lines
12. Low supply frequency
13. Poor recycling potential
14. Rapid technological advances
15. Declining use of material
16. Poor usage visibility
17. Declining production capacity
18. Small exploration effort
19. Extensive military use
20. Low research and development activity
21. Severe regulatory restraints
22. Increasing environmental restrictions
23. Important health and safety hazards
24. Foreign trade controls

native materials with regard to potential political risk whether or not conditions leading to a crisis are in existence (Table 15.1).

Lack of Domestic Resources

The availability of domestic reserves is among the most important factors in this analysis. The lack of domestic reserves or even resources that could be exploited at a higher cost in an emergency indicates a very high level of import dependence which implies the possibility of significant political risk and supply disruptions.

No Known Substitutes

Another very critical danger point is the lack of substitutes for a material that could replace it in case of a sudden cutoff, even at a cost in final product performance. For most materials some substitutes exist for some if not most of their applications. In some cases like the use of chromium for the production of high-quality stainless steels there are no known substitutes.

Small Number of Primary Producers

If only a few countries or a few firms produce a particular material the potential for the formation of a cartel and sudden price escalation is high. Because concerted action is required among various producers for the formation of a cartel the smaller the number of producers the easier it is to develop a consensus on production levels and prices.

Single or Sole Supplier

In some countries there is a single quasi-government agency or ministry responsible for the production and sales of one or more raw materials. If suppliers in the end-user country depend on their supplies from such a source they may be unable to meet their obligations if their sole source of supply is suddenly disrupted. This may cause an immediate shortage of a material in a country even though other foreign sources may continue in operation. Shortages of cobalt following the Zaire invasion of 1978 were in some measure due to the fact that one firm, the African Metals Corporation, was supplying most of the cobalt demand in the United States at the time.

Few Foreign Suppliers

Some minerals occur in only a few locations in countries outside of major consumption areas. A small number of foreign suppliers that control the distribution of such materials present the danger of an international marketing agreement often implemented in collaboration with the producers of such minerals. Antitrust legislation is effective mostly in the United States and does not necessarily prevent foreign firms from operating outside of its provisions as long as this is done under foreign jurisdictions.

Location of Foreign Sources

The remote and distant locations of some sources of minerals pose ordinary logistics problems, but the geography of the neighboring states and the nature of their political orientation are playing an increasingly important role. For example, rebel attacks on copper- and cobalt-producing areas of Zaire have been organized from bases in Angola.

Ideology of Foreign Suppliers

This is strictly a political factor that may have a very profound influence on the supply of raw materials to end-users. For example, the Islamic Republic of Iran under Ayatollah Khomeini took immediate steps to cut off the sales of Iranian oil to Israel and South Africa. This factor can change rapidly, depending on the predominant ideology of the government in power. The potential for unexpected government changes in supplier countries must be understood and monitored on a continuing basis. Events in Iran have shown that reliance on government assurances have proved to be inadequate.

Low Production Levels

The increasing costs of exploration, energy, and uncertain demand may discourage producers from keeping adequate production levels of some materials to insure uninterrupted supplies. On the other hand speculative hoarding or the existence of stockpiles may also be responsible for limiting production. Use of materials that are subject to such conditions increases the danger of spot shortages or supply disruptions.

Small Trade and Sales Volume

This is another danger point that may in fact be responsible for low production levels. There is only a limited use for some materials in very specific industries or applications. The relatively small business volume and lack of prospects of expansion of such trade may influence producers and suppliers to discard trade in such materials because it does not provide sufficient growth and profit incentives.

High Energy Requirements

This factor must be taken into account when considering substitutions for presently used materials. For example, aluminum is perceived as a substitute for steel in motor vehicles to effect fuel economies. But the production of aluminum in the first place consumes over four times the amount of energy required to produce the same amount of steel. The future of mining and processing operations in energy-poor countries is also in question. Escalating energy costs may force the shutdown or reduction of raw materials supplies from such regions unless the end-users are willing to pay considerably higher prices.

Extended Transportation Lines

The vulnerability of oil shipments from the Persian Gulf needs no comment. Other sources of raw materials may also be vulnerable because of the existence of very few roads and railway lines to transport the minerals from the mining areas to processing centers and shipping ports. Bridges, tunnels, international borders, ports, straits, and lengthy ocean shipments are all danger points increasing the probability of supply disruptions.

Low Supply Frequency

Low production levels and relatively small trade may both be the causes of low supply frequency of some materials. End-users not aware of this type of danger may find it very frustrating when commitments cannot be kept as a result of uncertain and infrequent materials supplies. Suppliers may be forced to resort to allocation to meet their obligations partially.

Poor Recycling Potential

This danger point means that continuing dependence on new supplies of the material will exist without the option of significant recovery from scrap when supplies are disrupted. For example, a considerable amount of gold is used in small quantities in electronic equipment, much of which is discarded after its useful life. It is fairly simple to separate gold from the other materials by electrolysis. But the collection and transportation of widely distributed electronics scrap is too expensive and time consuming to make extensive gold recovery from electronics worthwhile.

Technological Advances

There are two types of developments that create danger points for the supply of a particular material. One is the development of cheaper, more effective substitutes to replace the existing one, and a lot of research is being done in this area. The other involves the elimination of products that in turn endanger the continuing production of specific materials of which these products were major consumers.

Declining Use of Material

End-users may be unaware that the use of a material that is critical to their particular products is declining in other areas or industries. This may create a situation in which producers and suppliers are no longer interested in continuing to produce that material because of shrinking markets for its use. Product redesign or timely substitution may be the best way out if the situation is recognized ahead of time.

Poor Usage Visibility

This may be associated with the declining use of a material or applications that use only small amounts of it in the form of a catalyst or an alloy component. Suppliers who normally trade in several materials may concentrate on those for which obvious and growing markets continue to exist. End-users of such materials may be forced to search for sources or pay a premium for special processing required to produce such materials.

Declining Production Capacity

This may happen because of declining usage and other reasons. If the material in question is a by-product of another material whose production is being curtailed shortages may quickly develop. It is important to know how independent is the production of each critical material used in an enterprise to protect the operation against the threat of this type of shortage.

Reduced Exploration Efforts

Primary producers of specific materials are in a position to realize well in advance whether the markets for a material will continue to expand. If this is likely they will invest in exploration for new sources of those materials. If the opposite is true their new exploration investments will concentrate on different materials and could provide a good tip-off about the future of the material in question.

Extensive Military Use

Some materials may have predominantly military applications with no more than 5 to 10 percent of their supply being consumed in the civilian sector of the economy. The production of such materials may not be attractive to various private business enterprises, and the resulting availability of such materials would always be subject to sudden escalation of military demand, particularly in times of international tension and increased defense spending. For example, the use of cobalt increases much faster during a wartime economy than normal economic growth conditions would require.

Low Research and Development Efforts

The lack of significant research and development on new uses of a material may indicate its limited future potential as more versatile materials are being introduced. This may be a signal that production and supplies may decline in the future. On the other hand excessive research and development on new products may indicate the material is being phased out by the end-users.

Severe Regulatory Restraints

Government restrictions on mining, production, exports, and exploration are increasingly important to the availability of various minerals. Many of those restraints may be politically motivated to cater to specific interest groups.

In some foreign countries government regulation or the threat of it may be just a bargaining chip in an attempt to obtain better terms for resource exploitation for which the inputs of foreign capital and technology are being sought. In either case prolonged disputes and negotiations could cause delays and disruptions of supplies from such regions. Existing regulatory restraints must be considered as critical danger points, whereas the introduction of new regulations are events that may lead to a crisis in the future.

Environmental Restrictions

These danger points usually result from local citizen actions and local government regulation, but in many cases there are national laws already in existence that require local ratification or financing. In general the industrialized and populous countries of the West appear to be introducing the most severe environmental restrictions. However, takeovers of some Third World countries by various people's governments may use environmental controls in the future to curtail the production of minerals or to exact special payments toward environmental control. Such developments may cause the reduction or stoppage of production and may force end-users to look for new sources for some of their critical materials.

Health and Safety Regulations

These are often linked to the environmental restrictions, although the objectives of such regulations are primarily to insure the health and safety of workers involved in the production and use of specific materials. These regulations are more likely to be localized to a particular location or industry, but because metals in many forms exhibit a large degree of toxicity more often than not mineral and processing industries will be specifically affected. The restrictions against the use of lead in paints and gasoline and asbestos in construction are good examples of danger points affecting overall minerals production and availability.

Foreign Trade Restrictions

The existing trade restrictions may take many forms and must be evaluated by comparison with similar restrictions in existence in other countries that are also suppliers of the same materials. These danger points include existing import tariffs, export duties, quotas, licenses, specifications, shipping designations, and inspection requirements. All these are devices inhibiting the free flow of trade, and the introduction of new restrictions on trade in any particular country must be considered as an event leading to potential crisis in the future, depending on the new restrictions' effect on materials suppliers and distributors.

CONDITIONS LEADING TO CRISIS

Traditional supply disruptions result from war, labor disputes, civil unrest, and revolutions—all of which are classical conditions leading to a crisis of supply from the affected areas. In recent times additional factors have come into play, particularly on the international scene as a result of the rising tide of nationalism, human rights demands, and racial strife. The resulting political risks increasingly affect the availability of raw materials from foreign sources.

These forces have brought forth the formation of cartels, international marketing agreements, boycotts, embargoes, terrorism, hijacking, the taking of hostages, sabotage of transportation systems, and strikes. The forecasts for the rest of this century suggest that nationalistic pressures and international terrorism will increase in various parts of the world. This means that the possibility of protracted disruptions in raw materials supplies can be expected with even greater frequency than to date.

Another factor that may come into play in the future is nuclear terrorism. It is probably inevitable that sooner or later small and crude nuclear explosive devices will come into the hands of political groups seeking power in various countries. The use of nuclear threats against large population centers is not desirable politically by those who seek power within these countries. But nuclear blackmail against remote mining areas that provide raw materials to foreign end-users may find support not only among some populations but even governments that have been unable to meet the needs of their countries and are heavily indebted to foreign capital interests as many African countries are.

This could be a very serious threat if it occurs in some of the key southern African countries that control a large proportion of the global reserves of some strategic materials. Some African political and social scientists have already advocated nuclear power status for such key African countries as Nigeria and Zaire because they feel this would give those countries a greater voice in global politics to which Western powers will have to pay more attention. Niger, Namibia, and Gabon are already important African uranium producers outside of South Africa and could become a source of nuclear fuels and materials supply to such political forces in Africa.

Once the danger points inherent in the various materials in use have been identified the events and conditions leading to a potential crisis are regarded as "trigger points" that influence the availability of materials from affected areas. Such events when they occur modify the critical factors originally determined and indicate the possibility of a worsening or improving supply situation in the immediate future. Major events and conditions leading to a crisis have been listed in Table 15.2, but additional conditions may be used in specific situations as these apply to a particular end-user.

Table 15.2 Events and Conditions Conducive to a Crisis

1. Wars, revolutions, and civil unrest
2. Formation of cartels
3. Nationalization and state monopolies
4. Strikes
5. Embargoes and sanctions
6. Boycotts
7. Terrorism
8. Capital availability and cost
9. Labor availability and cost
10. Energy availability and cost
11. Transport availability and cost
12. New regulation
    Taxation
    Tariffs
    Trade controls
    Price and wage controls
    Currency exchange
    Health and safety
    Environment
13. Stockpiling and production controls
14. Corporate policy changes
15. Acts of God

Wars, Revolutions, and Civil Unrest

Wars, revolutions, and civil unrest are some of the traditional factors leading to the disruption of supplies, nationalization of foreign or private holdings, and change in previous conditions of doing business. These are important factors and are so obvious that they hardly need further explanation.

End-users should be more interested in being able to detect political, social, and economic activity with the potential to affect their supplies prior to the occurrence of such major disruptive events. The concept of developing a vulnerability index is basically to have a simple intelligence system designed to uncover conditions leading to major disruptions in time to take corrective action.

Formation of Cartels

The formation of cartels is unlikely to lead to the supply disruption because the primary purpose of a cartel is to maximize the revenues from the sale of raw materials by controlling prices and production. Nevertheless the formation of cartels may result in other political or economic action undertaken by some end-users that are affected adversely by such a move. Even if some end-users are willing to accept increased prices or materials allocations the availability of materials from a new cartel may be affected by production disruptions at the sources of supply.

State Monopolies

State monopolies are now in operation in many Third World countries and are in fact quasi- or national cartels controlling the production and distribution of raw materials. Basically this means that there is only one supplier or producer of one or more raw materials in a country that limits the choice of supply. The formation or expansion of state monopolies is an important event signaling potential changes in the price and availability of some raw materials. The coming to power of a Marxist or socialist government is almost tantamount with the formation of state monopolies to control raw materials within a country. In other cases state monopolies may control only individual resources, whereas the formation of a new ministry or state agency responsible for the production of all the minerals in a country would in fact signal a further centralization of such control.

Strikes

Strikes are designed to disrupt production or services to obtain better working conditions by the labor in an industry that may be influenced and used at the same time for other purposes quite unwittingly by other political forces. Strikes may occur directly at the mines where raw materials are extracted, at the processing plants and refineries, or within transportation systems and at ports of exporting and importing countries. Familiarity with the supply and transportation links is necessary to evaluate the significance of any particular strike to the availability of one or more raw materials.

Embargoes

Embargoes of trade are considered acts of war. The threat or imposition of an embargo by third countries against sources of raw materials supplies may affect all end-users regardless of whether they are in a country that participates or enforces such an embargo. Trade sanctions are also a form of selective embargoes.

Boycotts

Boycotts are politically motivated and are indicative of greater political risks developing in a country for some end-users. On the other hand boycotts are usually selective in nature and their effects can be sidetracked by the introduction of intermediaries and neutral third parties. Boycotts are not a serious long-term threat to supplies but may be indicators of more serious disruptions in the future.

Terrorism

Terrorism in all its forms is becoming increasingly problematic and can cause serious disruptions in supplies if it is directed specifically at the supply sources or transportation systems. It may take the form of attacks on mining and processing centers, hijacking of shipments, or holding hostage foreign executives and diplomats. The increase in terrorism occurring in a particular country, even in cases unconnected with raw materials supplies, may be a symptom of growing civil unrest and an indication of a worsening situation in the future.

It is well to remember that the largest number of terrorist attacks since 1968 have taken place in western Europe, the Middle East, and Latin America, but the largest number of victims were representatives of North American interests. As political disputes such as the North-South Dialogue heat up and attention centers on raw materials supply centers in African countries terrorism attacks may well escalate in those areas, creating serious raw materials supply problems to many strategic materials end-users.

Capital Availability and Cost

One of the first indications of increasing political risk in a country is the shortage and rising cost of capital to finance existing and future raw materials mining and processing projects. When capital availability is being evaluated it is important to identify the present and future sources of capital, since this may provide important clues to the ideological orientation of any changes that may be under way. Some foreign aid programs funded by the World Bank or other international agencies may still be traced back to their origins by discovering the specific country groupings or power blocs that promoted or opposed the programs.

Labor Availability and Cost

This condition is closely linked to the organized labor activity in a particular country, most of which are highly politicized. Labor availability and wage levels are obviously linked to strikes as events leading to a crisis. Specific union demands can provide an early indication of job actions contemplated in an industry or country that could have an effect on the materials supplies. In addition new wage settlements and the cost of labor increases may mean the withdrawal of private and international interests from mining activity and state takeover of the industry, leading to further supply uncertainties or disruptions. Most of the labor availability problems, however, are predictable and quantifiable because of the considerable media coverage such events receive.

Energy Availability and Cost

Sudden energy price escalations or supply disruptions could create conditions in some energy-poor countries under which mining output may be reduced or stopped altogether. Similarly various development programs being undertaken in Third World countries may create additional opportunities for exploration and mining in areas previously considered unprofitable because of a complete lack of energy supplies at whatever cost. The availability of energy in regions where richer ores can be extracted may cause the reduction or shutdown of operations in other areas as owners pursue higher profit opportunities.

Transport Availability and Cost

The opening of new roads, railways, and shipping lines or the increase in the frequency of transportation are the events that could significantly affect the availability of raw materials in a way similar to the effect created by expanding the availability of energy. On the other hand transportation facilities depend on the availability of energy, and escalating costs may equally well cause the termination or reduction of some transportation services. These events may therefore have both positive and negative effects on the availability of raw materials from the affected regions.

New Regulation

This condition comprises numerous events normally announced well in advance by official authorities. It is the effect of these events on specific end-users supplies that are not often understood. These events include the introduction of new taxes, wage and price controls, export and import duties, environmental controls, health and safety regulations, tariffs, and allocation quotas. These events are distinct from existing regulation contraints and are important only to the extent that they modify the regulation in effect.

All new regulation will have an impact on raw materials supplies, whether or not it is specially directed to promote or control the mining industry. National and international regulation must be taken into account when evaluating the effects of these events.

Stockpiling and Production Controls

Stockpiling materials at the sources of their production is primarily done for the purpose of stabilizing the market and maintaining price levels, and such activity may be an indication of cartel formation. On the other hand the existence of stockpiles during periods of civil unrest and labor actions may provide a cushion and assure the continuity of supplies. Production control by limiting output is another variant of stockpiling materials in the ground without the expenditure of energy and labor costs.

Sales or purchases of specific materials for the strategic stockpile maintained by the United States is also an event that affects the availability of some materials.

Corporate Policy

One of the most important and often ignored events is the corporate decision by producing or trading companies regarding their future plans to produce or distribute a particular raw material. For reasons of taxation, profitability, or regulation companies may abandon the production of one or more materials, creating a temporary shortage or even supply disruption. This is equally true of companies that engage in trading rather than producing materials. End-users must keep in mind that the business interests of producing and trading firms are not the same as those of materials-consuming enterprises.

Acts of God

The occurernce of droughts, floods, fires, earthquakes, hurricanes, and other natural disasters cannot be predicted in advance, but such events can influence the supplies from the affected areas. Familiarity with the major supply sources of your critical materials will allow the development of comparative data on the reliability of those sources under such circumstances. Acts of God may sometimes be conveniently seized on by political groups to continue a disruption that results from natural causes in order to exploit it for their own purposes without having to shoulder the blame for causing the disruption. The probability of the occurrence of acts of God must be assessed in conjunction with the political climate of the region in question.

NATIONAL VULNERABILITY INDEX

Using the critical danger points and the conditions conducive to crisis it is possible to develop an index rating all the materials used by a country, an industry, a company, or even a product manager or design engineer according to their vulnerability to supply disruptions. Most often such an index is developed on a national level to discover the exact exposure of a country to foreign sources of critical materials. Such an index is useful in guiding governments over thorny questions of allocating funds to develop strategic stockpiles of critical materials, promoting national minerals development policies, introducing taxation and investment incentives and trade controls.

Such a vulnerability index has been developed for the United States by the U.S. Army War College Strategic Studies Group that looked at materials of which at least 50 percent was imported from foreign sources during the mid-1970s. That index rated chromium, platinum, tungsten, manganese, aluminum, and titanium as the most critical materials for the United States (see Table 1.5 in Chapter 1).

A similar study was performed by West Germany in 1979 in which an attempt was made to quantify the estimates of future political risks with regard to certain critical materials. The German approach was to develop a "risk factor," ranging from 100 (low risk) to a high of 500 (high risk), for each material in question. The German index confirmed that even disruptions of supplies of minor materials like manganese would be very significant to the economy as a whole (see Table 15.3).

The most difficult task in developing such an index is the assignment of meaningful numerical values to the various critical factors that affect the supply availability of any particular material. Some of the critical factors are fairly easy to quantify. Import dependence, for example, can be simply recorded as the percentage of total consumption in the country that is being

Table 15.3   West German Raw Materials Political Risk Factor Index

High Risk	500
Chromium	370
Manganese	300
Asbestos	295
Tungsten	290
Cobalt	280
Vanadium	280
Titanium	270
Platinum	270
Aluminum	230
Nickel	225
Molybdenum	225
Copper	220
Tin	215
Lead	190
Zinc	180
Low risk	100

Source. Based on a report in the *Economist,* London, 1979.

met by imports from abroad, and such data are available from various international trade statistics. This can be expressed on a scale of 1 to 100 or 1 to 10, depending on the accuracy of the data available or the precision of the assessment required.

Other critical factors, such as the ideology of foreign suppliers, are not readily quantifiable. On a scale of 1 to 10 a free market capitalist economy may be considered the most desirable supply source, whereas a communist state monopoly would be the last choice, rated 10 in such an assessment. Other types of governments would then be given designations ranging from 2 to 9, depending on how centralized or market-oriented they are.

When two or more sources of the same material are controlled by governments with differing ideologies this fact should be reflected in the index by assigning weights to each ideology rating in proportion to the level of imports originating in that country. Similar judgments may be required for rating geography, location, regulation, and substitution potential impacts. Nevertheless, if consistent judgments are made with respect to all materials under study a useful comparative index will be developed.

As an example of a national vulnerability index chromium, nickel, and iron ore are shown evaluated in such a manner in Table 15.4. Several critical factors were chosen to illustrate the process of assigning index values ranging between 1 and 10 for each of the metals under analysis. In this rating system the highest "risk" score is 130 and would indicate the greatest relative vulnerability or political risk. The lowest risk, representing the most desirable conditions of materials supply would be 13 in this system.

Looking at the first critical factor, namely, domestic reserves, chromium was given a score of 10 reflecting the fact that there are no domestic chromite resources of practical value at present in the United States. Similarly

Table 15.4   National Vulnerability Index Example

Critical Factor	Chromium	Nickel	Iron Ore
Domestic reserves	10	9	1
Substitutes	8	6	1
Import dependence	9	7	2
Foreign sources	8	6	1
Location factor	10	4	1
Ideology factor	5	1	1
Cartel potential	5	1	3
Recycling potential	8	7	2
Military use	10	10	3
Stockpile position	10	5	2
Transportation factor	9	5	5
Regulation factor	1	1	2
Trade balance factor	2	4	8
Index total	95	66	32

nickel was given a score of 9 because some reserves exist in the United States. For iron ore the corresponding score is 1 because domestic reserves at present exist and are expected to last for some time.

On the other hand if this rating were to reflect the relative size of U.S. reserves to known global reserves it would be more appropriate to give it a score of 9 because the United States accounts for only 6 percent of iron ore reserves of the world. A score of 9 in this instance means that 90 percent or more of iron ore reserves of the world lies outside the United States.

This score would be further modified if the vulnerability factor were being developed for a long-range forecast. In such a case the ratio of domestic to global resources of iron ore rather than reserves would be compared, providing still another value. The choice of this score as of many others is clearly dependent on whether a short-term or a long-term vulnerability index is being constructed.

The import dependence score of 9 for chromium again reflects the fact that over 90 percent of chromium supplies comes from foreign sources. This score is slightly less in the case of nickel, reflected by a 7 because about 70 percent of that metal's demand is being met by imports from foreign sources. In the case of iron ore the score of 2 indicates imports of between 15 and 20 percent. If, for example, a scoring range of 1 to 100 were used the actual percentage could be assigned such as 17 percent or whatever the case may be at a particular point in time. On the other hand there is no reason why decimal points cannot be used within the 1- to 10-point range if required. The flexibility of this scoring system is really determined by the availability of the least-precise data for one of the critical factors.

All these ratings are relative, representing ratios of volumes or values, and some factors will reflect the relative importance between these values. For example, the relatively low iron ore import dependence of 2 in fact represents a much larger volume of imports and dollar value than the relatively high import dependence materials such as chromium and nickel. This is so because some materials are imported and used in much greater quantities than others. Nevertheless the high foreign trade impact of iron ore imports with a relatively low overall import dependence score is reflected by a high score (8) for iron ore under the trade balance effect factor.

The location factor of chromium is again being scored as 10, representing the relative instability of the major sources of chromite, namely, Zimbabwe and South Africa. The existence of alternative sources of this material in the Soviet Union and Albania, Turkey, and Iran does not improve the location factor rating from the political risk point of view.

By comparison sources of nickel in Canada, Norway, and Australia do not present such high political risk and are rated 4 in the example. In the case of iron ore the sources are much more numerous, and the choices of foreign suppliers even greater, meaning that the risk factor for this critical danger point is a low 1. Should some large iron ore sources like Brazil suddenly become unstable politically or change into a Marxist-type state the score for iron ore would increase to indicate a higher location of the supply risk factor.

By assessing individual risk levels for every critical factor and for every material under analysis it is then possible to obtain an index total that will be the arithmetic sum of all the risk factors assigned for each danger point for every material. Once this is done it is possible to compare all critical materials and rank them according to the highest vulnerability rating. If a more sensitive index is required that would indicate changes more dramatically from day to day or one event to another the summation can be done geometrically by arranging the risk factors as multipliers and divisors of a constant. Continuous computation of these risk factors will permit the study of trends and provide a basis for forecasts of future prospects.

In the case of chromium, nickel, and iron ore of the example the relative vulnerability index of each is 95, 66, and 32, respectively, of a total possible 130 points, representing the highest vulnerability possible under this scoring system.

As events and conditions conducive to a crisis take place they will influence the ratings assigned to each critical danger factor as they occur. This is not to say that some critical factors will not remain constant for weeks, months, or even years if no events of political significance take place, but the probability of this is low.

To keep track of the trends it is necessary to monitor these developments and change the scores to reflect the changing conditions. For example, the foreign sources for a particular material may suddenly come under attack as a result of revolution or a militant takeover, and this will immediately affect the vulnerability factor of all the materials that originate from that area.

The national strategic materials vulnerability index is a useful information system not only to materials end-users but also to foreign policy makers and international executives who must keep informed about the impact of political developments in foreign countries on their critical materials supply position.

A system of this type is only as good as the information it contains; therefore it is important that reliable and consistent sources of information are used to develop the risk factors for these applications. On the other hand the system is fairly simple to construct and relatively easy to use and maintain even on a daily basis if necessary.

INDUSTRY VULNERABILITY INDEX

The industry strategic materials vulnerability index is somewhat more specialized than the national vulnerability index and concentrates basically on materials of special significance to a particular industry. Most critical factors used in the construction of the national vulnerability index are available as a base, but additional factors pertaining to more specific substitutes, price stability, labor, capital, energy availability and cost, environmental, safety, health, and work hazard concerns, and specific taxation problems may be introduced to refine the vulnerability index and make it more meaningful to the industry in question (see Table 15.5).

This refinement can also take the form of more sensitive ratings, ranging from 1 to 100 for every critical factor. Analysis may also include specific alloys composed of several critical materials. This would allow a method of optimizing the selection of materials for industry uses that will include political risk factors and not just technological parameters.

The concept of an industry vulnerability index is illustrated by comparing aluminum, cobalt, and titanium, three metals of significance to the aircraft industry. Of the three cobalt shows the highest vulnerability because of high import dependence from relatively few sources located in politically unstable areas. The small number of suppliers, limited substitution in the aircraft industry, recent price instability, and trade controls all contribute to the relatively high vulnerability score of 132 for this metal. Aluminum and titanium have lower vulnerability ratings, but all three metals show high

Table 15.5   Industry Vulnerability Index Example Developed for Three Metals of Significance in the Aircraft Industry

Critical Factors	Aluminum	Cobalt	Titanium
Domestic reserves	10	9	9
Import dependence	9	10	5
Foreign sources	5	10	6
Location factor	5	10	3
Ideology factor	5	8	2
Cartel potential	7	5	1
Transportation	5	10	5
Number of suppliers	2	10	2
Military use	9	5	8
Substitutes	8	9	10
Recycling potential	7	8	9
Price stability	5	10	9
Labor factor	10	1	5
Capital factor	10	2	2
Energy factor	10	1	10
Environmental factor	1	1	3
Health and safety hazards	1	2	1
Taxation	1	1	5
Trade controls	2	10	4
Stockpile position	5	10	2
Index total	117	132	101

vulnerability when compared with other materials on the national vulnerability index.

In the case of the industry vulnerability index the difference between the national vulnerability index is best explained in terms of substitutes as one of the critical danger points. For a metal like aluminum the substitution factor on a national basis will show a relatively low rating because aluminum is used in many industries for a variety of applications. One of the industries using aluminum is of course the aircraft industry. But when the vulnerability index on an industry level is being developed for the same metal it will be given a high political risk rating for the substitution factor because it is very difficult to conceive of the aircraft industry having to use alternative materials to aluminum for the construction of modern high-speed aircraft.

Similar considerations are given to other factors and other materials used by varying industries. What it really means is that the perceived vulnerability of one material will vary from industry to industry and may even be different in each case from the index developed on a national level. It all depends on the values perceived by the end-users and their impact on the supply availability of a particular material that is critical to their industry.

CORPORATE VULNERABILITY INDEX

The corporate vulnerability index focuses on specific raw materials that provide the basic inputs for the manufacture of company products. Some form of monitoring of corporate raw materials needs is normally performed by materials managers, but their main concern is usually timely delivery and reasonable inventory levels. Since the availability of raw materials affects both, materials managers may do well to become more familiar with the political risks involved at the sources of supply of the materials they must buy.

Continuous monitoring of their company's critical materials supply availability trends by means of a corporate vulnerability index will give materials managers an advantage in dealing with materials suppliers and trading organizations and will allow them to make independent and informed decisions before shortages or disruptions take place.

An example of a corporate vulnerability index for a manufacturer of electronic components is shown in Table 15.6. This table rates three specific raw materials that are important to the manufacture of electronic components, namely, platinum, tantalum, and silicon. The number of critical factors in rating these materials may be even larger and more refined than that used to construct the national or the industry vulnerability index. In the example shown the high-risk factors associated with platinum danger points contrast dramatically with those for silicon that has very low-risk ratings on most counts. Silicon is a good example of an almost perfect raw material limited only by production capacity and market demand.

**Table 15.6   Example of a Corporate Vulnerability Index
Developed for Three Materials of Importance to a Typical
Electronic Components Manufacturer**

Critical Factor	Platinum	Tantalum	Silicon
Domestic reserves	10	9	1
Import dependence	10	10	2
Foreign sources	10	4	1
Location factor	10	5	1
Ideology factor	5	5	1
Cartel potential	10	1	1
Transportation	2	1	1
Number of suppliers	9	5	1
Military use	5	9	1
Stockpile position	10	10	1
Recycling potential	8	7	1
Price stability	10	8	1
Substitutes	10	5	1
Technology factor	1	10	1
Labor factor	1	1	1
Environment factor	10	1	5
Health and safety factor	1	1	1
Taxation	1	1	1
Trade controls	5	1	1
Index total	125	94	24

PRODUCT VULNERABILITY INDEX

In level of detail the product vulnerability index may not vary much from
the corporate vulnerability index, and in cases where a single product line
is the mainstay of the company it will essentially be the same. In multi-
product corporations with distinct and widely scattered divisions engaged in
the manufacture of several products requiring different sets of materials the
product or materials managers may choose to develop their own materials
vulnerability level at their plants.

The product vulnerability index may also be monitored by the production
and design departments in a corporation to assist them in choosing the best
mix of alternative materials for future products. For this purpose product
managers may access and use the same data base developed for the corporate vulnerability index but include additional factors of significance to the
design and production departments. They may also evaluate their materials
by assigning risk values based on their own judgments for comparison with
those developed in the corporate vulnerability index.

HOW TO SET UP YOUR OWN VULNERABILITY INDEX

The setting up of a strategic materials vulnerability index is fairly easy within a corporation because most of the resources that are required to do the job already exist within the corporation. What it entails is the organization and maintenance of a specialized information system that could be queried at will and could be used to alert the management in advance of potential problems in its critical materials availability. It must be understood that this is not a question of an inventory control system that has to optimize materials levels mostly on the assumption that access to all materials will continue uninterrupted at all times. Nor is this type of system comparable to the more common forecasting systems that predict the prices of materials based on assumptions of supplies and demands over the short term. The main objective of the vulnerability index is to inject the additional elements of the possibilities of political risk and supply disruption.

Much of the information required to develop a strategic materials vulnerability index is provided daily in the general and specialized media. However, reliance on these sources alone is not adequate because individual end-users depend on different mixes of critical materials, lead times, and substitutes and their margins to tolerate supply disruptions vary widely. Also most media cannot systematically monitor all the events that are critical to the critical materials of a particular corporation, each of which may have a different supply and transportation pattern, for example. However, end-users are responsible for categorizing and assigning risk values to the specific events as these occur, and they are best qualified to perform these tasks.

The major elements of a strategic materials vulnerability index information system are shown in Figure 15.1. The heart of the system is a small data base containing the basic critical factors associated with critical materials used in the company. This implies, of course, that an effort must first be made to identify all such critical materials used in the organization. A good starting point would be a list of materials that have repeatedly caused production problems in the past because of unexpected shortages or price escalation.

This data base may be computerized, particularly if on-line services and terminals are readily available as is the case in most large organizations today. Similar firms can also rely on rented space and terminals from numerous time-sharing companies offering on-line computing services, some of which are available on an international basis in many parts of the world. However, this is not mandatory, because initially only a small number of critical materials will be monitored. On the other hand this data may already exist in other information systems in the corporation in which case it could be accessed for use in developing the vulnerability index.

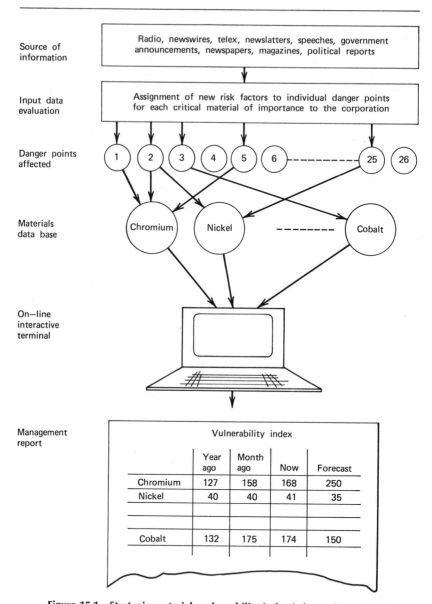

Figure 15.1 Strategic materials vulnerability index information system.

Crucial to the preparation of the index is the ability to assign risk-factor values for each critical danger point as conditions change and events take place in critical materials supply areas. For this purpose it is necessary to have current access to sources of information on the basis of which risk-factor values can be assigned. These sources may include radio, newswires, political reports, newsletters, trade magazines, newspapers, and corporate trade contacts in areas of interest.

As the information is being gathered either periodically or by exception, the existing risk-factor values are checked against the latest estimates, preferably developed independently by one or more persons within the company. These new risk factors are introduced into the system if they differ from those already assigned previously. At the same time additional information may force changes in some of the critical danger points under consideration, either adding new factors or eliminating others that are not pertinent anymore as a result of changed conditions.

Over a period of time vulnerability index values will accumulate for each critical material showing specific trends. These will indicate either increasing or decreasing vulnerability index values, reflecting political risks over time. When displaying the latest vulnerability index it will be useful to present also the value for each material that existed a year ago, a month ago, or at other intervals of significance to the management. In addition the data base will allow the user to present forecasts of vulnerability index values in the future based on various assumptions of possible developments that may take place in the affected areas. This in fact will give the user a useful tool to simulate political risk conditions at a future date.